The
Wine Lover's
Cookbook

The Wine Lover's Cookbook

GREAT RECIPES FOR THE PERFECT GLASS OF WINE

Sid Goldstein

foreword by JOHN ASH   photographs by PAUL MOORE

CHRONICLE BOOKS
SAN FRANCISCO

Library of Congress Cataloging-in-Publication Data:
Goldstein, Sid.
       The wine lover's cookbook: great meals for the perfect glass
of wine/by Sid Goldstein; foreword by John Ash; photographs by
Paul Moore.
          p. cm.
       Includes bibliographical references and index.
       ISBN-13: 978-0-8118-2071-4   ISBN-10: 0-8118-2071-8
       1. Cookery. 2. Wine and wine making. 3. Menus. I. Title.
TX714.G64926 1999
641.5–dc21   98-31671
                              CIP

Manufactured in China.

Prop and food styling by George Dolese.
Photography assistance by Jill Sorenson.
Design and typesetting by Anne Galperin.
The photographer wishes to thank his stylist, George Dolese, for
his creative talents and commitment to excellence; his assistant,
Jill Sorenson, for her ability to do everything and keep her humor;
and his wife, Deborah, for making his life so rich. Cheers!

Distributed in Canada by Raincoast Books
9050 Shaughnessy Street
Vancouver, British Columbia V6P 6E5

20 19 18 17 16 15 14 13 12 11

Chronicle Books LLC
85 Second Street
San Francisco, California 94105

www.chroniclebooks.com

Contents

Acknowledgments

As with all labors, particularly creative ones, a number of people helped this one come to fruition, either through the unselfish sharing of their palates and stomachs, through diligent testing of recipes, or through their contributions to the writing or editing process.

To all my pals who've enjoyed my food and wine (you know who you are), thanks for being there with open mouths to help devour the results.

To John Ash, for inspiration and vision.

To my enthusiastic testers, Sandy Rogers, Rami Rubin, Dorothy Woll, my sister, Ellen, and especially my mom, Lois Jamart, thanks for great support and critical feedback.

To Bill LeBlond, for believing in this project from Day One; to my copy editor, Laura Reiley, for her sensitive, constructive edit and for making me go the extra lengths to get it right; to Sarah Putman, the "glue" who keeps it all together at Chronicle Books; and to my photographer/stylist team, Paul Moore and George Dolese, who've brought to life what was not always beautifully conceived food, thanks for making this book what it is.

And, most of all, to my wife, Suzanne, for her endless faith, love, and support and for spectacularly delicious dessert recipes; to Zack, living proof that teenagers can be not only wonderful human beings, but articulate food critics as well; and to Ruby, my golden retriever ("angel in dog's clothes")—a truly terrible food critic but a passionate and skilled cleaner-upper.

Foreword

In America, the interest in pairing wine and food is a relatively recent phenomenon. It's really only been in the last couple of decades that most of us have thought much about how we merge the two together. I was reminded of this when I was asked to contribute to the recent revision of *Joy of Cooking*.

It was last revised in 1974, and between then and 1997, the world of food had changed dramatically. Ingredients, cooking techniques, and flavor combinations that we didn't even know existed in 1974 had become commonplace in 1997.

The world of wine has gone through a similar transformation. Not only have we discovered a whole new world of wine varietals, such as Viognier, Syrah, Sangiovese, and others, but winemakers, like cooks, have discovered new techniques and approaches for making wine that have opened up a whole new pantry of flavors. As a result, the traditional rules for pairing food and wine (e.g., "red wine with red meat; white wine with fish and white meats") really don't work very well anymore. The flavor palette of both food and wine have become so much more interesting and complex. It's an exciting time!

The downside (if there is one) to this explosion of options is that it's also become confusing for many of us: If the old rules don't work, what rules or guidelines can we use now? Both Sid and I have spent a good deal of our time in recent years trying to demystify the whole food and wine pairing issue. From my perspective, wine *is* food. It's best enjoyed in context with other food. At its simplest, it's just another element or flavor on the plate. With the exception of a tiny number of the world's greatest wines, wine should not be put on a pedestal. It's meant to be enjoyed daily as part of a healthy lifestyle. Above all, pairing food and wine "ain't rocket science."

The traditional method of marrying food and wine is to start with the food and then find a wine that goes with it. In this book, Sid has taken a unique approach by starting with the wine first. If you are a "wino" like me (in the Northern California wine country where I live, we use this term in a positive sense to identify those who are passionate about wine), then you're really going to enjoy this approach, especially if you have specific wines that you like to drink often.

As this book so clearly indicates, picking a grape varietal is only the first step. Skillful winemakers, who might as easily be called "wine chefs," can take a grape like Chardonnay and make it in a wide variety of styles from crisp, clean, and citrusy to rich and buttery with lots of vanilla notes. The foods that complement these different styles will vary tremendously.

This book does a masterful job of demystifying the marriage of wine and food, but it also unveils some really intriguing new flavor combinations along the way. I'm having a lot of fun with *The Wine Lover's Cookbook*, and I know you will, too.

JOHN ASH, MENDOCINO COUNTY, 1998

Introduction

To begin with, a promise and a caveat are in order: This is a very different type of cookbook from what you've probably encountered before, and I hope it will make you think about what you cook in a new way. The Bible mentions wine 650 times, starting with Genesis, but there are precious few food recommendations.

This book views wine as a source of divine culinary inspiration and as a guidepost for showcasing food in the very best possible light. It attempts to document my continuous journey to discover what I'll call great "wine food"—food that enhances the promise of the wine, wine that resonates with and amplifies the food.

As a dedicated wine lover and passionate cook, I find myself inspired in the kitchen by many things. Sometimes, it's the sweet scent of vine-ripened tomatoes in my garden at the height of summer. Or it might be memories of past winters that trigger the desire for a slowly braised veal stew to warm the cockles and kindle the spirit. But more often than not, I decide what to cook based on the type of wine that I want to serve with my meal. It's a peculiar but benign obsession. I call it "wine-first" cooking.

Throughout my years in the wine business with Fetzer Vineyards, I've had the pleasure of experiencing many sublime food and wine combinations. I've been fortunate to learn from some of the greatest chefs in the country through our culinary programs, both at the winery and throughout the United States. My personal mentor, John Ash, with whom I've collaborated on two cookbooks, probably has the best intuitive grasp of how food and wine interact of anyone I know. John's savvy in marrying foods with wine has been an invaluable source of learning for me, and he's had a profound impact on the way I think about food and on how I cook.

The principles of this type of cooking are pretty simple: Concentrate on great ingredients, keep the flavors simple and complementary, and don't allow the food to overwhelm the wine or vice versa. It's an effort to create harmony and synergy—the whole becomes greater than the sum of the parts.

I think you'll find these recipes to be reflective of a style that I consider distinctly "wine country." That is, you'll find an emphasis on fresh, lower-fat dishes with very little cream or butter. Although both cream and butter can be helpful bridge ingredients (ingredients that help connect the dish to the wine), I have chosen to largely avoid these types of dishes due to nutritional concerns and to stay on the good side of my lovely wife, Suzanne, to whom I often refer as the "food police."

In attempting to create great food and wine matches, I've relied on a few of the old rules to help. With each varietal type, I've tried to focus on at least one traditional or classic pairing to help best exemplify the connection. In many cases, the recipe is reflective of a regional connection to the wine, such as Rolled Veal with Prosciutto, Fontina, and Caper Sauce with Pinot Gris/Grigio (page 66), a personal interpretation of a traditional Italian food and wine marriage. In other cases, I've simply identified a dish that I feel captures the proper spirit of the pairing. Each of these "classic pairings" is indicated within the chapters.

In writing a book about food and wine pairing, I recognize some inherent challenges: First of all, not all Chardonnays, Pinot Noirs, etcetera are created equal. By that I mean that there are very different styles of each of the varietals we'll explore in this cookbook and that a recommendation for "Chardonnay" with a specific dish creates the option to select from about seven or eight hundred brands available on the shelves of retailers. Some of these are quite oaky, others are lighter and more fruity, while still others can be earthy, mineral-like, and more austere.

Rather than try to solve this problem with a specific wine recommendation, I've chosen to try to illuminate the differences in styles found in each of these varietal wines. Only experimentation (or the advice of a good wine merchant or a knowing friend) will ultimately resolve the answer to which is the perfect wine with the dish. At any rate, there are so many excellent choices within each varietal that it seems far too limiting to recommend a specific brand and vintage.

Furthermore, due to the laws of subjectivity, which ultimately dominate any food and wine pairing discussion, my perfect wine match might not be yours. Beauty is, after all, on the palate of the beholder. This is the reason I've recommended an alternative varietal with each dish as well. You might find it enjoyable to serve both wines simultaneously to see which works best for you and your guests. If nothing else, this should provide for good table conversation and lively debate.

The age of the wine is another variable that cannot be completely solved here, although I've tried to mention in the recipe introductions if an older, more mature wine or a younger, more vibrant one is best suited to the dish. There is a relatively big difference in the taste of most wines based on their age, and this factor can increase or decrease a wine's suitability for a given dish.

In writing this book, I have invariably left out some important varietals due to space limitations. Nebbiolo from the Piedmont region of Italy, Pinot Blanc from Alsace and California, Chenin Blanc from the Loire region of France (and the very little that remains in California), Sémillon from the Bordeaux region of France, and Tempranillo, a lesser-known grape from Spain, are a few of the varietal victims in this book.

All of the references in this book will be to varietal types as opposed to regions and appellations since my attempt here is to simplify and not confuse the selection process. This may be construed as a "California" approach (since in California we principally refer to wines by varietal type), but I'll accept that label willingly.

This all being said, my hope is that you'll experience as much delight in creating and presenting these food and wine combinations as I have had in discovering them. There is nothing more genuinely pleasing to me than close friends sharing great food, wine, and conversation at the table, involving themselves communally in one of life's most rewarding experiences. If this book helps to enhance this sublime connection of mind, palate, stomach, and spirit, I will be truly pleased with my work.

In vino veritas . . .

A Road Map to Great Food and Wine Pairings

THE RULES THEY ARE A-CHANGING

The pairing of food and wine is a complex and highly inexact science. It is fraught with outmoded rules and a propensity for generalizations. Much of what has guided the understanding in the past emerges from the traditions of regional dishes that are eaten with regional wines, such as tomato-based pastas with Chianti (primarily Sangiovese) or beef bourguignonne with French Burgundy (Pinot Noir).

This world has been turned absolutely upside down in the past fifteen to twenty years due to the rapid globalization of both food and wine. In the United States, in particular, we have absorbed the traditions of other food cultures—European, Asian, and Latin—and we have found ourselves in a quandary from a wine standpoint. Our varied, new cuisine includes Asian ingredients, such as cilantro, star anise, shiitake mushrooms, and pickled ginger, intermingling with classic European, Latin, and native ingredients.

The old wine rules simply weren't created with this diverse, cross-cultural culinary palette in mind. These changes have forced us to broaden the way we look at pairing food and wine, to be more open and experimental.

THE BASICS

There are a few basic tenets that I apply to the food and wine pairing process: I first consider the body of the wine that I'm going to serve. What is the texture or "mouthfeel" (weight and feel in the mouth) of the wine and what types of foods will most enhance it? While most wine tasting revolves around the aroma, bouquet, and flavor of

the wine, I can't emphasize enough how important "mouthfeel" is to successful food pairings.

Secondly, I consider the flavor of the wine. I think about the inherent fruit character that comes from the grape variety itself, as well as the flavors that are developed from aging the wine in oak barrels, if there's been any barrel aging. Zinfandel, for example, has a vibrant berry character that often meshes with a hint of spice from barrel aging. Chardonnay, in and of itself, contains apple, pear, and citrus notes; it's the barrel fermentation, malolactic fermentation (a process that converts harder acids to softer ones), and the aging process that contributes additional flavors to the wine, such as toast, vanilla, butter, and spice.

In addition to considering the body and flavor in both the food and the wine, I try to be aware of the level of intensity of each. Successful combinations come from creating relatively similar levels of intensity in both the food and the wine. An example would be a light, delicate white wine paired with fillet of sole with lemon-butter sauce, or a robust, heavy red with osso buco.

Lastly, I assess the basic taste of the wine. There are four basic tastes from which to choose: sweet, sour, bitter, and salty. (In fact, research dating back to 1909 in Japan has asserted that there is a fifth basic taste called *umami*, which refers to a savory taste, but this has never been uniformly accepted.)

Pairings work best when the basic taste (sweet, sour, bitter, salty) of both the food and the wine are relatively similar. This means making sure that a sauce doesn't get sweeter than the wine (see Mustard- and Sourdough-Coated Venison with Currant Sauce on page 195) or that the acid in the wine is sufficient to match the acidity found in a particular dish (see Mixed Greens with Thyme-Scented Goat Cheese Cakes and Balsamic-Dijon Vinaigrette on page 40). Occasionally, a contrast of basic tastes, such as a slightly sweet wine to offset saltiness in a dish (see

Baked Ham with Spicy Apricot-Orange Glaze on page 91) will work quite effectively.

Sweetness, in the case of wine, is a reflection of its residual sugar. Any wine above about 0.6 percent residual sugar has some apparent sweetness, although most wines don't start tasting sweet to many people until they reach about 1.5 percent residual sugar. These wines are often referred to as "off-dry," and are typically Riesling, Gewürztraminer, or Pinot Gris/Grigio. Sweet versions (above 5 percent) of all of these varietals are also produced. The problem is that residual sugar is not always indicated on the front or back label, so it can make selection a little tricky. See the Riesling section (page 68) for an explanation of how to select German-style Rieslings based on their nomenclature.

Sauternes (made from Sémillon and Sauvignon Blanc), sherry, and port are also produced as sweet wines. Some sweet dessert wines can be found in smaller, 375-milliliter bottles since a small taste of this liquid nectar goes a long way, particularly at the end of a meal that has included several other wines.

The basic taste of sourness as it relates to wine is experienced in the wine's natural acidity. Varietals that are particularly high in acid (Sauvignon/Fumé Blanc, Pinot Gris/Grigio, Sangiovese, and Pinot Noir) can balance more acidic dishes beautifully.

The basic taste of bitterness in wine is noticed primarily in its tannin structure. Tannin is that searing, back-of-the-tongue jolt that is experienced in many young red wines, such as Cabernet Sauvignon and some Merlot, Zinfandel, and Syrah. This is one of the many reasons that wines are aged in the bottle, both prior to release and in the buyer's cellar. Over time, tannins evolve and soften as red wines go through the bottle-aging process, adding complexity and flavor interest to the wines and making them far more pleasurable to drink.

Certain foods have tannins as well, most notably walnuts and pecans. These ingredients can help lessen the apparent effect of tannin in young Cabernet Sauvignon, Merlot, Syrah, and Zinfandel.

Saltiness is not an element found in wine, therefore it can be largely omitted from consideration. However, dishes that are slightly salty due to their use of anchovies, olives, soy, or Thai fish sauce can complement lighter, fruity wines, such as Gewürztraminer, Riesling, dry rosé, and some Pinot Noir. On the other hand, tannic red wines and oaky whites fare very poorly with salty dishes, which create a noticeable increase in the wines' apparent tannin and oak levels.

In evaluating these components of body, flavor, intensity, and basic taste, we can choose to find either similar elements in the food and wine pairing or contrasting ones. Successful combinations come from both. A similar match of flavor, for example, would be the Shrimp-Scallop Pâté with Cilantro, Dill, and Pine Nuts (page 34) with Sauvignon/Fumé Blanc. Herbal flavors in the dish match herbal flavors in the wine.

On the other hand, a pairing of Roast Pork with Holy Mole Sauce (page 174) with a dry rosé (one of the possible marriages with this dish) relies on a contrast of body and intensity between the rich chocolate mole and the light, fruity wine that refreshes and cleanses the palate.

If this all sounds a little daunting, or perhaps a bit too cerebral for something as fun as drinking wine with delicious food, then we can move on. However, an understanding of why some food and wine pairings harmonize in crescendo while others clang in discordance is very helpful, particularly as you begin to create your own pairings. Maybe Tony Hendra said it best in an amusing *Forbes FYI* article: "While you can assess certain aspects of a wine's merits in isolation, its apotheosis is at the table. . . . Wine separated from food is like a boxer who never goes into the ring; you can speculate all you want watching him work out how good he might be, but you'll never know for sure, till the bell sounds for Round One."

Ultimately, it's personal taste preference that rightfully dictates successful food and wine combinations, not arcane rules.

THE UGLY STEPSISTERS (FOODS TO AVOID)

So many ingredients are wine friendly (see Bridge Ingredients included in each wine section) that it seems only fair to point the proverbial finger at a few that are not. These ingredients don't mean to be this way, and, in fact, each of these foods is delicious on its own. These "ugly stepsisters" are simply best avoided when exploring successful pairings with wine.

Asparagus

OK, let's just say it: Asparagus is generally awful with wine. Not impossible, just difficult. It contains phosphorus and mercaptan, two components that twist the flavors in most wines in the wrong direction. If you must drink wine with asparagus, try Pinot Gris/Grigio or Sauvignon/Fumé Blanc as they have enough acidity to deal with this less-than-perfect wine food.

Artichokes

The enfant terrible of food and wine pairing, artichokes contain an acid called cynarin, which makes everything taste sweet after eating it. Think of your first sip of milk after eating artichokes. It tasted like someone poured sugar into it. With wine, artichokes simply notch up the apparent sweetness of the wine, and that's not such a good thing most of the time.

Chiles

The heat in chiles comes from a substance called capsaicin, which actually can be measured in what are called "Scovil units," named after the man who invented the process.

While small amounts of milder chiles, such as jalapeños, Anaheims, and poblanos, are not particularly problematic for wine matching, hotter chiles will wreak havoc with oaky white wines and tannic reds. Oaky wines will taste more oaky. High-alcohol wines will taste hotter, even burning. Tannic wines will seem more bitter. Overall, chiles numb the palate's ability to appreciate the subtleties of wine, particularly older reds. It's a pity, but it's true.

That does not rule out the possibilities, however, for successful wine pairings with chile-infused food. With spicier dishes, the best bets are fruity whites, such as Riesling, Pinot Gris/Grigio, Sauvignon/Fumé Blanc, and Gewürztraminer, and soft, fruity reds, such as Zinfandel, Pinot Noir, Rhône blends, and dry rosés. I hate to admit it, but white Zinfandel works well, too.

As much as I personally adore hot food, you'll find these types of recipes noticeably absent in this book, save for a few personal favorites, such as the Roast Pork with Holy Mole Sauce (page 174) and Clove-Infused Pork–Black Bean Stew with Tomatillo–Roasted Red Pepper Salsa (page 161), which marry well with a Syrah blend and Zinfandel, respectively.

Eggs

Eggs are notoriously difficult to match with wine because the yolks coat the palate and make it more difficult to taste wine. When eggs are used as part of quiches or hollandaise sauces, they are less intrusive. All in all, Champagne, Sauvignon/Fumé Blanc, Pinot Gris/Grigio, Riesling, Gewürztraminer, and fruitier styles of Chardonnay stand the best chance of working with eggs, but don't bet your entire meal on it.

Vinegar and Pickled Foods

Most vinegar is an enemy to wine, but there are exceptions: Balsamic vinegar, with its sweet, nutty character, can actually contribute complexity to sauces, but it must be used judiciously to avoid overpowering the wine. Other vinegars can rob wine of its fruit, making the wine seem astringent and unpleasant.

There are several salads in this book, which may come as a surprise due to popular thinking about not matching wines with salads. When matching salad dressings to wine, it's best to keep the ratio of oil to vinegar at least three parts to one. In general, white-wine vinegar works best with white wines and red-wine and balsamic vinegar with reds, but balsamic vinegar can adapt to white wine when used in salads.

Most pickled foods—save for capers, which I find to be an interesting complement when used sparingly with Sauvignon/Fumé Blanc and Pinot Gris/Grigio—present difficulty in pairing with wine, as well. The same can be said for pickled ginger, an ingredient so delicious that I go out of my way to find ways for it to work with aromatic, fruitier wines (Asian-Style Grilled Salmon with Fennel–Pickled Ginger Relish on page 78).

BRIDGE INGREDIENTS

Bridge ingredients are those which help connect the food and the wine through their interaction either in flavor, body, intensity, or basic taste (sweet, sour, salty, bitter). In each chapter, bridge ingredients are recommended to help make these connections come to life. Different varietals have different "friendly" ingredients; they can be very helpful in achieving harmony between food and wine.

It's amazing how slight adjustments of certain bridge ingredients (e.g., Dijon mustard added to a red-wine sauce or fresh herbs added at the last minute to a salsa or relish) can help accentuate the flavors of the dish and encourage greater affinity with the wine that is selected.

COOKING METHODS AS A FACTOR IN PAIRING FOOD AND WINE

While food and wine pairing is most often discussed in terms of how flavors, body, and basic tastes harmonize, there remains one more element to explore—the cooking method used.

While not always obvious, the technique used in cooking a dish will often affect how well (or poorly) it will partner with wine at the table. The following methods of cooking are the ones that seem to heighten food and wine pairings, although it can be argued that deep-frying, poaching, and steaming all have their places, too.

Grilling

Besides being my preferred cooking method, grilling offers a great opportunity to partner seafood, poultry, meats, and vegetables with wine. The main reason is that grilling is done quickly with the meat or vegetable in direct contact with its heat source. A tantalizing smoky flavor results, depending on what type of fuel is used (charcoal, mesquite, oak chips, or gas grills with flavorizing bars). This occurs because the juices drip down on the fuel source and cause smoke to be released back up to the meat or vegetable.

This caramelization of sugars and protein through grilling is similar to the process of toasting the inside of oak barrels that are used for aging wines. Most red wines are aged in either French- or American-oak barrels from six months to as long as two years. During this time, the wine picks up subtleties of aroma and flavor from the barrel that are often described as "smoky" or "toasty." Some white wines, Chardonnay in particular, are also aged in oak barrels and display aromas and flavors that result from the process. Chardonnay, barrel-aged Sauvignon/Fumé Blanc, Pinot Noir, Sangiovese, Zinfandel, Syrah, Merlot, and Cabernet Sauvignon all benefit from being paired with grilled dishes, making the connection seem more vivid and dramatic.

Roasting

Roasting is a dry-cooking method that browns the exterior of the meat while sealing the juices inside (assuming it's not overcooked). When roasting is done properly, it can have a very positive effect on wine pairing. The juiciness inside the meat, which is primarily protein and fat, helps coat the palate and soften the impression of both full-bodied red and white wines.

The browning of the outside skin also has a positive effect on wine pairing since this caramelizing process, whether it is accomplished by slow or fast roasting, helps connect the flavor of the meat to the barrel-aged characteristics of the wine.

Roasting meats, poultry, and certain seafood, such as salmon or sea bass, allows for the use of fresh or dried herbs, which can also help marry the meat to the wine. The flavor of the herbs is infused into the meat, adding depth that is the hallmark of simpler roasted fare.

Vegetables greatly benefit from roasting, which seals their moisture inside and dramatically intensifies their flavor. This has positive implications for wine pairing as it adds another element to a recipe that can support a pairing with a specific wine.

One of my favorite roasted ingredients is garlic. The caramelized, nutty character that develops when garlic is roasted (see page 164) seems to be a particularly friendly bridge ingredient to most wines. Because it is not nearly as sharp as raw garlic, I use roasted garlic in many relishes and sauce reductions as a helpful conduit to both red and white wines.

Sautéing

Sautéing meat, fish, or vegetables in a pan with fat (either butter or oil) also creates intriguing food and wine pairing possibilities. Because fat is being used in direct contact with the meat or fish, it adds a flavor and textural element that can help with some wines in particular.

Chardonnay, with its oily texture, is one very good example of a wine that can be helped by the sautéing process because it adds some fat (and "mouthfeel") to the dish. Cabernet Sauvignon and Syrah, with their higher tannin levels, will also often benefit from being paired with sautéed dishes containing some fat to help cut through the tannins. However, even delicate seafood (e.g., Zack's Pan-Seared "Spykick" Catfish on page 50) will benefit from quick sautéing that seals flavors and adds just a touch of fat to the fish.

The other benefit of sautéing is that it allows other ingredients and flavors to come in direct contact with the meat or fish during the cooking process. This allows flavors to become better integrated, which adds immeasurably to the success of the dish and to the wine with which it's being paired.

Braising

Braising is a cooking method that begins with the sealing of juices through a quick browning of the meat followed by the addition of a liquid, typically wine and/or stock. Once liquid is added, the dish simmers slowly under a covered top with all of the ingredients in one pot.

The obvious benefit of this type of cooking is the integration of flavors, which happens slowly but very surely. Specific flavors and ingredients are not the goal of braising, rather a merging and commingling of flavors and textures that views the whole as greater than the sum of the parts. Braising also allows wine to be used extensively in preparation of the dish, thereby suggesting a direct connection to a specific varietal.

Richer, more full-flavored whites such as Chardonnay and Viognier, as well as more full-bodied reds such as Zinfandel, Syrah, Cabernet Sauvignon, and Merlot harmonize beautifully with braised dishes. The fullness and weight of the wine are seemingly mirrored by the braising method (e.g., Braised Pork with Apples, Mushrooms, and Calvados, page 120, with a buttery Chardonnay). This makes good sense to the palate; it accepts both food and wine readily and with pleasure.

1

Spicy, salty, smoked, and highly seasoned dishes are best paired with wines that are fruity and lower in alcohol such as Riesling, Gewürztraminer, Pinot Gris/Grigio, dry rosés, and Pinot Noir. Avoid oaky and more tannic wines.

2

Richer, fattier foods pair best with heavier, full-bodied wines such as Chardonnay, Cabernet Sauvignon, Merlot, Zinfandel, and Syrah.

3

When pairing sweeter foods with wine, try to keep the sweetness in the dish less than the apparent sweetness of the wine. If necessary, sweetness in the dish can be curbed with a touch of citrus juice or vinegar.

4

Higher-acid foods, such as goat cheese, tomatoes, and citrus fruits, pair most effectively with higher-acid wines such as Sauvignon/Fumé Blanc, some Rieslings, Pinot Gris/Grigio, Zinfandel, and Pinot Noir. If the wine seems too tart for the dish, add a touch of lemon juice or vinegar to the dish.

5

In a meal progression where multiple wines will be served, serve lighter wines before more full-bodied ones. Serve dry wines before sweet ones, unless a dish with some sweetness is served early in the meal, in which case it should be matched with a wine of like sweetness. Serve lower-alcohol wines (Riesling, Sauvignon/Fumé Blanc, and Pinot Gris/Grigio) before higher-alcohol ones (Chardonnay, Viognier, Gewürztraminer, Zinfandel, Pinot Noir, Cabernet Sauvignon, and Syrah).

6

Help connect dishes to the specific wine you're serving by tasting a small amount of the wine as you're finishing a sauce or side dish so that the recipe can be "tweaked" to maximum effect. If the wine seems too tannic or bitter for the dish, a sprinkling of citrus zest or nuts can be added to the dish, for example.

7

When using wine in marinades or sauces, use a decent-quality wine. If possible, this should be the same varietal as will be matched with the dish, but it need not be the same exact wine if you wish to drink a better wine than the one with which you're cooking.

8

Grilling, roasting, sautéing, and braising are preferred cooking methods when matching dishes with most wines. Poaching and steaming are more delicate cooking methods that work best with more delicate wines such as Pinot Gris/Grigio and some Riesling. Smoking food works most effectively with lighter, fruitier wines—Riesling, Gewürztraminer, Pinot Noir, and Zinfandel.

9

Food and wine pairing is about synergy—the food should not overpower the wine, nor should the wine overpower the food.

10

Great food and wine combinations come from finding similarities and contrasts of flavor, body (texture), intensity, and basic taste. This is a highly subjective, inexact endeavor. Taste, and trust your own instincts.

White Wines

Champagne is truly like no other beverage made from grapes. Champagne represents gaiety, celebration, and success, and is capable of delighting us with its incomparable charm.

Champagne has been used for hundreds of years to celebrate important public events in the world and the no-less-great private accomplishments of mere mortals. Since it's mostly associated with special occasions, some of Champagne's real appeal — its ability to partner with food — is lost.

Because it is typically paired with appetizers, Champagne's role during the meal is not nearly as well understood as that of other wines. This has far more to do with the well-entrenched tradition of drinking Champagne out of the context of food than it does with its ability to be a compatible companion throughout the meal.

Champagne brings both effervescence and flavor to the party. The effervescence is, of course, unique to Champagne and is what allows it to partner with so many foods. It can refresh and cleanse like no other wine. Grapes for Champagne are picked very early, with higher acids, which creates added partnering potential, particularly with Asian and Latin dishes.

When it comes to smoky, salty, and spicy dishes, Champagne's capability is virtually unquestioned. However, when paired with more delicate main course dishes, like the Poached Swordfish with Champagne-Grape Sauce (page 27), it can be distinctively successful as well.

In California, the name "Champagne" is used interchangeably with "sparkling wine," but the latter is more correct since only wines produced in the French region of Champagne are theoretically real "Champagne." This is a relatively moot point because all of the better California "Champagne" and sparkling wine is made in the *méthode champenoise* style practiced in France.

The matter gets a little cloudy because there is a large quantity of inexpensive California "Champagne" produced that bears no resemblance to the elegant wines made in France. So, it's best to know your producer and look for the term *méthode champenoise* on the bottle as a sign of quality.

Champagne is produced in many different styles, ranging from bone dry to sweet. The nomenclature identifying these styles is a little confusing, but is worth knowing to ensure satisfaction with your purchase (see Champagne Styles on page 23). With French Champagne, a vintage date on a label ensures highest quality because vintages are declared only in excellent years.

Otherwise, a non-vintage Champagne will offer a very pleasant bottling, although perhaps without the complexity of a vintage-dated product.

Champagne is most often made from a blend of Pinot Noir and Chardonnay. When it is made from Pinot Noir alone, it is called *blanc de noirs*, and when it is produced from Chardonnay alone, it is called *blanc de blanc.* Rosé is produced primarily from Pinot Noir that has had a little contact with the skins so that it picks up a hint of color. Rosés can be particularly interesting wines—dry and rich with a little more complexity than golden bubbly. Most Champagne is classified as "brut" (meaning, roughly, "dry"), but a Champagne called *cremant,* or doux ("sweet"), is produced as a dessert wine. There is a range of styles between these extremes (see page 23).

Depending on the style selected, the Champagne will obviously interact very differently with food. Generally, bruts and especially *blancs de noirs* offer the greatest flexibility in partnering throughout the meal. Rosés offer surprising compatibility with meat and poultry dishes. In general, Champagne/sparkling wine offers far more potential at the table than is commonly acknowledged.

CHAMPAGNE/SPARKLING WINE

TYPICAL AROMAS & FLAVORS

Green Apple, Cherry, Strawberry, Raspberry,
Yeast, Toast, Nuts, Crab, Shrimp

BASE INGREDIENTS

*Base ingredients refer to the main ingredient
of the dish: meat, poultry, game, seafood, shellfish, or vegetable. These represent the core
ingredients that are most likely to be matched
with a varietal, although successful pairings
result as much from the other ingredients used
in the dish as they do the base ingredient.*

Lobster, Oysters, Clams, Mussels,
Shrimp, Salmon, Tuna, Monkfish,
Mackerel, Snapper, Sea Bass, Chicken,
Duck, Turkey, Quail, Veal, Pork, Eggs

BRIDGE INGREDIENTS

*Bridge ingredients help connect the food and
the wine through their interaction in flavor,
body, intensity, or basic taste.*

Smoked Salmon, Lox
Smoked Oysters
Smoked Mussels
Caviar
Sushi
Spices: Curry Powder, Ginger,
        Cayenne
Capers
Olives
Mushrooms
Soy Sauce
Avocado
Orange
Toasted Nuts: Hazelnuts,
        Almonds, Pine Nuts
Cream
Butter

BEST SOURCE REGIONS
CHAMPAGNE/SPARKLING WINE

The following is a list of countries, regions, and appellations (a wine word referencing specific growing locales) that produce the highest-quality versions of these wines.

This is not intended to be a complete list, only a reference for where the finest renditions can be found.

FRANCE
   Champagne
ITALY
   Moscato d'Asti/Asti
CALIFORNIA
   Napa
   Sonoma
   Mendocino
      Anderson Valley

CHAMPAGNE STYLES

Extra brut/blanc de blanc:
   Bone dry (under .6 percent residual sugar); delicate, austere

Brut/blanc de blanc *or* blanc de noirs:
   Off dry (under 1.5 percent sugar); medium-bodied

Extra dry:
   Off dry (1.2 to 2 percent sugar); full mouth

Sec:
   Medium-sweet (1.7 to 3.5 percent sugar); full mouth, lighter desserts

Demi-sec:
   Sweet (3.3 to 5 percent sugar); full mouth, dessert wine

Cremant or doux:
   Sweet (over 5 percent sugar); dessert wine

TIPS TO SUCCESSFUL MATCHES WITH CHAMPAGNE/SPARKLING WINE

1

Champagne/sparkling wine is the quintessential wine for smoky and salty foods as its acidity helps balance these flavors.

2

Champagne/sparkling wine is well suited as an aperitif because of its refreshing, appetite-stimulating effervescence, but it should not be disregarded as a wine for the main course as well.

3

Champagne/sparkling wine is an excellent accompaniment to brunch, particularly to egg dishes.

4

Asian foods can be served quite successfully with many Champagnes/sparkling wines because of the contrast of bold, often salty flavors with the brisk acidity of the wine.

5

Always serve Champagnes/sparkling wines well chilled.

Shrimp and Avocado Salsa in Pita Toasts (Classic Pairing)

RECOMMENDED WINE: Champagne/sparkling wine
ALTERNATIVE WINE: Pinot Gris/Grigio

THIS ZIPPY APPETIZER IS GREATLY ENHANCED BY A GOOD BRUT, WHICH CAPTURES AND HARNESSES THE SPICY, BUT NOT FIERY, JALAPEÑOS AND CONTRASTS THEM WITH BRIGHT EFFERVESCENCE. THE ACIDITY AND UNWAVERING FRESHNESS OF PINOT GRIS/GRIGIO IS ALSO QUITE EFFECTIVE IN MARRYING THE APPETIZER TO THE WINE.

¾ pound bay shrimp, drained but not rinsed

¼ cup finely chopped sweet or red onion

1½ cups chopped ripe red tomatoes

1 ripe avocado, peeled and cut into ¼-inch dice

1 jalapeño, seeded and minced

1 tablespoon fresh lime juice

2 tablespoons seafood cocktail sauce

½ cup coarsely chopped cilantro

Kosher salt

4 pita bread rounds, cut into 8 triangles each

GARNISH: cilantro sprigs (optional)

In a medium, nonreactive mixing bowl, combine shrimp, onions, tomatoes, avocado, jalapeño, lime juice, cocktail sauce, and chopped cilantro and mix thoroughly but gently. Refrigerate, covered, for 2 to 3 hours before using. Season to taste with kosher salt.

Lightly toast pita bread so that it is warmed through but not crispy. Spread pita open and spoon shrimp mixture into it. Serve on a large platter garnished with long sprigs of cilantro.

SERVES 6 TO 8 AS AN APPETIZER

Quesadillas with Smoked Mussels, Havarti, and Roasted Red Peppers

RECOMMENDED WINE: Champagne/sparkling wine
ALTERNATIVE WINE: Sauvignon/Fumé Blanc

CHAMPAGNE TRULY SPARKLES WITH MOST SMOKED FOODS. THESE QUESADILLAS FEATURE CREAMY HAVARTI CHEESE, SMOKED MUSSELS, AND DILL, WHICH ARE NATURAL FOILS FOR THE BUBBLY. A GOOD-QUALITY BRUT (OFF-DRY CHAMPAGNE) WILL WORK PERFECTLY HERE TO CONTRAST THE SMOKINESS OF THE MUSSELS AND THE SLIGHT SALTINESS OF THE CHEESE.

8 flour tortillas

1 ¾ cups shredded Havarti cheese

6 ounces smoked mussels or oysters

2 teaspoons chopped fresh dill
(1 teaspoon dried)

½ cup chopped roasted red bell peppers
(see page 116)

4 teaspoons seeded, chopped jalapeños

GARNISH: dill sprigs

Preheat oven to 350 degrees. Lay 4 tortillas out on a large baking sheet. Sprinkle cheese evenly on tortillas. Top with mussels, dill, roasted peppers, and jalapeños. Place remaining tortillas on top of each of the filled tortillas. Bake for 8 to 10 minutes or until cheese is melted. Press down tortillas after cheese begins to melt to help seal the top and bottom. Remove from oven and slice quesadillas into 4 pieces each.

Serve on a large platter with sprigs of dill.

SERVES 4 TO 6 AS AN APPETIZER

Poached Swordfish
with Champagne-Grape Sauce

RECOMMENDED WINE: Champagne/sparkling wine
ALTERNATIVE WINE: Pinot Gris/Grigio

CHAMPAGNE/SPARKLING WINE IS AN INTERESTING WINE TO USE IN COOKING BECAUSE IT HAS SO MUCH NATURAL ACIDITY. THIS RECIPE INTEGRATES IT IN A POACHING LIQUID WITH STOCK AND HERBS. THE FLAVORS ARE ON THE DELICATE SIDE, BUT THE AFFINITY IS OBVIOUS DUE TO THE CONNECTION BETWEEN THE SAUCE AND THE WINE. THE USE OF RED AND GREEN SEEDLESS GRAPES UNDERSCORES A COMMON GRAPEY CHARACTER THAT CAN BE FOUND IN MANY CHAMPAGNES/SPARKLING WINES.

1 ¼ cups fish stock

¾ cup Champagne/sparkling wine

1 tablespoon minced shallots

1 teaspoon chopped fresh thyme
(½ teaspoon dried)

½ teaspoon dry mustard

2 pounds fresh swordfish fillets

1 teaspoon drained capers

¼ cup halved green seedless grapes

¼ cup halved red seedless grapes

1 ½ tablespoons toasted chopped almonds

2 tablespoons unsalted butter at
room temperature

In a large sauté pan or skillet over medium high heat, reduce stock, Champagne, shallots, thyme, and mustard by half. Add the swordfish fillets, reduce heat to a simmer, cover, and poach for 10 to 12 minutes, until fillets are cooked through. Remove fillets and keep warm in foil.

Increase heat and reduce liquid to a consistency that coats the back of a wooden spoon. Add capers and grapes and cook for 1 to 2 minutes. Remove pan from heat and swirl in butter.

Serve swordfish with evenly divided grapes, sauce, and almonds on top. Serve with a squash purée.

SERVES 2 AS AN ENTRÉE

Sauvignon Blanc has encountered a long and winding road towards achieving real respect as a grape varietal. Part of this has to do with confusion over the name itself. The grape varietal is called Sauvignon Blanc; however, Robert Mondavi pioneered the name "Fumé Blanc" for it in the 1970s.

Subsequently, the name took hold with a number of wineries who were trying to increase interest in this lesser-known varietal and give it more cachet than it enjoyed at the time.

The Loire region in France produces "Pouilly-Fumé," an excellent wine made from Sauvignon Blanc, so the confusion is truly international in scope. To this day, the two names—Sauvignon Blanc and Fumé Blanc—are used interchangeably. They are the same wine.

Add to the confusion in nomenclature a profound difference in style in which the varietal is made, and we have an honest-to-goodness wine identity crisis. Vintners have made the wine in an overt, grassy-herbaceous style—an intense whiff of barnyard and freshly cut grass—or in a rich, barrel-fermented, almost Chardonnay style. The more herbaceous, strut-your-stuff style is controversial, but is enjoyed passionately by some wine drinkers.

Furthermore, the grape Sémillon is blended with many Sauvignon/Fumé Blancs in France, California, and Australia. Sémillon adds a rounder and fuller character to Sauvignon/Fumé Blanc that can be quite pleasant. Several wineries produce blends of these two varietals, which either have proprietary names or are called "Meritage White Table Wine." The term "Meritage" was coined by American wineries to codify a name for blends of red or white wines that are produced from several different Bordeaux varietals. The use of the name "Meritage" is decreasing rapidly.

This all being said, Sauvignon/Fumé Blanc is one of the most food-friendly wines made on the planet. Its lack of respect, to whatever extent this still exists, has precious little to do with its marvelous capabilities at the table. In terms of style and quality, significant progress is being made with this greatly underrated varietal. Wineries are learning a lot about growing the grape properly and avoiding the overtly grassy-herbaceous character that turns off some consumers.

Some of the more appealing things about Sauvignon/Fumé Blanc are that it's dry, lower in alcohol and relatively light in oak influence. For example, Sauvignon/Fumé Blanc can ably support spicy and assertively flavored dishes where Chardonnay, its big, very popular sister, falls apart completely. It also matches exceedingly well with many soups and salads, which are often tricky for wine pairing. Lastly, the varietal's prominent but not overpowering acidity allows it to balance higher-acid foods, such as goat cheese and tomatoes, quite effectively.

For all these reasons, we must pay due respect to Sauvignon/Fumé Blanc. We must forgive it for not being Chardonnay. We must allow it to be the "wild child" of the wine world. We should appreciate it for exactly what it offers: appealing aromas, a sassy fruit character, and excellent balance of fruit and acidity. And, lest we forget—the price of most Sauvignon/Fumé Blanc is very reasonable.

SAUVIGNON/FUMÉ BLANC

TYPICAL AROMAS & FLAVORS

Melon
Pear
Fig
Citrus: Grapefruit, Lemon, Lime,
    Orange
Tropical Fruit: Pineapple, Passion
    Fruit, Kiwi
Quince
Grassy
Lemongrass
Herbs: Dill, Thyme, Marjoram, Basil,
    Cilantro, Tarragon
Gooseberry
Fennel
Vanilla

BASE INGREDIENTS

*Base ingredients refer to the main ingredient
of the dish: meat, poultry, game, seafood, shellfish, or vegetable. These represent the core
ingredients that are most likely to be matched
with a varietal, although successful pairings
result as much from the other ingredients used
in the dish as they do the base ingredient.*

Shrimp, Clams, Oysters, Mussels, Scallops,
Catfish, Sole, Sea Bass, Snapper, Trout,
Swordfish, Chicken, Game Hens, Turkey

BRIDGE INGREDIENTS

*Bridge ingredients help connect the food and
the wine through their interaction in flavor,
body, intensity, or basic taste.*

Citrus: Orange, Lime, Lemon
Fennel (fresh or roasted)
Bell Peppers (fresh or roasted)
Herbs: Dill, Tarragon, Thyme, Basil,
    Chives, Cilantro, Sorrel
Spices: Curry Powder
Toasted Nuts: Hazelnuts, Pine Nuts,
    Almonds
Sour Cream, Yogurt
Mushrooms: Shiitake, Oyster, Crimini,
    Button
Cheeses: Goat, Swiss, Parmigiano-
    Reggiano, Ricotta, Brie, Feta,
    Fontina, Buffalo Mozzarella
Garlic (fresh or roasted)
Dijon Mustard
Capers
Green Olives
Ginger (fresh)
Prosciutto
Tomatoes, Sun-Dried Tomatoes
Eggplant

BEST SOURCE REGIONS
SAUVIGNON/FUMÉ BLANC

The following is a list of countries, regions, and appellations (a wine word referencing specific growing locales) that produce the highest-quality versions of these wines.

This is not intended to be a complete list, only a reference for where the finest renditions can be found.

CALIFORNIA
  Napa Valley
  Sonoma
  Mendocino
  Lake County
  Santa Barbara
WASHINGTON
FRANCE
  Loire
    Sancerre
    Pouilly-Fumé
  Bordeaux
    Graves
NEW ZEALAND
CHILE
SOUTH AFRICA

SAUVIGNON/FUMÉ BLANC STYLES

Lighter:
  Lighter body; often fermented in stainless steel rather than oak barrels; more delicate and fruity; excellent balance with good acidity

Barrel Aged:
  Medium body; richer with some toasty-oak flavors; not quite the same apparent acidity as the lighter style; sometimes blended with Sémillon

TIPS TO SUCCESSFUL MATCHES
WITH SAUVIGNON/FUMÉ BLANC

1

Sauvignon/Fumé Blanc fares well with foods that are aromatic, higher in acidity, and spicier than most.

2

Use fresh herbs whenever possible with Sauvignon/Fumé Blanc. They help complement the natural herbal quality in the wine.

3

Sauvignon/Fumé Blanc works well with many appetizers and first courses since it's light to medium bodied and sets the stage for fuller-bodied whites and heartier reds to follow.

4

Sauvignon/Fumé Blanc is the best white wine choice for many salads, soups, and green vegetable dishes.

Wild Mushroom
and Goat Cheese Bruschetta

RECOMMENDED WINE: Sauvignon/Fumé Blanc
ALTERNATIVE WINE: Champagne/sparkling wine

THIS TASTY BRUSCHETTA FEATURES THE DUO OF WILD MUSHROOMS AND GOAT CHEESE, TWO PARTICULARLY FRIENDLY INGREDIENTS TO SAUVIGNON/FUMÉ BLANC. THE EARTHY MUSHROOMS AND TANGY GOAT CHEESE MIRROR SIMILAR FLAVORS IN THE WINE AND ACCENTUATE ITS ACIDITY. A CHAMPAGNE/SPARKLING WINE WILL ALSO BENEFIT FROM THE PAIRING DUE TO ITS ACIDITY.

2 ounces oyster mushrooms

4 ounces shiitake mushrooms

5 ounces portobello mushrooms,
   inner gills removed

2 tablespoons olive oil

1 tablespoon unsalted butter

2 large garlic cloves, minced

1 shallot, minced

¼ cup dry sherry

¼ cup chicken stock

1 teaspoon dried thyme

½ teaspoon dried basil

   Kosher salt and red pepper flakes

16 thin slices of French sour baguette

3–4 ounces fresh goat cheese

GARNISH: minced lemon zest and minced
   chives, mixed together

Trim ends and coarsely chop mushrooms. In a large sauté pan or skillet over medium heat, heat olive oil and butter. Add garlic and shallot and sauté for 1 to 2 minutes, stirring frequently. Raise heat slightly and add mushrooms. Sauté for 7 to 8 minutes. Add sherry, chicken stock, thyme, and basil and cook until liquid is evaporated. Season to taste. Keep warm.

Preheat broiler. Put slices of baguette on a broiler pan and spread evenly with goat cheese. Spoon mushroom mixture evenly onto baguette slices. Broil for 3 to 4 minutes, or until mushrooms just begin to brown on top. Remove from the oven and place on serving dish. Garnish with a sprinkling of lemon zest–chive mixture.

SERVES 6 TO 8 AS AN APPETIZER

Shrimp-Scallop Pâté with Cilantro, Dill, and Pine Nuts

RECOMMENDED WINE: Sauvignon/Fumé Blanc
ALTERNATIVE WINE: Pinot Gris/Grigio

FRESH HERBS ARE AN EXCELLENT WAY TO MIRROR WHAT IS COMMONLY REGARDED AS A PLEASANTLY HERBAL NOTE IN MANY SAUVIGNON/FUMÉ BLANCS. THE COMBINATION OF SCALLOPS, SHRIMP, AND FRESH HERBS IS PERFECTLY MATCHED BY THE FRESH CITRUS FRUIT AND HERBAL FLAVORS IN THE WINE. SELECT FRUITIER, NON–BARREL FERMENTED SAUVIGNON/FUMÉ BLANC OR LIGHT, CRISP PINOT GRIS/GRIGIO, AS OAKIER WINES WILL OVERPOWER THIS DELICATE APPETIZER. THIS IS ADAPTED FROM AN OLD *SUNSET* MAGAZINE RECIPE.

4 ounces bay scallops

½ tablespoon unsalted butter

4 ounces bay shrimp

¾ cup spicy V-8 juice

1 envelope unflavored gelatin

2 tablespoons chopped fresh dill (1 tablespoon dried)

2 tablespoons chopped cilantro

1 tablespoon fresh lemon juice

¼ teaspoon white-wine Worcestershire sauce

¼ teaspoon Tabasco or other hot sauce

1 cup sour cream

¼ cup toasted pine nuts

Kosher salt and ground white pepper

GARNISH: thin slices of lemon, cilantro sprigs

In a medium sauté pan or skillet over medium heat, sauté scallops in butter for 3 to 4 minutes. Remove with a slotted spoon and coarsely chop in a food processor along with the shrimp. Reserve.

In a small pot, add V-8 juice and sprinkle in gelatin. Let stand for 7 to 8 minutes. Over medium heat, stir until the gelatin is dissolved. Remove from heat and cool. Add dill, cilantro, lemon juice, Worcestershire, Tabasco, sour cream, pine nuts, and scallop-shrimp mixture. Whisk thoroughly to combine. Season to taste and adjust with more hot sauce, if desired. The overall flavor should be delicate, not spicy.

Pour mixture into a plastic-lined 2½-cup mold (fish designs are particularly pretty) with the plastic well pressed into the mold design and over the top. This helps in removing the pâté. Cover and refrigerate for at least 4 hours or up to overnight. Remove cover from the top of mold.

To serve, unmold carefully onto a serving plate and garnish with lemon slices and cilantro sprigs. Keep chilled until ready to serve. Serve with crackers.

SERVES 10 AS AN APPETIZER

Roasted Eggplant-Garlic Soup

RECOMMENDED WINE: Sauvignon/Fumé Blanc
ALTERNATIVE WINE: Zinfandel

THIS RUSTIC SOUP, REDOLENT OF ROASTED GARLIC AND FRESH HERBS, PROVIDES A HEARTY FRAMEWORK FOR THE SASSY KICK OF SAUVIGNON/FUMÉ BLANC. THE FLAVORS OF THE WINE ACCENTUATE THE EGGPLANT, ROASTED GARLIC, AND FRESH HERBS, WHILE ITS FRUITINESS AND FRESH BURST OF ACIDITY CUT THROUGH THE RICHNESS OF THE SOUP AND PROVIDE REFRESHING CONTRAST. ZINFANDEL, WITH ITS RUSTIC CHARACTER AND GOOD ACIDITY, IS A RED WINE OPTION THAT'S PARTICULARLY EFFECTIVE WHEN THE SOUP IS BEING SERVED AS A MAIN COURSE WITH CRUSTY FRENCH BREAD.

1 large globe eggplant (about 1 pound)
Kosher salt and freshly ground black pepper
1 whole head garlic
Olive oil
1¾ cups chopped red onions
½ cup chopped fresh basil (¼ cup dried)

1 tablespoon chopped fresh thyme (½ tablespoon dried)
½ teaspoon red pepper flakes
3 cups seeded, chopped tomatoes
4½ cups chicken stock
GARNISH: basil sprigs, chopped red bell pepper

Preheat oven to 375°F. Trim ends of eggplant; leave skin on. Rinse, pat dry, and cut into ¼-inch rounds. Sprinkle with salt and pepper. Place on paper towels for 20 to 30 minutes to remove excess water.

Cut the top off of garlic head and sprinkle lightly with olive oil, salt, and pepper. Wrap in foil, leaving it a little open at top. Place eggplant and garlic on a lightly oiled baking sheet and roast for 15 minutes. Remove eggplant and continue roasting garlic for 35 minutes more. Chop eggplant into 1-inch pieces.

In a large soup pot, heat 1 tablespoon olive oil over medium heat. Add onions, basil, thyme, and pepper flakes and sauté for 5 to 6 minutes, or until onions are translucent. Squeeze garlic out of head, making sure that the flaky peel does not get mixed in, and add it to the pot. Add eggplant, tomatoes, and stock and bring soup to a boil. Reduce heat, cover, and cook for 10 to 12 minutes.

Remove from pot and transfer to a food processor or blender. Purée in batches. Soup can be refrigerated at this point.

Heat thoroughly before serving. Season to taste. Top with basil sprigs and chopped red bell pepper.

SERVES 8 AS AN APPETIZER OR 4 AS AN ENTRÉE

Black-eyed Pea and Tomato Soup with Cabbage

RECOMMENDED WINE: Sauvignon/Fumé Blanc
ALTERNATIVE WINE: Pinot Noir

M Y WIFE, ALTHOUGH NOT BORN IN THE SOUTH, IS A SUPERSTITIOUS BELLE IN HER OWN RIGHT. SHE CONVINCED ME LONG AGO THAT IT WAS GOOD LUCK TO HAVE BLACK-EYED PEAS AND CABBAGE ON NEW YEAR'S DAY. THIS SOUP IS A DELICIOUS WAY TO ENSURE GOOD FORTUNE. IT IS FRIENDLY TO SAUVIGNON/FUMÉ BLANC BECAUSE OF THE CONTRAST OF THE HEARTY SOUP AND THE FRUITY, YOUNG WINE, AND IT'S INCREDIBLY KIND TO HANGOVERS, SHOULD THAT BE AN ISSUE. SOUP AND WINE ARE NOT AN EASY PAIRING BECAUSE TWO LIQUIDS WITH DIFFERENT TEMPERATURES TEND TO CONFUSE THE PALATE. HOWEVER, THIS MATCH WORKS PARTICULARLY WELL, DUE TO THE COMPLEMENTARY FLAVORS. IT IS PARTICULARLY ENJOYABLE WHEN FIRST COOKED BECAUSE OF THE FRESH CRUNCH OF THE SLIGHTLY UNDERCOOKED VEGETABLES. REHEATED, IT LOSES A LITTLE OF THE CRUNCH, BUT THE FLAVORS BLEND TOGETHER SEAMLESSLY.

2 cups fresh or frozen black-eyed peas

4 ounces diced ham

3 tablespoons olive oil

3 cloves garlic, chopped

1 large red onion, peeled and chopped (about 2 cups)

1¼ cups chopped carrots

3 celery stalks, chopped (about 2 cups)

1 teaspoon dried chervil or thyme

1 teaspoon *fines herbes* (see NOTE)

1 teaspoon caraway seed

1 14½-ounce can chopped tomatoes with juice

1 11½-ounce can spicy V-8 juice

4 cups chicken stock

1½ cups chopped green cabbage

Kosher salt and red pepper flakes

GARNISH: chopped parsley, grated Parmesan cheese

In a large stockpot, cover black-eyed peas in cold, salted water and add diced ham. Bring to a boil, reduce heat and simmer, covered, for 15 minutes. Peas should be tender and slightly al dente. Drain and reserve peas and ham.

In the same large stockpot over medium-high heat, heat oil. Add garlic, onions, carrots, celery, herbs, and spices and sauté for 6 to 7 minutes, until onions are translucent. Don't overcook; the vegetables should remain al dente. Add tomatoes, juice, and stock. Bring to a boil, then reduce heat, and simmer, covered, for 10 minutes. Add cabbage and reserved black-eyed peas and ham for last 4 to 5 minutes. Don't overcook; part of the pleasure of the dish is the crispness of the cabbage.

Spoon into soup bowls and garnish with chopped parsley and grated Parmesan. Season to taste. Serve with crusty, sourdough garlic French bread.

NOTE: *Fines herbes* is a mixture of chervil, chives, tarragon, and parsley and can be purchased bottled in the spice aisle of most grocery stores.

SERVES 6 TO 8 AS AN APPETIZER

Sid's Caesar

RECOMMENDED WINE: Sauvignon/Fumé Blanc
ALTERNATIVE WINE: Pinot Gris/Grigio

I SUPPOSE THAT A CAESAR SALAD IS NOT A CULINARY REVELATION, BUT I MUST SHARE THIS ONE WITH YOU. ORIGINALLY INSPIRED BY TWO CULINARY FRIENDS, MARY SUE MILLIKEN AND SUSAN FENIGER FROM SANTA MONICA'S BORDER GRILL, THIS CROWD-PLEASING CAESAR IS NOT ONLY DELICIOUS, BUT IT IS AN INSPIRING FOOD AND WINE COMBINATION TO BOOT. THE TART, CRISP FRUIT OF A GOOD SAUVIGNON/FUMÉ BLANC OR PINOT GRIS/GRIGIO CONTRASTS BEAUTIFULLY WITH THE SALTY ANCHOVIES AND PARMESAN.

7 anchovy fillets, chopped

⅓ teaspoon freshly ground black pepper

¾ tablespoon chopped roasted garlic (see page 164)

¾ cup extra-virgin olive oil

½ cup grated Parmesan cheese

4 slices sourdough or other hearty French or Italian bread

1 egg

2 tablespoons red-wine vinegar

1½ tablespoons fresh lemon juice

1½ teaspoons dry mustard

½ teaspoon celery salt

1 teaspoon minced lemon zest

⅛ teaspoon Tabasco or other hot sauce

½ teaspoon white-wine Worcestershire sauce

1¾ pounds romaine lettuce, cut into bite-sized pieces

Preheat oven (or toaster oven) to 375°F.

In a food processor or blender, combine anchovies, pepper, roasted garlic, and olive oil and process for 1 minute until smooth. Add grated Parmesan and process for 30 seconds. Remove 3 tablespoons of dressing.

Using a brush, spread mixture evenly on both sides of sliced bread. Bake bread for 20 minutes, or until a nice crust develops. Do not burn. Break or cut toast into bite-sized, "crouton-like" pieces.

In a small saucepan filled more than halfway with water, bring water to boil. Place a refrigerated egg into water and boil for 1 minute and 15 seconds. Remove with a slotted spoon and let cool.

Place anchovy–olive oil mixture in a large, nonreactive bowl and add red-wine vinegar, lemon juice, mustard, celery salt, lemon zest, Tabasco, and white-wine Worcestershire. Spoon entire egg carefully out of shell and add to the mixture. Whisk thoroughly and refrigerate until ready to toss salad.

To serve, place cold romaine in a large salad bowl. Whisk dressing thoroughly and adjust seasoning, if necessary. Add to salad and toss vigorously. Add croutons and continue tossing to coat croutons. Serve on well-chilled salad plates.

SERVES 6 AS AN APPETIZER

Chilled Leeks with Green Olives, Capers, and Sun-Dried Tomato Vinaigrette (Classic Pairing)

RECOMMENDED WINE: Sauvignon/Fumé Blanc
ALTERNATIVE WINE: Pinot Gris/Grigio

THIS RECIPE IS REMINISCENT OF THE RUSTIC FARE OF PROVENCE IN ITS USE OF MEDITERRANEAN INGREDIENTS, BUT IT'S VERY "CALIFORNIA" AT THE SAME TIME. THIS IS A PERFECT WARM-WEATHER DISH SINCE IT'S SERVED CHILLED. AS A FLAVOR SHOWCASE FOR THE CRISP, SLIGHTLY "GREEN" CHARACTER OF SAUVIGNON/FUMÉ BLANC, THIS DISH OFFERS SUN-DRIED TOMATOES, OLIVES, AND CAPERS—ALL FRIENDLY INGREDIENTS TO THE WINE. PINOT GRIS/GRIGIO OFFERS SIMILARLY BRIGHT ACIDITY, ALTHOUGH NOT QUITE THE FLAVOR INTEREST.

4 medium leeks

2 eggs

⅔ cup thinly sliced sun-dried tomatoes packed in oil

3 tablespoons balsamic vinegar

2 teaspoons Dijon mustard

¼ teaspoon kosher salt

¼ teaspoon black pepper or more to taste

1¼ tablespoons capers

¼ cup pitted, chopped green olives

⅓ cup olive oil

Kosher salt

GARNISH: chopped hard-boiled egg

Trim dark green tops of leeks so that only a tiny part of the green remains. Leave slightly trimmed root attached to keep leeks held together.

Bring a large pot of salted water to a steady boil. Add leeks and simmer, covered, for 10 to 12 minutes. Leeks should be tender and cooked through. Remove from water with tongs and place in an ice bath. Place eggs in the same boiling water and cook for 10 minutes, until hard-boiled. Remove with tongs and let cool. Chop eggs and reserve for garnish.

When leeks are cooled, slice in half lengthwise without cutting all the way through. Remove outer part of leeks. Pull top green part of leeks apart and rinse out any grit under cold water. Drain leeks and chill for 2 hours. If a quick chill is needed, leeks can be placed in the freezer for 20 to 30 minutes.

In a small, nonreactive mixing bowl, combine sun-dried tomatoes, vinegar, mustard, salt, pepper, capers, and green olives. Drizzle oil into bowl while whisking thoroughly. Season to taste. Adjust balance of vinaigrette if necessary. Refrigerate.

To serve, divide leeks evenly on chilled plates, fanning out leaves slightly and leaving them attached to the root. Whisk vinaigrette thoroughly and drizzle over top of leeks. Any remaining vinaigrette can be used as a topping for seafood or salad. Garnish with chopped hard-boiled egg.

SERVES 4 AS AN APPETIZER OR SIDE DISH

Mixed Greens with Thyme-Scented Goat Cheese Cakes and Balsamic-Dijon Vinaigrette

RECOMMENDED WINE: Sauvignon/Fumé Blanc
ALTERNATIVE WINE: Pinot Gris/Grigio

Matching salads and salad dressings with wine is nothing short of a trick. Vinegar, for the most part, robs wine of its apparent acid and strips it of its flavor. The exception is balsamic vinegar, which has a sweeter quality than other vinegar, making it far more wine-friendly. This simple but delicious salad relies on tart, creamy goat cheese, a particularly harmonious ingredient with good acidity, to partner with the tangy taste of Sauvignon/Fumé Blanc. The brisk acidity of Pinot Gris/Grigio allows it to be a natural pairing partner as well.

8 ounces fresh goat cheese

2 tablespoons olive oil

3 teaspoons chopped fresh thyme
(1 ½ teaspoons dried)

¼ cup plain bread crumbs

1 teaspoon dried thyme

⅛ teaspoon crushed black pepper

⅛ teaspoon kosher salt

¼ cup balsamic vinegar

1 teaspoon Dijon mustard

¾ cup olive oil

Kosher salt and freshly ground black pepper

12 ounces mixed salad greens

GARNISH: edible flowers (optional)

Form 12 small rounds of goat cheese and put in a small, low-rimmed glass dish. Top with olive oil and chopped fresh thyme and let sit for 1 hour, refrigerated.

In a small mixing bowl, combine bread crumbs, dried thyme, ⅛ teaspoon pepper, and ⅛ teaspoon salt. Coat goat cheese rounds with bread crumb mixture on top and bottom.

In another small mixing bowl, add vinegar and mustard and whisk thoroughly. Slowly drizzle in olive oil while whisking. Season to taste and reserve.

Preheat oven to 350°F. Place goat cheese rounds on a baking sheet and bake for 15 minutes, until golden brown. Remove with a spatula.

To serve, place salad greens in a large bowl. Combine with vinaigrette and mix thoroughly. Divide salad evenly on 6 salad plates. Top with 2 goat cheese cakes per plate. Garnish with edible flowers.

SERVES 6 AS AN APPETIZER

Radish Slaw with Rémoulade and Pistachios

RECOMMENDED WINE: Sauvignon/Fumé Blanc
ALTERNATIVE WINE: Pinot Gris/Grigio

THE TANGY BITE AND BITTERNESS OF RADISHES PROVIDE INTERESTING FLAVOR COMPONENTS FOR WINE MATCHING, PARTICULARLY WHEN AMPLIFIED BY A LIGHTLY SPICY RÉMOULADE. IN THIS CASE, THE CRISP, FRUITY CHARACTER OF SAUVIGNON/FUMÉ BLANC IS THE PERFECT COUNTERPOINT TO THE BITTERNESS AND CREAMY TEXTURE OF THE "SLAW." AN OREGON PINOT GRIS WITH A HINT OF FULLNESS AND A CRISP ACID BACKBONE IS A WORTHWHILE OPTION. THIS DISH IS A GREAT ACCOMPANIMENT TO A SUMMER BARBECUE, PARTICULARLY WITH GRILLED LAMB OR PORK DISHES.

RÉMOULADE

1 egg

2 tablespoons fresh lemon juice

1½ tablespoons coarse-grained mustard

¼ teaspoon kosher salt

¼ teaspoon freshly ground black pepper

½ cup olive oil

2 teaspoons tomato paste

1 tablespoon chopped parsley

1 tablespoon minced chives

½ tablespoon chopped fresh thyme
  (¼ tablespoon dried)

1 tablespoon capers

2 tablespoons chopped cornichons
  or dill pickles

½ teaspoon liquid from canned chipotle
  chiles in adobo or hot sauce (optional)

———

1 large daikon radish (about 8 ounces),
  peeled and diced

1 bunch red radishes (about 10 radishes),
  stemmed and thinly sliced

3 stalks celery, diced

⅓ cup shelled pistachios

6 ounces mixed greens (optional)

To prepare the rémoulade, place egg in a slotted spoon and place in boiling water for 90 seconds to cook egg slightly.

Scoop out egg and put into a food processor or blender along with lemon juice, mustard, salt, and pepper. With motor running, slowly add olive oil and process until mixture becomes emulsified. Add tomato paste, parsley, chives, thyme, capers, cornichons, and chile liquid and continue to process until well mixed. Adjust seasonings.

Combine radishes and celery in a large bowl. Add ½ cup or slightly more of the rémoulade to coat completely. Mix thoroughly. Save the remaining rémoulade for sandwiches or as a condiment for seafood dishes (will keep in refrigerator for 3 to 5 days). Mix thoroughly and refrigerate for 2 to 3 hours.

Prior to serving, add pistachios and mix thoroughly, saving a few pistachios to garnish on top. Serve on top of evenly divided mixed greens if serving as a plated salad.

SERVES 6 AS AN APPETIZER OR ACCOMPANIMENT

Roasted Potato and Carrot Salad
with Basil-Citrus Dressing

RECOMMENDED WINE: Sauvignon/Fumé Blanc
ALTERNATIVE WINE: Riesling

T HIS IS A CONTEMPORARY SPIN ON POTATO SALAD WITH A FRESH, CLEAN, CITRUS-HERBAL TASTE AND A LUSH TEXTURE, MAKING IT A GREAT ADDITION TO SUMMER BARBECUES. THE VEGETABLES ARE ALL ROASTED, WHICH BRINGS OUT A NATURAL SWEETNESS IN THEM THAT WORKS WELL WITH SAUVIGNON/FUMÉ BLANC. A CITRUS-BASED SOUR CREAM DRESSING REPLACES THE MORE TRADITIONAL MAYONNAISE-BASED ONE AND HELPS ACCENTUATE THE CITRUSY FLAVORS IN THE WINE. THE FRUITINESS AND FRESHNESS OF A GOOD GERMAN OR ALSATIAN RIESLING IS ALSO AN EXCELLENT COUNTERPOINT TO THE DRESSING.

3 pounds small new or purple potatoes, rinsed

1½ pounds carrots, peeled

2 tablespoons olive oil

¾ teaspoon kosher salt

½ teaspoon freshly ground black pepper

1 pound cherry tomatoes, halved (mixed red and yellow, if available)

DRESSING

3 green onions, minced

¾ cup chopped fresh basil

1 tablespoon fresh lemon juice

3 tablespoons fresh orange juice

½ tablespoon fresh lime juice

¾ cup sour cream

1 tablespoon Dijon mustard

½ tablespoon honey

¼ teaspoon jalapeño Tabasco or other hot sauce

¼ cup olive oil

Kosher salt and freshly ground black pepper

Preheat oven to 375°F. Prick potatoes in several places with a fork. Place potatoes and carrots in a large ovenproof dish or baking sheet. Drizzle with oil, using hands to coat the vegetables, and sprinkle with salt and pepper. Roast for 1 hour.

Remove from oven and cool. Quarter potatoes and cut carrots into 1-inch, bite-sized pieces. Place in a large, nonreactive bowl. Add tomatoes.

To prepare the dressing, combine green onions, basil, citrus juices, sour cream, mustard, honey, and Tabasco and whisk thoroughly. Add olive oil in a slow drizzle while whisking. Season to taste.

Add dressing to potato mixture and mix thoroughly to coat vegetables. Season to taste. Refrigerate for 2 to 3 hours, covered, before serving. Serve at room temperature.

SERVES 6 AS AN APPETIZER OR SIDE DISH

Prawn–Celery Root Salad with Ruby Grapefruit and Toasted Pine Nuts

RECOMMENDED WINE: Sauvignon/Fumé Blanc
ALTERNATIVE WINE: Pinot Gris/Grigio

THE INTERPLAY OF SWEET PRAWNS, TART GRAPEFRUIT, REFRESHINGLY BITTER CELERY ROOT, AND A BALANCING TOASTED-NUT NOTE CREATES A BACKGROUND OF DELICATE SWEET-TART-BITTER COMPONENTS TO HEIGHTEN THE CITRUS-HERBAL FLAVORS OF SAUVIGNON/FUMÉ BLANC. TEXTURALLY, THE WEIGHT OF THE DISH SUPPORTS THE BODY OF THE WINE QUITE NICELY.

DRESSING

⅓ cup fresh ruby grapefruit juice

2 teaspoons honey

½ teaspoon hot sauce (Inner Beauty brand preferred)

1 cup sour cream

¼ teaspoon white-wine Worcestershire

½ teaspoon celery salt

———

1 pound cooked, peeled, and deveined prawns

2 heads celery root (about 1¾ pounds), peeled and shredded

3 tablespoons minced green onions

3 tablespoons chopped parsley

4 plum tomatoes, seeded and chopped

3 whole ruby grapefruit, peeled and sectioned with white membrane removed

Kosher salt and freshly ground black pepper

1 large head butter lettuce

GARNISH: toasted pine nuts

To make dressing, in a small, nonreactive mixing bowl, combine all ingredients and whisk thoroughly.

In a larger bowl, combine prawns, celery root, green onions, parsley, tomatoes, and grapefruit sections and mix together thoroughly. Add whisked dressing and refrigerate, covered, for 2 to 3 hours. Season to taste.

Gently pull off whole leaves of lettuce, rinse, and dry. Place lettuce cups on chilled salad plates. Spoon prawn–celery root mixture into lettuce cups and top with toasted pine nuts.

SERVES 4 AS AN APPETIZER

Pizza with Peppered Shrimp, Canadian Bacon, Mushrooms, and Feta Cheese

RECOMMENDED WINE: Sauvignon/Fumé Blanc
ALTERNATIVE WINE: Zinfandel

THIS FLAVORFUL PIZZA, FEATURING PEPPERY SHRIMP, SMOKY CANADIAN BACON, MUSHROOMS, AND TANGY FETA CHEESE, IS A GREAT EXAMPLE OF HOW A DISH CAN MARRY ALMOST EQUALLY WELL WITH A DRY WHITE WINE AND A ROBUST, FRUITY RED. THE SAUVIGNON/FUMÉ BLANC COMBINATION CLICKS AS THE CRISP, FRUITY WHITE WINE CONTRASTS WITH THE SMOKY HAM, WHILE ACCENTUATING THE SHRIMP AND FETA CHEESE. THE ZINFANDEL MATCH PLEASES WITH THE WINE'S ABILITY TO HARMONIZE WITH ALL OF THESE FLAVORS IN ADDITION TO AMPLIFYING THE LIVELY TOMATO SAUCE. AN INTRIGUING FOOD AND WINE CONUNDRUM—TRY BOTH! IF HOMEMADE PIZZA DOUGH IS NOT WORTH IT, A PRE-MADE CRUST WILL SUFFICE. HOWEVER, THIS IS A TASTY DOUGH RECIPE.

PIZZA DOUGH

- 1 cup warm tap water (110° to 115°F on an instant-read thermometer)
- 2 teaspoons granulated sugar
- 1 envelope (¼ ounce) active dry yeast
- ¼ cup plus ½ tablespoon extra-virgin olive oil
- 3 cups all-purpose flour
- 1½ teaspoons kosher salt
- ¼ teaspoon ground white pepper
- 2½ tablespoons chopped mixed herbs (parsley, basil, oregano)
- 2½ tablespoons chopped sun-dried tomatoes packed in oil
- Sprinkling of cornmeal

TOPPING

- ¾ cup tomato sauce
- 2 cloves chopped roasted garlic (see page 164)
- 4 teaspoons chopped fresh dill (2 teaspoons dried)
- ⅛ teaspoon kosher salt
- ½ teaspoon freshly ground black pepper
- 1 teaspoon fresh lemon juice
- ¼ cup diced Canadian bacon or ham
- ¾ cup sliced crimini or shiitake mushrooms
- ¼ cup chopped roasted red peppers (see page 116)
- 2 ounces crumbled feta cheese
- 10 large shrimp, shelled and deveined
- Red pepper flakes, crushed

To make pizza dough, in a small mixing bowl, combine warm water, sugar, and yeast, stirring to make sure yeast dissolves. Let stand at room temperature until a foam begins to appear, about 8 to 10 minutes. The color will be a nutty beige. Add ¼ cup of the olive oil to the yeast mixture while stirring for 15 to 20 seconds.

In a food processor fitted with a steel blade, add flour, salt, and pepper. Process for 10 seconds to mix. Add the herbs and sun-dried tomatoes and process for a few seconds. With the machine running, slowly pour in the olive oil–yeast mixture and process until the mixture comes together in a ball, about 30 to 45 seconds.

Remove dough from the food processor and place on a lightly floured surface. Knead the dough by pressing it down and away from you with the back of your hand for about 5 to 8 minutes, or until the

RECIPE CONTINUES

Pizza with Peppered Shrimp, Canadian Bacon, Mushrooms, and Feta Cheese
CONTINUED

dough is smooth and elastic. This can be tested by placing your thumb in the middle of the dough. It should rise back up slowly. If dough is too dry, add more warm water and knead until dough achieves the proper consistency. If it is too sticky, add small amounts of flour.

Place dough in a large mixing bowl coated with ½ tablespoon olive oil. Roll dough in oil so that a thin layer covers it. Cover bowl with plastic and let dough rise in a warm place for about 1½ hours (an unheated oven works well), or until it has doubled in size.

Place dough on a lightly floured surface and punch it down several times to remove air bubbles. Place dough on a 12-inch pizza pan that has been dusted lightly with flour and cornmeal. Using hands, stretch dough out and press it down to a ½ -inch thickness to fill the pan, keeping the edges a little thicker.

To make topping, in a small mixing bowl, whisk together tomato sauce, roasted garlic, dill, salt, ¼ teaspoon black pepper, and lemon juice. Spread evenly on to pizza. Top pizza with Canadian bacon, mushrooms, peppers, and feta cheese. Sprinkle ¼ teaspoon black pepper on to shrimp and space them evenly on pizza. Sprinkle with red pepper flakes.

Preheat oven to 450°F. Bake pizza on the top rack of the oven for 16 to 18 minutes or until crust is golden brown. Slice into pieces and serve.

SERVES 2 TO 3 AS AN ENTRÉE

"May you never want for wine, nor for a friend to help drink it."

FRENCH PROVERB

Risotto with Lemon Shrimp, Roasted Garlic, and Goat Cheese

RECOMMENDED WINE: Sauvignon/Fumé Blanc
ALTERNATIVE WINE: Chardonnay

P LAYING OFF THE CITRUS CHARACTER FOUND IN MANY SAUVIGNON/FUMÉ BLANCS, THIS DISH MARRIES LEMONY SHRIMP AND TART GOAT CHEESE WITH THE NUTTY CHARACTER OF ROASTED GARLIC, WHICH ADDS A HEADY PERFUME TO THE DISH. A LIGHTLY OAKED CHARDONNAY WILL ALSO WORK WITH THIS DISH, OFFERING A SLIGHTLY MORE FULL-BODIED CHARACTER ALONG WITH CITRUS-LIKE FLAVORS TO ACCENT THE LEMONY SHRIMP.

MARINADE

- 1 ½ tablespoons fresh lemon juice
- 1 teaspoon chopped lemon zest
- ¼ teaspoon red pepper flakes
- ⅛ teaspoon kosher salt
- ¼ teaspoon dried dill
- 1 tablespoon olive oil
- 1 tablespoon white wine

———

- 12 ounces medium shrimp, peeled and deveined
- 2 tablespoons olive oil
- 2 tablespoons unsalted butter

- ½ cup chopped shiitake mushrooms
- 2 tablespoons chopped shallots
- 1 ½ cups Arborio rice
- ¾ cup white wine
- 2 tablespoons lemon juice
- 2–3 cups hot chicken stock
- ⅓ cup crumbled goat cheese
- 2 tablespoons chopped roasted garlic (see page 164)
- 1 teaspoon minced lemon zest
- 2 tablespoons chopped green onions
- GARNISH: 12 cherry tomatoes, halved

To make marinade, combine all ingredients in a medium, nonreactive bowl and whisk thoroughly. Add shrimp and marinate, covered and refrigerated, for 1 to 2 hours.

Just prior to cooking the risotto, pour contents of marinade with shrimp into a medium sauce pan and cook for 3 to 4 minutes, or until shrimp are pink and just cooked through. Remove shrimp from pan with a slotted spoon and keep warm.

To make risotto, in a large saucepan over medium heat, heat olive oil and 1 tablespoon butter. Add mushrooms and shallots and sauté for 3 to 4 minutes, stirring frequently. Add rice and continue cooking for 4 to 5 minutes, stirring continuously to coat rice with oil-butter mixture.

Carefully add the wine and lemon juice (as it may steam up when poured into the hot pan) and simmer until it is nearly evaporated. Start adding the heated stock in ½ cup increments and slowly stir until each addition of stock is absorbed into the rice. After 2 cups have been added, taste the rice to see if it is cooked al dente (cooked completely through but slightly firm). If not, continue adding small amounts of stock until the rice is al dente. Add the goat cheese, roasted garlic, lemon zest, green onions, warm shrimp, and 1 tablespoon butter and stir thoroughly while still on heat.

To serve, heat large soup bowls and place risotto in the middle of the bowls. Place 3 to 4 shrimp alternated with 4 halved cherry tomatoes around the perimeter of each bowl.

SERVES 6 AS AN APPETIZER OR 4 AS AN ENTRÉE

Pappardelle Frutti di Mare "Mediterraneo"

RECOMMENDED WINE: Sauvignon/Fumé Blanc

ALTERNATIVE WINE: Pinot Gris/Grigio

THIS IS A RELATIVELY TRADITIONAL SEAFOOD PASTA THAT PACKS A LOT OF FLAVOR INTO ITS TOMATO-BASED SAUCE. THE INTENSITY OF THE SAUCE AND SLIGHT SPICINESS FROM THE RED PEPPER FLAKES ARE BEAUTIFULLY COMPLEMENTED BY AN UN-OAKY SAUVIGNON/FUMÉ BLANC OR A CRISP PINOT GRIS/GRIGIO IN A CLASSIC FOOD AND WINE MARRIAGE. THIS RECIPE CONJURES UP BEAUTIFUL MEDITERRANEAN FISHING VILLAGES, BUT WILL CREATE PLEASURE WHEREVER YOU MAY BE.

- 2 tablespoons olive oil
- 2 teaspoons chopped shallots
- 1 tablespoon chopped garlic
- 1 pound mixed seafood (cleaned calamari, cut into rings, bay scallops, rock shrimp)
- 12 ounces fresh sea bass, cut into small pieces
- ½ cup dry white wine
- ½ cup fish or chicken stock
- 1 cup chopped fresh tomatoes
- 2 tablespoons tomato paste
- ½ cup chopped sun-dried tomatoes packed in oil
- ½ cup tomato sauce
- ½ teaspoon toasted fennel seed, crushed
- 1 teaspoon dried oregano
- ½ teaspoon saffron threads (optional)
- ½ teaspoon red pepper flakes
- Kosher salt and freshly ground black pepper
- 1 pound fresh pappardelle or fettuccine
- GARNISH: freshly grated Parmesan, chopped parsley

Bring a large pot of salted water to a boil.

In a large sauté pan or skillet over medium heat, add oil, shallots, and garlic and cook for 1 to 2 minutes, stirring to prevent shallots and garlic from browning. Add mixed seafood and sea bass and continue sautéing for 3 to 4 minutes, stirring frequently. Add wine, stock, tomatoes, tomato paste, sun-dried tomatoes, tomato sauce, fennel seed, oregano, saffron, and red pepper flakes. Bring to a boil, then reduce heat, and simmer for 7 to 8 minutes, stirring occasionally. Season to taste.

Add pappardelle to the boiling water and cook for 3 to 4 minutes, until al dente. Strain noodles. Immediately distribute noodles evenly onto 4 plates. Top with sauce. Sprinkle with freshly grated Parmesan and chopped parsley.

SERVES 6 TO 8 AS AN APPETIZER OR 4 AS AN ENTRÉE

Zack's Pan-Seared "Spykick" Catfish with Tomatillo–Root Vegetable Gratin

RECOMMENDED WINE: Sauvignon/Fumé Blanc
ALTERNATIVE WINE: Pinot Gris/Grigio

M Y SON, ZACK, COINED THE WORD "SPYKICK" (PRONOUNCED "SPY-KICK") TO REFER TO ANYTHING THAT IS SPICY AND HAS A LITTLE KICK TO IT. I'VE DEDICATED THIS DISH TO HIM–AN INTRIGUING COMBINATION OF SPICY, PAN-SEARED CATFISH WITH A SWEET-TART-SMOKY GRATIN. THE FRUITY, TART, AND OFTEN SMOKY CHARACTER OF SAUVIGNON/FUMÉ BLANC ECHOES THE TART FLAVORS OF THE TOMATILLOS AND THE SMOKY MOZZARELLA AND HELPS TAME THE "SPYKICK" CATFISH WITH ITS CRISPNESS.

GRATIN

- 2 tablespoons olive oil
- 2 cups sliced yellow onions
- 3 cloves garlic, chopped
- 1 pound tomatillos, husked, rinsed, and quartered
- 2½ tablespoons minced jalapeños
- 2 teaspoons chopped fresh basil (1 teaspoon dried)
- 2 teaspoons chopped fresh thyme (1 teaspoon dried)
- ½ cup white wine
- 1 pound rutabagas or parsnips, peeled and sliced horizontally into ½-inch pieces
- 1 pound Yukon Gold or other yellow-fleshed potatoes, thinly sliced

- 8 ounces smoked mozzarella cheese, grated (about 1½ cups)

—

- 1 tablespoon sweet paprika
- ½ teaspoon dried thyme
- ¾ tablespoon dried basil
- 1 teaspoon cayenne pepper
- ½ teaspoon kosher salt
- ¼ teaspoon freshly ground black pepper
- 1¾ pounds catfish fillets
- 2 tablespoons unsalted butter

GARNISH: chopped roasted yellow pepper (see page 116)

To make gratin, in a large sauté pan or skillet over medium-high heat, heat oil. Add onions, garlic, tomatillos, jalapeños, and herbs and sauté for 8 to 10 minutes. Add wine, cover, and simmer for 3 to 4 minutes.

Preheat oven to 375°F. In a large, 9-by-13-inch rectangular, lightly oiled Pyrex baking dish, place a thin layer of tomatillo mixture on bottom. Then place a layer of rutabagas on top, followed by a layer of cheese and then a layer of potatoes. Repeat sequence again and top with a sprinkling of cheese.

Put in the oven and bake for 45 minutes. Cover and continue cooking for 10 minutes more. Remove and let rest, covered, for 8 to 10 minutes before serving.

Meanwhile, combine paprika, herbs, cayenne, salt, and black pepper in a small bowl and mix thoroughly. Rub onto catfish on both sides. In a large sauté pan or skillet over high heat, melt butter. Add catfish and quickly sear for 3 to 4 minutes. Turn and continue searing for 2 to 3 minutes, or until done. Remove from pan and place on plates. Place squares of gratin on the side. Garnish with chopped roasted yellow pepper.

SERVES 4 AS AN ENTRÉE

Grilled Sea Bass with Mango–Roasted Red Pepper Relish

RECOMMENDED WINE: Sauvignon/Fumé Blanc
ALTERNATIVE WINE: Chardonnay

HERE'S A NICE WEEKNIGHT SEAFOOD DISH FOR TWO, WHICH CAN BE DOUBLED OR TRIPLED AS NEED BE. THE RICH, MEATY QUALITY OF SEA BASS (PARTICULARLY CHILEAN SEA BASS, WHICH IS INCREASINGLY AVAILABLE IN GOOD MARKETS) IS A NICE TEXTURAL CONTRAST FOR SAUVIGNON/FUMÉ BLANC, WHILE THE USE OF EXOTIC MANGO TO MIRROR TROPICAL FLAVORS IN BOTH SAUVIGNON/FUMÉ BLANC AND CHARDONNAY IS QUITE EFFECTIVE. THE SWEET ROASTED PEPPER FLAVORS HELP TIE THE DISH TO SAUVIGNON/FUMÉ BLANC IN PARTICULAR. PAIRING WITH A LESS OAKY CHARDONNAY IS ALSO A FLATTERING COMBINATION, BUT CUT THE AMOUNT OF JALAPEÑOS IN HALF SO THAT THEY DON'T CLASH WITH THE OAK IN THE CHARDONNAY.

1 tablespoon rice- or white-wine vinegar

1 tablespoon toasted sesame–chile oil

1/2 tablespoon white-wine Worcestershire sauce

Kosher salt and freshly ground pepper

2 sea bass (Chilean, if possible) fillets (about 1 pound)

RELISH

1 cup diced fresh or frozen mango

1/4 cup halved cherry tomatoes

1/4 cup diced roasted red bell pepper (see page 116)

1/4 cup chopped sweet onion (Maui, Walla Walla, or Vidalia preferred)

1 tablespoon minced jalapeños

2 tablespoons chopped fresh cilantro

1/4 teaspoon ground ginger

1/2 teaspoon chopped fresh thyme (1/4 teaspoon dried)

1/8 teaspoon ground white pepper

Kosher salt

In a glass dish, combine vinegar, oil, Worcestershire, and salt and pepper to taste. Marinate sea bass for 2 hours, covered and refrigerated.

To make relish, in a small mixing bowl, combine all ingredients and stir thoroughly. Season to taste. Cover and refrigerate for 2 hours.

Remove sea bass from marinade. Over a hot charcoal fire or under the broiler, cook for 3 to 4 minutes per side, or until fish is just done. Don't overcook or the fish will dry out.

To serve, place sea bass on plate and top with relish. Serve with curried couscous.

SERVES 2 AS AN ENTRÉE

Turkey Piccata with Hot-Sweet Mustard–Lime Sauce

RECOMMENDED WINE: Sauvignon/Fumé Blanc
ALTERNATIVE WINE: Pinot Gris/Grigio

THIS IS A TERRIFIC NATURAL PAIRING FOR SAUVIGNON/FUMÉ BLANC, WHICH OFTEN EXHIBITS CITRUS FLAVORS, USING LIME AS A TOP NOTE. THE HOT-SWEET MUSTARD LENDS A TANGY, SWEET ELEMENT TO THE SAUCE AND CONNECTS BEAUTIFULLY TO THE FRUIT CHARACTER OF THE WINE. VEAL CAN REPLACE THE TURKEY IN THIS DISH, IF DESIRED.

1	teaspoon dried basil	2	tablespoons chopped shallots
½	teaspoon dried tarragon	2½	tablespoons fresh lime juice
½	teaspoon dried thyme	⅓	cup white wine
½	teaspoon crumbled dried rosemary	2	teaspoons hot-sweet mustard
¼	teaspoon kosher salt	¼	teaspoon white-wine Worcestershire sauce
¼	teaspoon freshly ground black pepper	6	drops Tabasco or other hot sauce
1	tablespoon all-purpose flour	1½	tablespoons drained capers
1¾	pounds turkey breast slices		GARNISH: chopped parsley, lime slices
2	tablespoons extra-virgin olive oil		

In a small mixing bowl, combine basil, tarragon, thyme, rosemary, salt, pepper, and flour and mix thoroughly. Place turkey on waxed paper and sprinkle it evenly on both sides with herb mixture.

In a large, nonstick sauté pan or skillet over medium-high heat, heat olive oil. Add shallots and turkey slices and sauté for 2 minutes. Turn turkey and add lime juice, wine, mustard, Worcestershire, Tabasco, and capers. Sauté for an additional 2 minutes. Remove turkey and keep warm. Simmer the sauce for an additional 1 to 2 minutes to reduce slightly.

Place turkey slices on plates and top with sauce. Garnish with parsley and lime slices. Serve with roasted garlic mashed potatoes.

SERVES 4 AS AN ENTRÉE

Ricotta-Stuffed Chicken Breast
with Roasted Red Bell Pepper Sauce

RECOMMENDED WINE: Sauvignon/Fumé Blanc
ALTERNATIVE WINE: Pinot Noir

T HIS IS A RUSTIC ITALIAN-STYLE DISH THAT HARMONIZES WITH SAUVIGNON/FUMÉ BLANC THROUGH THE COMBINATION OF
ROASTED PEPPER AND RICOTTA CHEESE FLAVORS, WHICH ACCENTUATE THE HERBAL NOTES IN THE WINE. THIS VERSATILE
DISH COMPLEMENTS PINOT NOIR AS WELL, RELYING ON THE MATCH BETWEEN THE SWEET CHERRY FLAVORS OF THE WINE WITH
SWEET ROASTED NOTES OF THE PEPPERS. IF SERVING WITH PINOT NOIR, MAKE THE SAUCE WITH RED WINE, NOT SHERRY.

SAUCE

1½ tablespoons olive oil

2 teaspoons chopped garlic

1 cup chopped roasted red bell peppers
  (see page 116)

½ cup dry sherry

¼ cup chicken stock

1 tablespoon tomato paste

1 teaspoon chopped fresh oregano
  (½ teaspoon dried)

1 teaspoon chopped fresh basil
  (½ teaspoon dried)

Kosher salt and red pepper flakes

—

4 large (7–8 ounces each) bone-in chicken
  breasts

Kosher salt and red pepper flakes

2 cups ricotta cheese

6 tablespoons chopped sun-dried tomatoes
  packed in oil

2 tablespoons chopped fresh basil
  (1 tablespoon dried)

2 tablespoons chopped fresh thyme
  (1 tablespoon dried)

1 tablespoon chopped shallots

1 tablespoon minced chives

1 tablespoon flour

2 tablespoons butter or olive oil

GARNISH: minced chives

To make sauce, in a large sauté pan or skillet, heat olive oil over medium heat. Add garlic and roasted peppers and sauté for 3 to 4 minutes. Add sherry, stock, tomato paste, oregano, and basil, increase heat to simmer, and reduce mixture slightly for 4 to 5 minutes. Transfer to a food processor or blender and process until well combined. Season to taste, reserve, and keep warm.

Rinse chicken breasts and pat dry. With a sharp knife, carefully cut a deep incision horizontally into each breast. Sprinkle with salt and red pepper flakes.

In a mixing bowl, combine ricotta, sun-dried tomatoes, basil, thyme, shallots, and chives and mix thoroughly. Using your fingers, stuff ricotta mixture equally into each breast. Dust with flour.

Preheat oven to 375°F. In a large, ovenproof sauté pan or skillet, melt butter over medium heat. Sauté chicken breasts for 3 to 4 minutes on each side until lightly browned. Transfer to the oven and roast for 15 to 18 minutes. Remove from oven and keep warm until ready to serve.

To serve, spoon hot sauce into a pool on each plate. Place breast on top. Garnish with chopped chives and serve. Serve with linguine with chopped fresh basil and extra-virgin olive oil.

SERVES 4 AS AN ENTRÉE

Every wine has its special moment, and Pinot Gris, also known as Pinot Grigio, is surely no exception. Time and place are important to Pinot Gris/Grigio because the wine is uniquely suited to certain occasions. Pinot Gris/Grigio fares well as an afternoon sipping wine, but also shines as a partner to seafood dishes that require more acidity than what most other white wines offer. Therefore, its place on the table is unquestioned.

Think of Pinot Gris/Grigio as being similar to Sauvignon/Fumé Blanc without the herbal character. It is innocence, purity, and laughter. Not to be taken too seriously, Pinot Gris/Grigio doesn't intrude; it slips right in.

Pinot Gris is the name given to the grape that grows in Oregon and in Alsace in France. The same grape is called Pinot Grigio in Italy; it's as simple as that. Wherever it is grown, Pinot Gris/Grigio is best suited to cool climates where its natural acidity can remain in check with a lively fruit character.

In Italy, Pinot Grigio is typically fermented in stainless-steel fermentation tanks and is lean, somewhat neutral, and relatively high in acid. It is commonly sipped as an aperitif at sidewalk cafés or served at lunch with simple, fresh seafood dishes. Perhaps lacking in complexity, Pinot Grigio is nevertheless incredibly refreshing, full of verve, and is particularly well suited to being enjoyed in warm weather.

The Pinot Gris of Alsace has a remarkably different character due to its different location and soil type. Fuller, richer, and more emphatic than its Italian counterpart, Alsatian Pinot Gris can range from very dry to quite sweet, but it is always driven by forward fruit. It resembles Gewürztraminer in body and Pinot Blanc in its steely character. Often, these wines take on an almost copper hue. When produced as dessert wines, they are quite opulent and are called Tokay Pinot Gris.

In Oregon, Pinot Gris is sometimes barrel-aged after an initial fermentation in stainless steel, giving the wines more flavor interest, yet with the insistent fruit and noticeable acidity of the Alsatian versions.

As a companion to food, Pinot Gris/Grigio offers its steely-minerally character and brisk acidity to help counter fattier seafood and higher acid foods such as tomatoes.

Oregon Pinot Gris has often been considered the perfect foil for salmon (see page 64). It is also extremely flexible with a wide range of spicier dishes, such as the racy "TDF" Gumbo Ma-Gumbo (page 60).

PINOT GRIS/GRIGIO

TYPICAL AROMAS & FLAVORS

Peach, Dried Peach
Lime
Lemon
Tangerine
Pear
Apple
Nuts
Lemongrass
Mineral
Herbs: Thyme, Oregano

BASE INGREDIENTS

Base ingredients refer to the main ingredient of the dish: meat, poultry, game, seafood, shellfish, or vegetable. These represent the core ingredients that are most likely to be matched with a varietal, although successful pairings result as much from the other ingredients used in the dish as they do the base ingredient.

Shrimp, Clams, Oysters, Mussels, Scallops, Salmon, Smoked Salmon, Sea Bass, Snapper, Trout, Swordfish, Sole

BRIDGE INGREDIENTS

Bridge ingredients help connect the food and the wine through their interaction in flavor, body, intensity, or basic taste.

Citrus: Lime, Lemon
Fennel (roasted)
Bell Peppers
Garlic, Shallots, Onions
Herbs: Dill, Tarragon, Thyme, Basil,
    Chives, Cilantro, Sage
Toasted Nuts: Pine Nuts, Almonds
Cheeses: Goat, Ricotta, Mozzarella,
    Fontina
Sour Cream, Yogurt
Dijon Mustard
Capers
Green Olives
Bacon
Prosciutto
Tomatoes, Sun-Dried Tomatoes

BEST SOURCE REGIONS
PINOT GRIS/GRIGIO

The following is a list of countries, regions, and appellations (a wine word referencing specific growing locales) that produce the highest-quality versions of this varietal. This is not intended to be a complete list, only a reference for where the finest renditions can be found.

OREGON
  Willamette Valley
  Umpqua Valley
WASHINGTON
FRANCE
  Alsace
ITALY
  Alto-Adige
  Friuli
CALIFORNIA
  Santa Barbara
  Napa Valley

PINOT GRIS/GRIGIO STYLES

Pinot Grigio (Italy):
  Typically lighter in color and body;
  bright, crisp acidity; light and fruity with
  no barrel aging

Pinot Gris (Oregon and Alsace):
  Pale straw in color; occasionally copper-
  hued; slightly rounder and fuller; sometimes barrel-aged

*Late Harvest Pinot Gris
(Vendange Tardive/Sélection de Grains Noble):*
  Darker in color; full-bodied; luscious,
  and sweet but with balancing acidity; a
  dessert wine

TIPS TO SUCCESSFUL
MATCHES WITH
PINOT GRIS/GRIGIO

1
Pinot Gris/Grigio matches best with foods that are higher in acid.

2
Italian Pinot Grigio is ideally suited to lighter-bodied dishes, particularly delicate seafood and shellfish.

3
Oregon and Alsatian versions of Pinot Gris can withstand more full-bodied seafood, such as salmon or sea bass.

4
Pinot Gris/Grigio is an excellent all-purpose wine for appetizers and lunches.

5
Drink Pinot Gris/Grigio when the weather is warm, since its refreshing acidity can be most appreciated then.

Marinated Mussels and Roasted Red Bell Peppers (Classic Pairing)

RECOMMENDED WINE: Pinot Gris/Grigio
ALTERNATIVE WINE: Sauvignon/Fumé Blanc

THIS TASTY MUSSEL AND ROASTED RED BELL PEPPER CONCOCTION, HIGHLIGHTED BY AN HERB-INFUSED MARINADE, BECKONS PINOT GRIS/GRIGIO QUITE SUCCESSFULLY. THE FRESHNESS AND SIMPLICITY OF THIS APPETIZER IS ACCENTUATED BY THE CRISP ACIDITY AND RACY FRUIT IN THE WINE. BECAUSE OF THE SIMILAR TANGY FRUIT AND GOOD ACID STRUCTURE OF SAUVIGNON/FUMÉ BLANC, THE PAIRING WILL WORK ALMOST AS WELL.

1 1/4 cups cold water

1/2 cup white wine

2 1/2 pounds fresh mussels, debearded and rinsed in cold water (see NOTE)

2 red bell peppers, roasted, seeded, peeled, and julienned into 2-inch-long strips (see page 116)

2 1/2 tablespoons white-wine vinegar

6 tablespoons extra-virgin olive oil

2 teaspoons chopped fresh oregano (1 teaspoon dried)

1/4 teaspoon kosher salt

1/2 teaspoon red pepper flakes

1 teaspoon minced shallots

4 ounces mixed greens (optional)

In a large stockpot, combine water and wine. Place mussels in a steamer basket inside the pot above the liquid. Cover pot, bring heat to high, and steam mussels for 8 minutes, until they open. Remove mussels from the pot, and with a spoon, scoop meat gently out of the shells into a medium glass bowl. Add 1 cup of roasted peppers to the bowl, and reserve the rest for another use.

In a separate small mixing bowl, combine the vinegar, oil, oregano, salt, red pepper flakes, and shallots and whisk thoroughly. Add the vinaigrette to the mussels and peppers and combine thoroughly. Adjust seasonings as necessary. Cover and refrigerate for at least 1 hour. The flavors will continue to blend over several days.

Serve on an antipasto plate with toothpicks or on top of chilled salad greens with mussels, peppers, and marinade evenly divided among four plates.

NOTE: Mussels can often be purchased without their stringy "beards." If they have not been cleaned, simply run the mussels under cold water and pull the bearded part of the mussel out from its shell.

SERVES 4 TO 6 AS AN APPETIZER

"TDF" Gumbo Ma-Gumbo

RECOMMENDED WINE: Pinot Gris/Grigio
ALTERNATIVE WINE: Sauvignon/Fumé Blanc

THIS WAS THE FIRST DISH I WAS EVER TAUGHT TO COOK—AN AUTHENTIC CAJUN GUMBO TAUGHT TO ME BY A CHINESE COOKING INSTRUCTOR IN SAN FRANCISCO. IT IS A CHALLENGING MATCH FOR WINE, BUT NOT AN IMPOSSIBLE ONE. THE SPICY, TONGUE-TINGLING FLAVORS AND HEARTY WEIGHT OF THE DISH ARE TAMED AND CONTRASTED BY THE BRIGHT, TANGY FRUIT OF PINOT GRIS/GRIGIO OR BY A FRUITY, UN-OAKY SAUVIGNON/FUMÉ BLANC. THE "TDF" MEANS "TO DIE FOR," WHICH IT MOST ASSUREDLY IS—THE BEST GUMBO I'VE TASTED OUTSIDE OF NEW ORLEANS!

12 ounces medium shrimp with shells

1 whole cooked Dungeness crab, meat removed (or 8 ounces cooked crab meat)

6 chicken legs (drumettes)

½ cup fresh or frozen okra, sliced in half lengthwise

2 tablespoons unsalted butter

3 tablespoons vegetable oil

3 tablespoons flour

1 large green pepper, cored, seeded, and chopped

2 stalks celery, ends removed and chopped

2 cups chopped yellow onions

4 cloves garlic, chopped

2 ounces ham, tasso, or smoked bacon, diced

4 cups fish stock (or 2 cups clam juice plus 2 cups water)

1 28-ounce can chopped tomatoes with liquid

1¼ teaspoons red pepper flakes

1½ teaspoons filé powder (see NOTE)

1 tablespoon Worcestershire sauce

1 bay leaf

1½ teaspoons dried thyme

3 tablespoons dried oregano

1 tablespoon dried basil

2 tablespoons tomato paste

1 cup white wine

1 andouille or other spicy sausage, thinly sliced

4 cups cooked white rice

Kosher salt and cayenne pepper

GARNISH: chopped parsley, minced green onions

Shell and devein shrimp. Shell crab, if using whole crab. Lightly salt and pepper chicken and set aside.

In a small sauté pan over medium heat, sauté okra in 1 tablespoon of butter for 5 to 6 minutes, until lightly browned. Set aside.

In a large stockpot, heat 2 tablespoons of oil over medium heat. Add shrimp and sauté for 2 to 3 minutes until they turn pink. Remove with a slotted spoon and set aside. Add chicken and sauté for 10 minutes, turning frequently, until the skin browns. Remove chicken, place on paper towels, and pat dry.

Add 1 tablespoon oil and 1 tablespoon butter to the stockpot. Add flour. Cook slowly, stirring frequently, until the roux mixture turns a nutty brown, but is not burnt. Increase heat slightly and add green pepper, celery, onions, garlic, okra, and ham. Sauté for about 8 minutes until vegetables are softened.

Add stock along with tomatoes, red pepper flakes, filé powder, Worcestershire, bay leaf, thyme, oregano, basil, tomato paste, and wine. Bring to a boil and stir well. Reduce to a simmer and cook, covered, for 1½ hours to develop flavor. (Can be made ahead to this point and refrigerated.)

Thirty minutes prior to serving, add sausage and chicken and prepare rice. Ten minutes prior to serving, add shrimp and crab. Season to taste. Stir thoroughly and serve over rice in large soup bowls. Garnish with chopped parsley and minced green onions.

NOTE: Filé powder is made of ground sassafras leaves and is often used as a thickening agent in Cajun gumbos. It can be found in gourmet sections of grocery stores.

SERVES 6 AS AN APPETIZER

"One barrel of wine can work more miracles than a church full of saints."
ITALIAN PROVERB

Scallop Salad with Anchovies, Radishes, and Almonds

RECOMMENDED WINE: Pinot Gris/Grigio
ALTERNATIVE WINE: Sauvignon/Fumé Blanc

THIS INTERESTING SALAD OFFERS UP SWEET, JUICY SCALLOPS, SALTY ANCHOVIES, TART LIME JUICE, BITTER RADISHES, ALMONDS, AND THE BEGUILING FLAVOR OF SAFFRON. THE RESULTING COMBINATION OF COMPLEX FLAVORS IS NICELY CONTRASTED BY THE CRISPNESS AND FORTHRIGHT FRUITINESS OF PINOT GRIS/GRIGIO OR AN EQUALLY APPEALING, FRUIT-DRIVEN SAUVIGNON/FUMÉ BLANC.

¼ cup walnut oil

¼ cup extra-virgin olive oil

1½ tablespoons white-wine vinegar

4 teaspoons lime juice

½ teaspoon saffron threads

2 tablespoons chopped shallots

3 teaspoons chopped anchovy fillets

¼ cup chopped fresh basil

1½ pounds sea scallops

4 ounces mixed salad greens

½ cup thinly sliced radishes

¼ cup toasted slivered almonds

GARNISH: cherry tomatoes, halved

In a nonreactive mixing bowl, combine oil, vinegar, lime juice, saffron, shallots, anchovies, and basil and whisk thoroughly. Add scallops and marinate, refrigerated, for 1 hour. Remove scallops from marinade and reserve marinade. Adjust marinade, if necessary.

Preheat oven to broil. Place scallops on a broiling pan and broil for 2 to 3 minutes. Turn and continue broiling for 2 to 3 minutes, until cooked through but not overcooked.

To serve, divide greens, radishes, almonds, and cherry tomatoes evenly on four plates. Divide scallops evenly. Drizzle reserved marinade over scallops and greens.

SERVES 6 AS AN APPETIZER

Dragon-Fire Noodles with Shrimp

RECOMMENDED WINE: Pinot Gris/Grigio
ALTERNATIVE WINE: Riesling

THIS DISH IS AN ADAPTATION OF A RECIPE FROM MY FRIEND BARBARA TROPP, WHOSE FORMER CHINA MOON RESTAURANT AND INCREDIBLY WONDERFUL COOKBOOKS SET THE STANDARD IN CONTEMPORARY CHINESE COOKING. THIS FIERY NOODLE RECIPE DEMONSTRATES HOW WELL A FRUITY WINE WITH GOOD ACIDITY CAN COUNTERBALANCE CHILE HEAT. A VERY LIGHT, CRISP ITALIAN PINOT GRIGIO WOULD BE THE BEST CHOICE HERE.

¼ cup hot chile oil

1 tablespoon toasted sesame oil

¼ teaspoon Thai chile paste

2½ tablespoons reduced-salt soy sauce

2 tablespoons chopped pickled ginger (see page 78)

2 tablespoons juice from pickled ginger

1½ tablespoons fresh lemon juice

2½ tablespoons seasoned rice-wine vinegar

1½ tablespoons chopped fresh mint

Minced zest of 1 lemon

1 pound shrimp, shelled and deveined

1 pound Chinese egg noodles

1 roasted red bell pepper, peeled and chopped (see page 116)

1 roasted yellow bell pepper, peeled and chopped

1 cup loosely packed cilantro leaves

GARNISH: white or black sesame seeds and minced green onions

In a large mixing bowl, combine oils, chile paste, soy sauce, pickled ginger and juice, lemon juice, vinegar, mint, and lemon zest and whisk together. Adjust seasonings; mixture should be hot and spicy but not tongue-numbing. Add shrimp to mixture and refrigerate for 1 to 2 hours.

In a large soup pot, bring salted water to a gentle boil. Carefully add the noodles and cook for 2 minutes, or until the noodles are al dente. Strain noodles thoroughly and return them to the pot. Add about a tablespoon of the marinade to the noodles to prevent them from sticking, and combine well. Cover.

In a large sauté pan or skillet over medium-high heat, add shrimp along with marinade and simmer for 1 to 2 minutes until shrimp are just cooked through. Add shrimp and marinade to the noodles and heat the entire mixture.

Just prior to serving, add the roasted peppers and cilantro leaves and mix thoroughly. Garnish with the sesame seeds and green onions. Serve immediately.

This dish can be served in smaller portions in a wine-friendly Asian meal with the Asian-Style Grilled Squab with Fennel, Bok Choy, and Chanterelle Mushrooms (page 134).

SERVES 2 TO 3 AS AN ENTRÉE OR 4 TO 6 AS AN APPETIZER

Grilled Salmon with Roasted Poblano–Lime Butter

RECOMMENDED WINE: Pinot Gris/Grigio
ALTERNATIVE WINE: Sauvignon/Fumé Blanc

I N OREGON, WHERE PINOT GRIS IS BEING PRODUCED WITH GREAT SUCCESS, SALMON IS CONSIDERED TO BE THE QUINTESSENTIAL MATCH. THE BRISK ACIDITY OF THE WINE, COMBINED WITH A LUSHNESS IN SOME STYLES, WEAVES ITS WAY AROUND THE OILY RICHNESS OF SALMON BEAUTIFULLY AND CLEANSES THE PALATE. THIS RECIPE FEATURES A COMPOUND BUTTER WITH MILDLY HOT ROASTED POBLANO CHILES AND LIME, A FLAVOR I FIND IN MANY OREGON PINOT GRIS.

4 fresh salmon fillets (about 2½ pounds)

2½ teaspoons Thai fish sauce or soy sauce

1 teaspoon white-wine Worcestershire sauce

1 tablespoon fresh lime juice

1½ teaspoons toasted sesame oil

1 poblano (or Anaheim) chile

4 teaspoons (½ stick) unsalted butter

2 teaspoons fresh lime juice

1 teaspoon minced chives

Place salmon fillets skin side down in a large glass dish. In a small nonreactive bowl, mix together the fish sauce, Worcestershire, lime juice, and sesame oil. Pour over salmon, cover, and refrigerate for 2 hours, turning once.

Preheat oven to 375°F. Place chile in the oven and roast for 45 minutes, turning once. Place in a paper bag for 15 minutes. Peel and seed as thoroughly as possible. Mince the pepper.

In a food processor or blender, place butter, lime juice, chives, and 1 tablespoon minced chile. (Save remaining poblano for spicing up a salad dressing or adding to a braised dish.) Process for 20 to 30 seconds until mixture is well combined. With a spatula, remove the butter from the processor and place on a piece of waxed paper. Gently form into a cylinder by rolling paper over the butter. Using hands, push ends of butter together to form a small log. Refrigerate until 30 minutes prior to using.

To prepare salmon, create a hot fire on the grill. Place salmon, skin side down, and grill for 5 minutes. Turn and grill for an additional 4 to 5 minutes or until salmon is cooked through. Place a slice of butter on top of salmon just prior to removing from the grill so that it melts slightly. This is great with polenta cakes and sautéed bok choy on the side.

SERVES 4 AS AN ENTRÉE

Grilled Swordfish with Tomatillo-Cilantro Salsa Verde

RECOMMENDED WINE: Pinot Gris/Grigio
ALTERNATIVE WINE: Sauvignon/Fumé Blanc

THIS FOOD AND WINE FLIRTATION RELIES ON THE INTRIGUING MATCH OF TART TOMATILLOS AND UNIQUELY BITTER CILANTRO WITH THE BRISK ACIDITY OF PINOT GRIS/GRIGIO, WHICH OFTEN SHOWS HINTS OF BITTERNESS AS WELL. I PARTICULARLY LIKE THIS COMBINATION SINCE THE FRUITY, ZESTY WINE SEEMS TO BE AN ALMOST PERFECT MIRROR FOR THE DISH. AN UN-OAKY SAUVIGNON/FUMÉ BLANC IS EVERY BIT AS SUCCESSFUL AS IT MIRRORS THE SAUCE WITH ITS "GREEN" FLAVORS.

MARINADE

½ cup firmly packed cilantro leaves

2 tablespoons extra-virgin olive oil

2 tablespoons fresh lemon juice

1 tablespoon honey

1½ tablespoons seeded, minced jalapeño

1 cup sliced yellow onions

2 cloves garlic

1 teaspoon ground cumin

½ teaspoon kosher salt

¼ teaspoon red pepper flakes

—

6 8-ounce swordfish steaks

2 pounds tomatillos, husked and rinsed

1 jalapeño

4 cloves garlic, peeled

1 shallot, peeled

⅓ cup chopped cilantro

3 tablespoons white wine

¼ teaspoon ground cumin

1½ teaspoons honey

⅓ teaspoon kosher salt

⅛ teaspoon freshly ground black pepper

⅛ teaspoon red pepper flakes

GARNISH: cilantro sprigs, toasted sesame seeds

To make marinade, mix all ingredients together in a food processor or blender until smooth. Place swordfish in a glass or plastic baking dish and cover with marinade. Marinate, refrigerated, for 1 to 2 hours.

Preheat oven to 350°F. Place tomatillos, jalapeño, garlic, and shallot on a baking sheet and roast for 30 to 35 minutes. Remove from oven. Seed jalapeño.

In a food processor or blender, purée tomatillos, jalapeño, garlic, and shallot until smooth. Add cilantro, wine, cumin, honey, salt, pepper, and red pepper flakes and continue processing until ingredients are well integrated.

Transfer to a small pot and bring to a boil. Reduce heat, cover, and simmer for 25 to 30 minutes. Season to taste. Adjust with a little more honey if sauce is too tart.

Remove swordfish from marinade. Over a hot charcoal fire, grill swordfish for 4 to 5 minutes. Turn and continue grilling for 3 to 4 minutes, or until cooked through but not dried out.

To serve, spoon portions of sauce onto plates and top with a piece of grilled swordfish. (Save any remaining sauce for future use with grilled chicken.) Garnish with cilantro sprigs and a sprinkling of toasted sesame seeds.

SERVES 6 AS AN ENTRÉE

Rolled Veal with Prosciutto, Fontina, and Caper Sauce

RECOMMENDED WINE: Pinot Gris/Grigio
ALTERNATIVE WINE: Sauvignon/Fumé Blanc

THOROUGHLY ITALIAN IN ITS INSPIRATION, RESEMBLING VEAL SALTIMBOCCA, THIS TASTY DISH IS ACCENTUATED BY A CRISP, FULL PINOT GRIS/GRIGIO. AN OREGON PINOT GRIS IS ACTUALLY BETTER SUITED THAN THE ITALIAN VERSION BECAUSE IT IS FULLER BODIED, PROVIDING A TEXTURAL AFFINITY TO THE CHEESE AND HARMONIZING WITH THE SAGE, PROSCIUTTO, AND LIME FLAVORS.

1⅓ pounds veal scaloppini	1 cup white wine
¼ teaspoon freshly ground black pepper	2 tablespoons fresh lime juice
4 ounces thinly sliced prosciutto	¾ teaspoon Dijon mustard
4 ounces thinly sliced Fontina or mozzarella cheese	2 tablespoons capers
10–12 whole sage leaves	¼ teaspoon red pepper flakes
	2 tablespoons unsalted butter

Between two sheets of waxed paper, pound veal slightly to tenderize. Sprinkle with pepper and top each piece with prosciutto, cheese, and sage leaves. Roll veal up from the end and hold together with short skewers or toothpicks.

In a small, nonreactive mixing bowl, mix together wine, lime juice, mustard, capers, and pepper flakes. Reserve.

Preheat oven to 350°F. In a large sauté pan or skillet over medium heat, melt butter. Add veal and brown on both sides. Transfer veal to a large baking sheet and cook for 7 to 8 minutes or until cheese is melted but not oozing out of rolls.

While veal is baking, add wine mixture to the sauté pan and simmer to reduce slightly. Place veal rolls on plates and top with sauce. Serve with baked polenta wedges and herbed roasted tomatoes.

SERVES 2 TO 3 AS AN ENTRÉE

"The gods made wine the best thing for mortal man to scatter cares."

STASINUS OF CYPRUS, *THE CYPRIA*

Riesling is one of the less-appreciated grape varietals in the Western world. Considered one of the world's great white wines since the nineteenth century, Riesling currently enjoys precious little popularity among American wine drinkers.

When Riesling is grown in the right locale and made with a judicious hand, it is an elegant and often impressive wine. Stylistically, Riesling couldn't be further from Chardonnay, which may, in part, explain why it's not terribly popular with the Chardonnay-crazed American wine consumer.

Forward fruit, crispness, purity, and low alcohol are Riesling's hallmarks—all characteristics that support its remarkable ability at the table. Riesling is also one of the few white wines that benefits from aging, due to its excellent acidity and fruit. It is also one of the lowest-alcohol wines available.

One factor contributing to the indifference towards German Riesling in the United States may have to do the complex labeling and varying levels of sweetness that are offered. German Rieslings range from bone-dry aperitif wines to incredibly sweet dessert versions. They are noted on the front label with the following nomenclature (from driest to sweetest): *Kabinett, Spätlese, Auslese, Beerenauslese, Trockenbeerenauslese,* and *Eiswein.*

Of these, *Kabinett* wines are quite dry and best suited to appetizers, including spicy ones,

while *Spätleses* are fuller in body, a touch sweeter, and better suited to Asian dishes as well as seafood and poultry dishes with cream sauce. *Auslese, Beerenauslese, Trockenbeerenauslese,* and *Eiswein* are considered dessert wines, although they are a sublime pairing with foie gras or a rich pâté.

In general, German Rieslings tend to be far more complex and flavorful than those made in California or Washington, the two primary areas of Riesling production in the United States. In particularly excellent vintages, German Rieslings can be absolutely stunning wines. Wherever it is grown, Riesling relies on a very cool climate and a long growing season to ripen properly.

In California, Riesling has been referred to as "Johannisberg Riesling" for many years. However, new regulations ensure that in the future only "Riesling" or "White Riesling" will be the appropriate nomenclature. Both in California and Washington, where perfectly enjoyable Riesling is produced, the styles range from dry (under 1 percent residual sugar), to off-dry (about 1.5 to 3 percent residual sugar), on through to sweet dessert wines, which are often produced in smaller 375-milliliter bottles and are most commonly called "Late-Harvest Riesling." In Australia, Riesling is sometimes labeled "Rhine Riesling" and is made both dry and sweet. Riesling is also produced in New York State, primarily in the drier style.

Along with Gewürztraminer, with which it shares the characteristic of a high fruit note and no oak-barrel aging, Riesling is extraordinarily flexible with Asian and Latin dishes, particularly with those exhibiting spicier flavors. It is also infinitely capable with smoked and saltier dishes, which makes it a superb partner to a holiday ham or a companion to the perfect picnic. Riesling will also flatter salads with fruit (Harvest Salad with Pears, Blue Cheese, and Pomegranates on page 74) and main course dishes with fruit sauces.

Riesling is, in a word, special. It is a wine of quiet and enlightened persuasion and pleasure. It is both a refreshing quaff that can delight in warm weather like no other varietal, as well as a more sublime, intriguing potion that can demand sensory investigation and thought. It's hard to imagine that Riesling will not gain more favor in the future as its considerable charms become better understood and appreciated.

RIESLING

TYPICAL AROMAS & FLAVORS

Apple
Pear
Peach, White Peach
Apricot
Floral: Jasmine, Rose, Orchid
Honey
Petroleum, Rubber Band
Mineral, Stone
Chalk
Mint
Juniper
Lime
Lychee Nut
Guava

BASE INGREDIENTS

Base ingredients refer to the main ingredient of the dish: meat, poultry, game, seafood, shell-fish, or vegetable. These represent the core ingredients that are most likely to be matched with a varietal, although successful pairings result as much from the other ingredients used in the dish as they do the base ingredient.

Shrimp, Scallops, Mussels, Trout, Smoked Trout, Salmon, Smoked Salmon, Snapper, Sole, Sea Bass, Chicken, Ham, Pork, Smoked Pork

BRIDGE INGREDIENTS

Bridge ingredients help connect the food and the wine through their interaction in flavor, body, intensity, or basic taste.

Apple
Pear
Lime
Orange, Orange Zest
Corn
Leeks, Sweet Onions
Peas
Mushrooms
Bacon, Pancetta, Prosciutto
Green Olives, Black Olives
Herbs: Mint, Tarragon, Cilantro
Spices: Ginger, Curry Powder, Nutmeg
Honey
Soy Sauce
Cheeses: Roquefort, Blue Cheese,
        Cambazola, Feta

BEST SOURCE REGIONS
RIESLING

The following is a list of countries, regions, and appellations (a wine word referencing specific growing locales) that produce the highest-quality versions of these wines.

This is not intended to be a complete list, only a reference for where the finest renditions can be found.

GERMANY
   Mosel-Saar-Ruwer
   Rheingau
   Rheinhessen
   Pfalz
FRANCE
   Alsace
AUSTRIA
CALIFORNIA
   Mendocino
   Monterey
   Napa
WASHINGTON
SOUTH AUSTRALIA

RIESLING STYLES

Dry (Kabinett *and* Spätlese):
   Lighter body; crisp and delicate with
   good acidity; lower alcohol

Medium-sweet (Spätlese, Auslese):
   Light-medium body; forward, ripe fruit
   with good concentration, often quite rich

Sweet (Beerenauslese, Trockenbeerenauslese, Eiswein):
   Medium body; lush mouthfeel; sweet
   dessert wines

TIPS TO SUCCESSFUL
MATCHES WITH RIESLING

1

Riesling is an ideal choice with many appetizers because it is a perfect "set up wine" for fuller wines to follow.

2

Riesling is particularly adept at contrasting with smoked, salty, and spicy dishes; however it is also well suited to more delicate and subtle dishes.

3

Riesling can work well with hearty dishes when it's used to contrast them in weight and body.

4

Riesling, because of its refreshing, low-alcohol character, is an ideal outdoor, summer wine.

Chilled Summer Peach Soup

RECOMMENDED WINE: Riesling
ALTERNATIVE WINE: Gewürztraminer

WHAT MORE COULD YOU ASK FROM A SUMMER SOUP THAN FOR IT TO BE REFRESHING AND REQUIRE VIRTUALLY NO TIME ON THE STOVE? DESPITE THE FACT THAT SOUPS IN GENERAL ARE DIFFICULT TO MATCH WITH WINE, THIS LUSCIOUS PEACH SOUP IS A TANTALIZING, APPETITE-STIMULATING SUMMER BEAUTY THAT MARRIES PERFECTLY WITH THE PEACHY QUALITY IN MANY RIESLINGS. THE FLAVOR MATCH IS ALMOST EQUALLY GOOD WITH OFF-DRY (SLIGHTLY SWEET) GEWÜRZTRAMINER.

6 large, ripe peaches

1 tablespoon honey

1 cup plain yogurt

⅓ cup peach nectar

⅛ cup Riesling

1 tablespoon minced crystallized ginger

1 tablespoon chopped fresh mint

1 tablespoon chopped fresh chives

½ teaspoon minced orange zest

1 teaspoon five-spice powder or curry powder (see NOTE)

GARNISH: mint sprigs, plain yogurt, 24 raspberries

Place peaches in boiling water for 2 minutes. Remove and place in an ice-water bath. Gently pull off skin. Halve and pit peaches.

In a food processor or blender, purée peaches, honey, yogurt, nectar, wine, crystallized ginger, mint, chives, orange zest, and five-spice powder.

Refrigerate, covered, for at least 2 hours. Adjust sweetness level, adding a little more yogurt to make sure that the soup is not so sweet that it will overpower the wine. Ladle into soup bowls. Garnish with mint sprigs, a small dollop of yogurt, and 4 raspberries per bowl placed carefully on top of yogurt.

NOTE: Five-spice powder is a combination of cinnamon, star anise, fennel, cloves, and Szechwan pepper and is found in the Asian grocery sections of most markets.

SERVES 6 AS AN APPETIZER

Wilted Red Cabbage Salad with Tangerines, Bay Shrimp, and Almonds

RECOMMENDED WINE: Riesling
ALTERNATIVE WINE: Gewürztraminer

THIS "SLAW" WORKS WITH RIESLING THROUGH SIMILAR TASTE PROFILES, WHICH IS TO SAY THAT BOTH THE DRESSING AND THE WINE ARE A LITTLE SWEET. THE TANGERINES HEIGHTEN THE FRUITY CHARACTER OF OFF-DRY RIESLING. GEWÜRZTRAMINER, WITH ITS FORWARD SPICY-CITRUS CHARACTER, IS ALSO AN ABLE PARTNER TO THIS DISH. THIS IS A GOOD CHOICE BEFORE HEAVIER ENTRÉES.

2 pounds red cabbage (1 large head)

DRESSING

2 tablespoons white-wine vinegar

1 tablespoon tangerine juice

2 tablespoons balsamic vinegar

½ teaspoon honey

1 tablespoon soy sauce

½ teaspoon curry powder

⅛ teaspoon red pepper flakes

2 teaspoons minced fresh ginger

2 tablespoons minced green onions

2 tablespoons chopped cilantro

6 tablespoons extra-virgin olive oil

Kosher salt and freshly ground black pepper to taste

¼ cup toasted slivered almonds

¼ cup freshly grated Parmesan or Asiago cheese

6 ounces bay shrimp

1 cup tangerine sections, seeded

Cut cabbage in half and remove core. Shred finely, rinse with cold water and dry.

To make dressing, in a small nonreactive mixing bowl, whisk all ingredients together thoroughly. Adjust balance and seasoning to taste.

Heat a large wok, sauté pan, or skillet until very hot. Carefully add 2 to 3 tablespoons of well-mixed dressing. Stir-fry a portion of cabbage for 30 seconds or until lightly wilted. Cabbage should be crunchy and turn a beautiful purple-red. With a slotted spoon, remove cabbage to a serving bowl. Continue stir-frying cabbage in batches, adding a little whisked dressing each time. Use only as much dressing as needed to coat and flavor cabbage.

When finished wilting cabbage, add as much remaining dressing as desired. Reserve remaining dressing for another use. Mix in almonds, cheese, shrimp, and most of tangerine sections, reserving a few to garnish top of salad. Serve warm immediately by dividing evenly and garnishing with remaining tangerine slices.

SERVES 6 TO 8 AS AN APPETIZER OR SIDE DISH

Harvest Salad with Pears, Blue Cheese, and Pomegranates

RECOMMENDED WINE: Riesling

ALTERNATIVE WINE: Sauvignon/Fumé Blanc

COME AUTUMN, SEASONAL INGREDIENTS LIKE PEARS, POMEGRANATES, AND WALNUTS START APPEARING IN FARMERS' MARKETS AND GROCERY STORES. THIS SALAD IS A GREAT WAY TO CELEBRATE THE CHANGING OF THE SEASON WITH A COMBINATION OF INGREDIENTS THAT IS QUITE FLATTERING TO OFF-DRY, SLIGHTLY SWEET RIESLING. THE SALTINESS AND TANG OF THE BLUE CHEESE PROVIDES A COUNTERPOINT TO THE FRUITY WINE WHILE THE PEARS CAPTURE THE PEAR-LIKE QUALITY IN MANY RIESLINGS.

DRESSING

1 cup Riesling, simmered, reduced by half, and cooled

1 tablespoon Dijon mustard

2 tablespoons white-wine vinegar

¼ teaspoon kosher salt

¼ teaspoon freshly ground black pepper

6 tablespoons olive oil

1 pound mixed greens

½ cup crumbled blue cheese

⅓ cup toasted walnuts

½ cup pomegranate seeds

1 cup peeled and diced Anjou or Bosc pears

In a small, nonreactive mixing bowl, whisk all dressing ingredients together thoroughly.

On small plates, evenly divide greens and top with blue cheese, walnuts, pomegranate seeds, and pear. Top with whisked dressing.

SERVES 4 AS AN APPETIZER

Grilled Vegetable Salad with Major Grey Chutney Dressing

RECOMMENDED WINE: Riesling
ALTERNATIVE WINE: Gewürztraminer

———————————————

THIS SLIGHTLY SWEET AND SPICY VEGETABLE SALAD CAN BE SERVED COLD AS A FIRST COURSE OR WARM AS A SIDE DISH WITH MEAT OR FISH. AS A FIRST COURSE, ITS BEGUILING SWEET-TART FLAVORS REQUIRE A WINE WITH SOME SWEETNESS TO MATCH IT EFFECTIVELY. A NICELY CHILLED, MEDIUM-SWEET STYLE CALIFORNIA RIESLING, GERMAN RIESLING, OR GEWÜRZTRAMINER WILL WORK WONDERS.

3 Japanese eggplants (about 1¼ pounds), ends trimmed, sliced lengthwise in ¼-inch-thick pieces

2 medium radicchio heads, cored, and halved lengthwise

1 bulb fresh fennel, cored, stalks removed, and halved crosswise

1 red bell pepper, cored, seeded, de-ribbed, and halved lengthwise

1 green bell pepper, cored, seeded, de-ribbed and halved lengthwise

1 yellow bell pepper, cored, seeded, de-ribbed, and halved lengthwise

DRESSING

4½ tablespoons Major Grey mango chutney

1 teaspoon Szechwan chile sauce (see NOTE)

1 teaspoon five-spice powder (see NOTE)

3 tablespoons rice-wine vinegar

2½ teaspoons Thai fish sauce (see NOTE)

⅔ cup olive oil

Arrange prepared vegetables in a large, flat glass dish.

To make dressing, place all ingredients in a food processor or blender and process until well mixed. Pour dressing over vegetables and coat all sides. Allow vegetables to marinate for 2 to 3 hours.

Prepare a hot barbecue fire. When coals are very hot, place all vegetables on grill and grill for 15 to 18 minutes, turning once. Fennel will take a few minutes longer than the rest of the vegetables. It will also fall apart a little on the grill so care needs to be taken that it doesn't slip through the grates.

When vegetables are cooked, refrigerate for a couple of hours or serve warm. When ready to serve, slice peppers and fennel into ½-inch-wide strips. Divide equally on plates and arrange in an attractive manner.

NOTE: Szechwan chile sauce, five-spice powder, and Thai fish sauce are found in most Asian food sections of grocery stores or in specialty Asian markets.

SERVES 6 AS AN APPETIZER OR SIDE DISH

Creole-Style Prawns

RECOMMENDED WINE: Riesling
ALTERNATIVE WINE: Sauvignon/Fumé Blanc

THIS CREOLE-STYLE PRAWN DISH IS A TERRIFIC SHOWCASE FOR AN OFF-DRY, FRUITY RIESLING. THE DECIDEDLY NON-GOURMET INGREDIENT OF CATSUP (YES, HUMBLE BOTTLED CATSUP), WITH ITS SWEET-TART-TANGY FLAVORS, WRAPS ITSELF AROUND RIESLING WITH UNEXPECTED GRACE. SAUVIGNON/FUMÉ BLANC IS A TART, FRUITY CONTRAST TO THE SLIGHTLY SWEETER QUALITIES OF THE DISH. REDOLENT OF HERBS AND SPICES, THE SAUCE PROVIDES A FLAVORFUL BED FOR THE SWEET SUCCULENCE OF THE PRAWNS. SERVE OVER WHITE RICE.

3 tablespoons unsalted butter

2 tablespoons all-purpose flour

1½ cups fish or chicken stock

1 cup chopped green pepper

2 cloves garlic, minced

¾ cup chopped sweet onions

1 large tomato, seeded and diced, or one 14½-ounce can chopped tomatoes, drained

½ cup catsup

¼ cup pitted, chopped Kalamata olives

⅓ teaspoon cayenne

1 teaspoon sweet paprika

1 teaspoon dried thyme

1 teaspoon dried basil

1 teaspoon dried marjoram

2 pounds prawns, shelled and deveined

Kosher salt and cayenne pepper

GARNISH: chopped green onions

In a medium sauté pan or skillet over medium heat, melt 2 tablespoons butter. Add flour and stir with a wooden spoon until smooth and slightly brown. Slowly add stock and stir until thickened slightly. Reserve.

In a large sauté pan or skillet over medium heat, melt 1 tablespoon butter and sauté green pepper, garlic, and onions for 3 to 4 minutes, until onions are translucent and green pepper is tender. Add tomatoes, catsup, olives, cayenne, paprika, and herbs and simmer for 5 minutes. Add reserved stock mixture to onion-pepper mixture and stir until well blended. Add prawns and simmer for 20 minutes, covered. Season to taste.

To serve, spoon white rice into large soup bowls. Divide prawns and sauce over rice. Sprinkle green onions over top.

SERVES 4 AS AN ENTRÉE

Asian-Style Grilled Salmon with Fennel–Pickled Ginger Relish

RECOMMENDED WINE: Riesling

ALTERNATIVE WINE: Gewürztraminer

ONE OF RIESLING'S MOST PLEASING CHARACTERISTICS IS ITS INTRIGUING FLORAL SCENT (KNOWN AS "BOUQUET" IN WINE-SPEAK). I'VE FOUND THAT DISHES WITH GINGER AND OTHER ASIAN SEASONINGS CAN ACCENTUATE THIS QUALITY QUITE NICELY. THE SWEET CHARACTER OF FENNEL (KNOWN ALSO AS SWEET ANISE) IS ANOTHER FLATTERING FLAVOR TO THIS PAIRING. A FAIRLY DRY GERMAN-STYLE RIESLING (ONE LABELED *KABINETT* OR *SPÄTLESE*) WILL CAPTURE THESE FLAVORS ADEPTLY. GEWÜRZTRAMINER ALSO ADAPTS VERY WELL TO THIS DISH.

MARINADE

- 2 tablespoons reduced-salt soy sauce
- 1 tablespoon rice-wine vinegar
- ½ tablespoon sesame chile oil
- 2 tablespoons minced green onions
- ½ tablespoon white-wine Worcestershire sauce
- ½ teaspoon ground ginger

- 4 fresh salmon fillets (about 2 pounds)

RELISH

- 1 fennel bulb, cored and halved lengthwise
- 1 tablespoon chopped fresh fennel fronds (see NOTE)
- 5 tablespoons chopped pickled ginger (see NOTE)
- 3 tablespoons minced green onions
- 1 teaspoon fresh lime juice
- 1 tablespoon seasoned rice-wine vinegar
- ¾ cup peeled, diced cucumber
- 1 teaspoon toasted sesame seeds
- Kosher salt and freshly ground black pepper

To make marinade, in a small mixing bowl, whisk all ingredients together. In a medium glass dish, put salmon skin side down and top with marinade. Cover and refrigerate for 1 to 2 hours, turning once.

To prepare relish, preheat oven to 350°F. Place fennel on a baking sheet and roast for 30 minutes. Let cool slightly and chop coarsely.

In a medium nonreactive mixing bowl, combine ¾ cup of chopped fennel with fennel fronds, pickled ginger, green onions, lime juice, vinegar, cucumber, and sesame seeds and mix thoroughly. Season to taste with salt and pepper. Cover and refrigerate for 1 to 2 hours.

When ready to serve, grill salmon skin side down over hot coals for 5 to 6 minutes. Turn and cook for an additional 4 to 5 minutes. Do not overcook; salmon should remain pink and juicy on the inside.

To serve, place salmon on plates and divide relish evenly on side.

NOTES: Fennel fronds are the dark green, leafy part of the fennel stalk. Pickled ginger can be found in the produce section of many grocery stores. It is bottled (or sometimes packaged) and kept cool in the produce section. Make sure you find the light pinkish, natural-looking pickled ginger called *shoga amasu zuke* as opposed to the very unnatural-looking, red-dyed version that is often found in Asian sections of grocery stores.

SERVES 4 AS AN ENTRÉE

Hoisin Barbecued Game Hens with Chinese-Style Vegetables

RECOMMENDED WINE: Riesling

ALTERNATIVE WINE: Gewürztraminer

———————————————

RIESLING GETS ITS REPUTATION FOR PAIRING WELL WITH ASIAN FOOD BECAUSE OF THE FRUITY, LOW-ALCOHOL CHARACTER OF THE WINE—THE WAY IN WHICH THE FORWARD FRUIT ACTUALLY ACCENTUATES RATHER THAN OBLITERATES SPICES. THIS SIMPLE GRILLED CHICKEN IS A DANDY FOIL FOR DRY TO OFF-DRY RIESLING. IT PROVIDES A BRIGHT, CLEANSING CONTRAST FOR THE COMBINATION OF SALTY (SOY AND FERMENTED BLACK BEANS), SWEET (HONEY), AND SPICY (SESAME CHILE OIL AND GINGER) FLAVORS IN THE DISH. THE MARINADE IS ACTUALLY A HOMEMADE HOISIN SAUCE.

3 Cornish game hens

MARINADE

½ cup reduced-salt soy sauce

¼ cup mirin (see NOTE), sweet sake, or Riesling

2 tablespoons honey

2 tablespoons seasoned rice-wine vinegar

1 tablespoon fermented black beans, rinsed and chopped (see NOTE)

2 teaspoons sesame chile oil (see NOTE)

2 teaspoons fresh lime juice

3 garlic cloves, chopped

2 tablespoons ground ginger

⅓ cup chopped cilantro

———

3 tablespoons vegetable oil

1 cup sliced yellow onions

1 tablespoon minced garlic

1½ tablespoons peeled, minced ginger

1 cup thinly chopped carrots

½ cup diced celery

¾ cup julienned red bell pepper

¾ cup julienned yellow bell pepper

½ cup thinly chopped green cabbage

8 ounces bok choy, ends trimmed and halved horizontally

2 teaspoons five-spice powder (see page 72)

3 tablespoons reduced-salt soy sauce

¼ cup chicken stock

1 tablespoon brown sugar or honey

Remove neck, giblets, and livers from cavity of game hens and rinse hens thoroughly in cold water and pat dry. Halve the hens by cutting firmly through the breast and backbone with a sharp knife. Pound each half hard a couple of times with the palm of your hand to flatten the hens.

To make marinade, in a medium sauté pan or skillet, combine all ingredients and simmer for 7 to 8 minutes. Cool in refrigerator (or freezer, if time is short). In a large sealable plastic bag, marinate hens for 2 to 3 hours. Remove hens from marinade and reserve marinade.

Prepare a charcoal fire. When coals are very hot but not flaming, carefully separate them to the sides of the grill so that the hens can cook in the middle part of the grill using indirect heat. It's important that fire is not flaming so that it doesn't burn the honey in the marinade, but it needs to be hot enough to last for an hour of cooking time. Gas grills work quite well for this purpose.

Place hens on grill skin side down and cook, covered, for 25 to 30 minutes, basting frequently with marinade. Turn and continue to cook and baste for 25 to 30 minutes, or until juices run clear when poked with a fork. Remove from grill and keep warm.

RECIPE CONTINUES

In a large sauté pan or wok, heat oil over high heat. Add onions, garlic, ginger, carrots, celery, peppers, cabbage, bok choy, and five-spice powder. Stir-fry for 3 to 4 minutes, tossing constantly. Add soy sauce, stock, and brown sugar and continue to stir-fry for 2 to 3 minutes more. Do not overcook.

To serve, divide vegetables evenly on plates and top with game hen halves.

NOTE: Mirin (rice wine), fermented black beans, and sesame chile oil are sold in Asian sections of groceries or in Asian markets. If not using fermented black beans, add 1 extra tablespoon reduced-salt soy sauce.

SERVES 6 MODEST APPETITES OR 3 GOOD ONES

Smoked Pork Chops with Sauerkraut and Green Apples (Classic Pairing)

RECOMMENDED WINE: Riesling
ALTERNATIVE WINE: Pinot Gris/Grigio

THIS IS A SPIN ON AN ALSATIAN CHOUCROUTE (WITHOUT THE GOOSE FAT), WHICH IS CONSIDERED TO BE A CLASSIC MATCH WITH OFF-DRY RIESLINGS. IN THIS CASE, THE TONGUE-TINGLING SAUERKRAUT AND SWEET-TARTNESS OF GREEN APPLES PROVIDE A STIMULATING MATCH WITH THE PLEASANT ACIDITY OF THE WINE, WHILE THE SLIGHT SWEETNESS OF THE RIESLING CONTRASTS THE SMOKY, SALTY PORK. THE MIXTURE SLOWLY SIMMERS IN A BOTTLE OF RIESLING AS WELL, GIVING THE MATCH EXTREMELY GOOD ODDS OF SUCCESS–A PERFECT SUNDAY NIGHT WINTER DINNER DISH.

3 ounces pancetta or bacon, chopped

3 cloves garlic, chopped

1 medium yellow onion, sliced

6 whole juniper berries, crushed with the back of a knife

4 whole black peppercorns

1 teaspoon dried thyme

1 bay leaf

6 whole cloves

¾ teaspoon caraway seeds

1 750-milliliter bottle Riesling

3 tablespoons apple cider vinegar

1 22-ounce jar sauerkraut, rinsed with cold water and squeezed

¾ pound boneless pork loin chops (about ¾-inch thick)

1 pound smoked chicken or pork sausage, halved crosswise

¾ pound Yellow Finn or other yellow-fleshed potatoes, quartered

1½ cups sliced green apples

In a large stockpot, sauté pancetta in its own fat for 4 to 5 minutes. Add garlic and onions and continue sautéing for 5 to 6 minutes. Add juniper berries, peppercorns, thyme, bay leaf, cloves, caraway seeds, wine, and cider vinegar. Put sauerkraut into the pot and carefully place pork chops, sausage, and potatoes into the sauerkraut and liquid so that they're well covered. Cover pot and simmer for 50 minutes. Add the apples and continue cooking for 4 to 5 minutes.

Divide meat, sauerkraut, and potatoes evenly onto plates or serve in large soup bowls.

SERVES 4 TO 6 AS AN ENTRÉE

Simply stated, Gewürztraminer is an enigma. Probably the least understood of all varietals, Gewürztraminer has a small following of incredibly dedicated fans who love the wine for its aromatic brilliance and its lush, exotic fruit flavors.

Gewürztraminer is a hedonistic wine with little subtlety and a lot of pizzazz. The great versions of the wine are produced in the Alsace region of France; they range from quite dry to very sweet. Regardless of style, they are spectacularly fragrant, displaying exotic floral and spice notes. In fact, *Gewürz* means "spice" in German, and this is the quality that makes the wine so attractive to some wine drinkers.

Alsatian Gewürztraminers can be quite "over the top" in some cases, but they are never lacking for either aromatic or flavor interest. The dry style is particularly interesting: it smells as if it is sweet, but hits the palate dry and fruity with a full mouthfeel.

The dessert versions are quite exotic and lushly flavored, excellent for matching with apricot, peach, and apple desserts. These wines have typically been infested with *Botrytis cinerea*, a beneficial rot that occurs naturally in vineyards in humid conditions after an autumn rain. (This same rot can favorably affect Riesling as well.) The nomenclature *"vendange tardive"* or *"sélection des grains nobles"* (even sweeter) is used to signify the "late-harvest" character of these wines. They are always quite sweet.

In the United States, the wine is made in California and Washington in a range of styles, typically off-dry (1.5 to 3.5 percent residual sugar). Unfortunately, due to its lack of broad popular acceptance, many growers are pulling the grape out of their vineyards in California and opting for other varietals that generate more revenue and enjoy greater consumer demand. This bodes poorly for the future of Gewürztraminer in California.

Where most other varietals fall flat with smoked, spicy, salty, and slightly sweet dishes, Gewürztraminer and Riesling accentuate them with tremendous success. Sweet-tart chutneys, relishes, and smoky salsas are but a few of the flavors that are captured brilliantly by Gewürztraminer, thus establishing the wine's uniqueness and versatility at the table.

In matching wines to Asian and Indian cuisines, particularly where soy sauce or spice is used, Gewürztraminer can be nothing short of an epiphany. The exotic fruitiness and mild sweetness in many versions of the wine contrast the saltiness and spice of these dishes with great effectiveness. Dishes such as chicken curry, sweet-and-sour pork, tandoori chicken, stir-fried, spicy seafood, and poultry dishes are other examples of dishes that benefit greatly from being paired with Gewürztraminer.

GEWÜRZTRAMINER

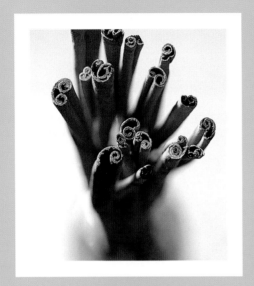

TYPICAL AROMAS & FLAVORS

Apricot
Peach
Nectarine
Pineapple
Lychee Nuts
Guava
Honey
Carnation
Jasmine
Honeysuckle
Rose
Gardenia
Spices: Cinnamon, Clove, Nutmeg

BASE INGREDIENTS

Base ingredients refer to the main ingredient of the dish: meat, poultry, game, seafood, shellfish, or vegetable. These represent the core ingredients that are most likely to be matched with a varietal, although successful pairings result as much from the other ingredients used in the dish as they do the base ingredient.

Crab, Mussels, Shrimp, Poultry,
Turkey, Squab, Pork

BRIDGE INGREDIENTS

Bridge ingredients help connect the food and the wine through their interaction in flavor, body, intensity, or basic taste.

Orange
Tropical Fruit: Pineapple, Passion Fruit,
    Mango, Guava, Papaya
Lychee Nuts
Spices: Curry Powder, Ginger, Fennel
    Seed, Cinnamon, Clove
Sweet Onions
Coconut
Cheeses: Jalapeño Jack, Smoked Gouda,
    Smoked Mozzarella
Soy Sauce
Sugar, Honey

BEST SOURCE REGIONS
GEWÜRZTRAMINER

The following is a list of countries, regions, and appellations (a wine word referencing specific growing locales) that produce the highest-quality versions of these wines.

This is not intended to be a complete list, only a reference for where the finest renditions can be found.

CALIFORNIA
WASHINGTON
FRANCE
  Alsace
GERMANY
  Pfalz

GEWÜRZTRAMINER
STYLES

Dry:
  Lighter body; lower alcohol; fruity

Off-Dry:
  Medium body; lush, noticeable sweetness

Sweet:
  Full-bodied; lush, opulent, exotic; dessert wine

TIPS TO SUCCESSFUL
MATCHES WITH
GEWÜRZTRAMINER

1
Pair Gewürztraminer with smoked, salty, slightly sweet, and spicy dishes for best results.

2
Avoid pairing Gewürztraminer with dishes that have too much acidity. It's a lower-acid wine, and it will seem lifeless.

3
When making sweet dishes, don't let the dish get sweeter than the wine because it will flatten the impression of the wine.

4
Don't pair Gewürztraminer with delicately flavored seafood or poultry as it will overwhelm the dish.

5
Serve Gewürztraminer well chilled.

Arugula, Smoked Trout, Roasted Beets, and Caramelized Cashews with Ginger-Chile Dressing

RECOMMENDED WINE: Gewürztraminer

ALTERNATIVE WINE: Riesling

THE SPICY CHARACTER OF GEWÜRZTRAMINER PROVIDES A PARTICULARLY NICE FOIL FOR SMOKED AND SPICIER FOODS. THIS TASTY, FULL-FLAVORED SALAD FEATURES SMOKED TROUT, ROASTED BEETS, AND CARAMELIZED SPICY CASHEWS, ALL OF WHICH HELP CONNECT WITH THE UNIQUE FLAVORS OF GEWÜRZTRAMINER. AN OFF-DRY, FRUITY CALIFORNIA GEWÜRZTRAMINER WORKS BEST WITH THIS DISH, BUT AN OFF-DRY RIESLING WILL ALSO PAIR QUITE NICELY. ROGER DIKON, A TALENTED CHEF FROM HAWAII, PROVIDED THE ORIGINAL INSPIRATION FOR THIS SALAD.

5½ ounces small beets, rinsed and ends trimmed

DRESSING

2 eggs

⅓ cup peeled, finely chopped fresh ginger

1½ tablespoons chopped shallots

2 tablespoons reduced-salt soy sauce

3 tablespoons seasoned rice-wine vinegar

1 teaspoon toasted sesame oil

2½ tablespoons honey

1 tablespoon Dijon mustard

2 serrano chiles, seeded and diced

1 cup olive oil

2 tablespoons water

Juice of ½ lemon

Kosher salt and freshly ground black pepper

⅔ cup raw, unsalted cashew halves or macadamia nuts (about ¼ pound) (see NOTE)

2 tablespoons honey

½ teaspoon Tabasco or other hot sauce

2 tablespoons water

1 pound arugula, rinsed and dried

8 ounces smoked trout, skin removed and cut into 1-inch pieces

Roast beets in a 350°F oven for 1 hour. Remove from oven, peel, and dice.

To make dressing, with a slotted spoon, place eggs in boiling water and cook for 90 seconds in order to cook slightly through. Peel the eggs, separate yolks, and discard whites. In a blender or food processor, blend egg yolks, ginger, shallots, soy sauce, vinegar, sesame oil, honey, mustard, and chiles for about 20 seconds. With motor running, slowly add the oil and process until thick. Add water and lemon juice. Season to taste.

Toast cashews in a 350°F oven until golden brown. Discard any nuts that turn black.

In a medium sauté pan or skillet, heat honey over low to medium heat for 2 to 3 minutes. Add the nuts, Tabasco, and water and cook until the nuts are fully coated and the liquid has fully evaporated. Remove from pan, place on waxed paper, and separate nuts slightly so that they don't stick together. Cool to room temperature.

To assemble, divide arugula on chilled salad plates. Top with evenly divided smoked trout, diced beets, and caramelized nuts. Spoon dressing over and serve. Reserve remaining dressing for another use.

NOTE: Unsalted cashews and macadamias are available at health food stores. If unsalted nuts are not available, rinse salted ones in cold water and let dry. In this event, the toasting process is not necessary.

SERVES 8 TO 10 AS AN APPETIZER

Indian Chicken with Nectarine Chutney

RECOMMENDED WINE: Gewürztraminer
ALTERNATIVE WINE: Riesling

IT'S NOT SURPRISING THAT MANY INDIAN, MOROCCAN, THAI, AND OTHER ASIAN RESTAURANTS FEATURE GEWÜRZTRAMINER AND RIESLING ON THEIR WINE LISTS. THIS DISH IS A GOOD EXAMPLE OF WHERE CHARDONNAY SIMPLY WILL NOT DO. IN FACT, A CHARDONNAY WOULD BE TOTALLY OBLITERATED BY THESE FLAVORS. INSTEAD, YOU'LL FIND HARMONY IN THE INTERMINGLING OF AROMATIC, TONGUE-TINGLING SPICE, TARTNESS, AND SWEETNESS IN THE DISH SUPPORTED BY THE SPICY, FRUITY CHARACTER OF A SLIGHTLY SWEET GEWÜRZTRAMINER. DON'T LET THE LONGER INGREDIENT LIST DISSUADE YOU; THIS DISH IS QUITE EASY TO MAKE.

1 5- to 6-pound whole roasting chicken

1½ teaspoons kosher salt

2 whole shallots, peeled and halved

3 whole garlic cloves, peeled

MARINADE

1½ cups plain yogurt

3 tablespoons lemon juice

2 teaspoons ground coriander

½ teaspoon ground cinnamon

2 teaspoons ground cumin

1 teaspoon ground ginger

¼ teaspoon ground cloves

4 teaspoons ground sweet paprika

½ teaspoon crushed red pepper flakes

CHUTNEY

1½ cups sliced yellow onions

¾ cup apple-cider vinegar

1 tablespoon fresh lemon juice

1 cup brown sugar

3 tablespoons golden raisins

2 teaspoons ground coriander

½ teaspoon ground cardamom (optional)

1 4-inch cinnamon stick

½ teaspoon dried orange peel

1 teaspoon mustard seed

2 tablespoons peeled, minced fresh ginger

¼ teaspoon ground cloves

½ teaspoon kosher salt

¾ teaspoon red pepper flakes

2 pounds ripe nectarines, pitted and sliced into 6 pieces each

¼ cup chopped fresh cilantro

GARNISH: cilantro sprigs

Remove skin from breast, thighs, and legs of chicken by peeling it away from flesh carefully. Discard skin. Rinse chicken in cold water and pat dry with paper towels. Using a small knife, make two incisions in each breast and thigh of chicken. Rub salt inside and outside the chicken, including inside the incisions. Place shallots and garlic inside the cavity of the chicken.

To make marinade, in a medium mixing bowl, combine all ingredients and whisk together thoroughly. Line a large ovenproof baking dish with aluminum foil and put chicken in dish. Using your hands, rub marinade inside and outside the chicken, including into the incisions. Refrigerate, covered, for 4 to 6 hours, or up to overnight.

To make chutney, in a heavy, 4-quart nonreactive pot, combine onions, vinegar, lemon juice, brown sugar, raisins, coriander, cardamom, cinnamon, orange peel, mustard seed, ginger, cloves, salt, and red pepper flakes and bring to a boil, stirring thoroughly. Reduce heat to a simmer and cook for 10 minutes, stirring occasionally.

Add nectarines and cook for 12 to 14 minutes, until liquid begins to reduce and thicken and nectarines are cooked through but not mushy. Discard cinnamon stick. Add chopped cilantro. Mix thoroughly and refrigerate for 3 to 4 hours before serving. Makes about 2½ cups and will keep, covered and refrigerated, for 1 to 2 weeks. Makes an excellent condiment for grilled pork, barbecued ribs, and baked ham.

To serve, preheat oven to 375°F. Roast chicken for 70 to 80 minutes, basting frequently with excess marinade until internal temperature of chicken is 165° to 170°F. Remove chicken from oven, cover with foil, and let rest in a warm place for 10 minutes. Cut chicken into serving slices. Divide evenly and serve with chutney on the side. Garnish with cilantro sprigs.

NOTE: The chicken can be cooked spectacularly well on a gas grill. Use indirect heat with the temperature set at 375°F. Put chicken on a large piece of foil with ends curled up. Cook for 70 to 80 minutes, covered, basting frequently, until internal temperature of chicken is 165° to 170°F. Cover and let rest as above.

SERVES 4 AS AN ENTRÉE

"I wonder often what the Vintners buy one half so precious as the goods they sell."

OMAR KHAYYAM, *THE RUBIYAT*

Spicy Gingered-Carrot Soup

RECOMMENDED WINE: Gewürztraminer
ALTERNATIVE WINE: Pinot Gris/Grigio

THE USE OF ASIAN SPICES AND FLAVORINGS IN THIS SOUP PROVIDES A CLASSIC SHOWCASE FOR THE UNIQUE CHARACTER OF AN OFF-DRY GEWÜRZTRAMINER. THE FRUITY WINE WEAVES A CONNECTING WEB BETWEEN THESE EXOTIC SPICES AND, AT THE SAME TIME, CONTRASTS THE CREAMY RICHNESS OF THE PEANUT BUTTER, WHICH IS A KEY ELEMENT IN THIS BRIGHTLY COLORED SOUP. AN OREGON PINOT GRIS, WITH ITS FLESHY BODY AND CRISP, FRUITY CHARACTER, ALSO WORKS WELL BUT DOES NOT PROVIDE QUITE THE FLAVOR INTEREST OF GEWÜRZTRAMINER.

1½ tablespoons olive oil

1 large yellow onion, chopped

2 stalks celery, ends trimmed and diced

3 cloves garlic, chopped

3 tablespoons peeled, chopped fresh ginger

1 pound carrots, peeled and chopped

4½ cups chicken stock

¼ teaspoon red pepper flakes

¼ teaspoon ground coriander

½ teaspoon turmeric

1½ tablespoons Thai fish sauce

3 tablespoons fresh lime juice

2 teaspoons seasoned rice-wine vinegar

2 tablespoons smooth peanut butter

2 tablespoons brown sugar

1 teaspoon toasted sesame oil

½ cup coconut milk (see NOTE)

½ cup milk

Kosher salt and freshly ground black pepper

GARNISH: chopped fresh cilantro, toasted sesame seeds

In a large stockpot, heat oil over medium-high heat. Add onions, celery, garlic, ginger, and carrots and sauté for 5 to 6 minutes, until onions are translucent. Add stock, red pepper flakes, coriander, turmeric, fish sauce, lime juice, vinegar, peanut butter, brown sugar, sesame oil, coconut milk, and milk and bring to a simmer. Cover and lightly simmer for 25 to 30 minutes. Let cool slightly.

Transfer the mixture to a food processor or blender and pulse several times. This may need to be done in batches. Purée until smooth. Season to taste.

Store, covered, in refrigerator until ready to serve. To serve, bring soup to low boil. Ladle into soup bowls and sprinkle with chopped cilantro and toasted sesame seeds. This soup can be served chilled as well.

NOTE: Coconut milk, used extensively in Thai cooking, is finding its way into more mainstream grocery stores in addition to being available in Asian food stores. If unavailable, use whole milk instead.

SERVES 6 AS AN APPETIZER

Baked Ham with Spicy Apricot-Orange Glaze and Curried Apple Couscous (Classic Pairing)

RECOMMENDED WINE: Gewürztraminer
ALTERNATIVE WINE: Riesling

GEWÜRZTRAMINER IS A FAR MORE VERSATILE WINE AT THE TABLE THAN MOST COOKS REALIZE, BUT IT IS CLASSICALLY PAIRED WITH SMOKED AND SALTIER FOODS, SUCH AS THIS BAKED HAM. THE FLAVORS PULL TOGETHER HARMONIOUSLY BECAUSE OF THE SPICY ORANGE GLAZE, WHICH ADDS SOME SWEETNESS TO THE DISH, ALONG WITH THE AROMATIC CURRIED COUSCOUS.

1 8- to 9-pound smoked ham

20 whole cloves

GLAZE

1½ cups fresh orange juice

1 tablespoon minced orange zest

4 cups Gewürztraminer or Riesling (two 750-milliliter bottles required)

1 tablespoon Dijon mustard

½ teaspoon ground ginger

1 teaspoon dried sage

5 tablespoons apricot jam

¼ teaspoon minced chipotle chiles in adobo (see page 175)

¾ cup brown sugar

1 tablespoon unsalted butter

1 medium green apple, cored, peeled, seeded, diced, and sprinkled with lemon juice

1½ teaspoons curry powder

2 cups chicken stock

⅛ teaspoon cayenne pepper

1 10-ounce box couscous (1½ cups)

¼ cup minced green onions

⅛ cup diced toasted almonds

Kosher salt

½ cup golden raisins

1 teaspoon cornstarch mixed with 1 teaspoon cold water

Trim ham of fat down to a ¼-inch layer. Score crisscross slashes into fat and stick cloves into ham, evenly distributed throughout. Put ham in a large, foil-lined, ovenproof baking dish.

To make glaze, in a medium sauté pan or skillet, combine all ingredients and bring to a boil. Reduce heat, stir, and simmer for 7 to 8 minutes. Transfer to a plastic bowl and let cool.

Preheat oven to 350°F. Place ham in the dish and pour glaze over the top. Press brown sugar over top of entire ham. Bake ham for 1¼ hours, basting frequently with the glaze.

In a small sauté pan or skillet, heat butter. Add apple and ½ teaspoon curry powder and sauté for 7 to 8 minutes. Keep warm.

In a small sauté pan or skillet, bring the stock, remaining 1 teaspoon curry powder, and cayenne to a boil. Stir in the couscous and remove from heat. Cover and let stand for 10 minutes to absorb liquid. Fluff couscous with a fork. Add apples, green onions, and almonds and mix thoroughly. Add salt to taste. Keep warm.

Remove ham from oven and keep warm under foil. Add pan drippings to a sauce pan and bring to a steady simmer. Add raisins and cornstarch mixture and thicken for a couple of minutes.

To serve, carve ham into slices. Top with sauce and serve couscous alongside.

SERVES 10 AS AN ENTRÉE

Viognier (pronounced "VEE-oh-nyay") is a relatively new grape to most wine drinkers, although it has existed for many years on the rugged, granite slopes in Condrieu in the northern Rhône region of France, where it arrived via either Roman legionnaires or Greeks from Marseilles around 600 B.C.

Viognier from Condrieu in France is limited in availability since acreage is extremely small. Subsequently, there is relatively little production, and the wines are quite rare. More Viognier has been planted in last few years in the southern regions of France. These wines are considerably less expensive than those from Condrieu, but they are not nearly as complex or interesting as the real thing.

Only in the past ten years has Viognier been grown in California, and really only in the past five years has its acreage grown beyond the miniscule stage. There are, in fact, a little over five hundred acres of Viognier planted in all of California, but acreage is expanding steadily. Surprisingly, there is some fine Viognier being grown in Virginia as well.

Viognier is quite difficult to grow because it is susceptible to rot and climatic variables. In order to achieve high quality in certain locales, it must be severely pruned in order to control its vigorous growth and minimize yields. Viognier is relatively late to ripen, which also makes for unpredictability during harvest. All of these variables contribute to its scarcity.

Like many other varietals, California Viognier is more approachable than its French counterpart. It varies in style from those fermented in stainless steel and not introduced to oak, to heavily barrel-fermented, Chardonnay-like bottlings, which can display as much oak as they do fruit. Most California Viogniers, regardless of where they are made, are also fairly expensive due to their scarcity. They generally range in price from fifteen to thirty dollars, with very few bottles under twelve dollars.

So, why bother with Viognier if it's so rare and expensive? Simply, Viognier is an exotic, fragrant grape with an alluring array of smells and flavors that make it quite intriguing to drink. There is a certain mystery to Viognier: Its fullness and richness, which are natural characteristics of the grape itself, are similar to Chardonnay, while its bouquet is more reminiscent of Gewürztraminer. Most of all, Viognier is about fruit and mouthfeel; it has distinctive flavors, an opulent texture, and it is fairly heady stuff.

Despite being high in alcohol (often over 14 percent), fat in the mouth (full-bodied), and lower in acidity, Viognier can be an interesting wine to pair with more aromatic, full-flavored foods. While typically made in a dry style, its floral bouquet and high alcohol often give it the perception of being sweet, which it is not. In the end, you can enjoy Viognier for its incomparable, exotic character.

VIOGNIER

TYPICAL AROMAS & FLAVORS

Peach, Dried Peach
Apricot, Dried Apricot
Honeysuckle
Orange Blossom
Spiced Orange
Vanilla
Oak
Honey
Mineral

BASE INGREDIENTS

Base ingredients refer to the main ingredient of the dish: meat, poultry, game, seafood, shell-fish, or vegetable. These represent the core ingredients that are most likely to be matched with a varietal, although successful pairings result as much from the other ingredients used in the dish as they do the base ingredient.

Salmon, Mahi-Mahi, Halibut, Sea Bass, Shrimp, Crab, Lobster, Mussels, Smoked Mussels, Smoked Oysters, Chicken, Duck, Pork, Veal

BRIDGE INGREDIENTS

Bridge ingredients help connect the food and the wine through their interaction in flavor, body, intensity, or basic taste.

Corn
Squash
Dried Fruit: Apricot, Peach
Tropical Fruit: Pineapple, Coconut,
    Mango, Papaya
Citrus Fruit: Orange, Blood Orange
Spices: Ginger, Curry Powder, Sweet
    Paprika
Herbs: Rosemary, Lavender, Basil,
    Thyme, Fennel Seed
Toasted Nuts: Macadamia, Almonds,
    Pine Nuts, Cashews
Honey
Cream, Sour Cream
Butter
Olive Oil

BEST SOURCE REGIONS
VIOGNIER

The following is a list of countries, regions, and appellations (a wine word referencing specific growing locales) that produce the highest-quality versions of these wines.

This is not intended to be a complete list, only a reference for where the finest renditions can be found.

FRANCE
Rhône
Condrieu
Château-Grillet
Languedoc-Rousillon
CALIFORNIA
San Luis Obispo
Santa Barbara
Napa Valley
Sonoma
Mendocino
VIRGINIA

VIOGNIER STYLES

Fruity:
Medium to medium-full body; focus on fruit with little or no oak; exotic and aromatic with fairly intense flavors; can be powerful and high in alcohol

Barrel-Aged:
Medium to medium-full body; exotic aromas and flavors with hints of vanilla and spice from barrel fermentation and aging; powerful and rich, yet elegant; can be high in alcohol

TIPS TO SUCCESSFUL
MATCHES WITH VIOGNIER

1

Because of its full body, Viognier matches best with foods that have some richness.

2

Dishes with a smoky character often pair quite successfully with Viognier.

3

Because of the overt and pleasant peachy, apricot character of the wine, dishes with either of these fruits can support the wine beautifully.

Louis-Style Shrimp in Endive "Boats"

RECOMMENDED WINE: Viognier

ALTERNATIVE WINE: Gewürztraminer

THESE TASTY "SHRIMP BOATS" WORK EQUALLY WELL PASSED AS AN APPETIZER OR SERVED AS A FIRST COURSE. THE SWEET, SPICY ZING OF THE DRESSING, COUPLED WITH ITS CREAMY TEXTURE, HEIGHTENS THE EXOTIC FLAVORS AND LUSH BODY OF VIOGNIER EXTREMELY WELL. A FRUITY, OFF-DRY GEWÜRZTRAMINER WORKS ALMOST AS WELL AS VIOGNIER TO MIRROR THESE FLAVORS.

¾ cup sour cream

⅓ cup prepared seafood cocktail sauce

2 tablespoons minced cornichons
   or dill pickles

1 tablespoon minced green onions

2 teaspoons chopped fresh tarragon
   (1 teaspoon dried)

1 tablespoon chopped fresh parsley

⅛ teaspoon kosher salt

   Pinch of white pepper

   Dash of hot sauce

1½ pounds bay shrimp

1¼ pounds Belgian endive

GARNISH: chopped parsley

In a large mixing bowl, combine sour cream, cocktail sauce, cornichons, green onions, tarragon, parsley, salt, pepper, and hot sauce and mix thoroughly. Add shrimp and mix well. Season to taste. Refrigerate, covered, for at least 1 hour.

Trim ends from endive and gently pull off outer leaves so that they remain in one piece. Discard the smaller, inner leaves. Rinse in cold water and dry. Keep endive chilled until ready to use.

To serve, distribute endive leaves evenly in a circle on six large appetizer plates. Alternatively, these can be presented on a large platter. Spoon a small amount of shrimp into endive leaves. Sprinkle with chopped parsley.

SERVES 6 AS AN APPETIZER

Smoked Oyster–Cream Cheese Wontons

RECOMMENDED WINE: *Viognier*
ALTERNATIVE WINE: *Champagne/sparkling wine*

THIS TASTY LITTLE APPETIZER OFFERS A TEXTURAL CONNECTION TO THE SILKY CHARACTER OF VIOGNIER. WHILE THE CREAMY FILLING SLIDES ACROSS THE PALATE AND INTERTWINES WITH THE WINE, THE SMOKY OYSTERS ARE COMPLEMENTED BY VIOGNIER'S EXOTIC FRUIT FLAVORS. CHAMPAGNE/SPARKLING WINE PLAYS A DIFFERENT ROLE, OFFERING CRISP ACIDITY AS A CONTRAST TO THE FILLING. THIS RECIPE CAN BE HALVED FOR SMALLER GROUPS.

24 round wonton wrappers

7½ ounces (2 cans) smoked oysters, drained of oil

8 ounces cream cheese

1 teaspoon white-wine Worcestershire sauce

½ teaspoon jalapeño Tabasco or other hot sauce

¾ teaspoon minced lemon zest

1½ teaspoons minced fresh chives

1½ teaspoons fresh lemon juice

White pepper

GARNISH: minced lemon zest, minced fresh chives

Preheat oven to 350°F. Lightly oil a mini-muffin tin and press wonton wrappers into the holes in the tin so that the wrappers come up the sides of each hole. Bake wontons for 8 to 10 minutes. Remove and let rest.

In a food processor or blender, combine oysters, cream cheese, Worcestershire, Tabasco, lemon zest, chives, and lemon juice and process for about 15 to 20 seconds until well blended. Do not overprocess. Season to taste.

With a spatula, remove the mixture from the processor bowl or blender and place in another small bowl. Carefully spoon the mixture into the wonton cups.

Place the wontons back in the oven at 375°F and bake for an additional 10 to 15 minutes, until they are golden. Remove the wontons from the tin and place on a decorative serving plate. Garnish each wonton with a light sprinkling of lemon zest and chives.

Reserve additional oyster–cream cheese mixture as a spread for crackers. It will keep well in the refrigerator for a week to ten days.

MAKES 24; SERVES 12 AS AN APPETIZER

Lobster Salad with Apricot-Walnut Vinaigrette

RECOMMENDED WINE: Viognier
ALTERNATIVE WINE: Chardonnay

VIOGNIER RELIES A GREAT DEAL ON ITS UNIQUE APRICOT-PEACH FRUIT FLAVORS AND SENSUOUS MOUTHFEEL TO ACHIEVE ITS BEGUILING EFFECT. THIS RECIPE FEATURES RICH LOBSTER WITH A LUSCIOUS APRICOT-WALNUT VINAIGRETTE TO CAPTURE THE VERY ESSENCE OF FLAVOR AND TEXTURE IN THE WINE. CHARDONNAY, BECAUSE OF ITS FULL BODY AND NATURAL AFFINITY WITH THE RICHNESS OF LOBSTER, IS ALSO A NICE MATCH. THE RECIPE WILL SERVE TWO HEALTHY APPETITES OR FOUR LIGHTER ONES.

1 2-pound fresh live Maine lobster

1 tablespoon white-wine vinegar

2½ tablespoons apricot nectar

1 tablespoon walnut oil

¼ cup extra-virgin olive oil

⅛ teaspoon white-wine Worcestershire

1 teaspoon dried tarragon

Kosher salt and freshly ground black pepper

3–5 ounces mixed salad greens

GARNISH: 8 to 12 cherry tomatoes

In a large soup pot, bring water to a rolling boil and place live lobster in the pot. Cover and boil for 7 to 8 minutes. Remove lobster with tongs and let drain in the sink. Place lobster on a large plate and refrigerate for 1 to 2 hours.

In a small, nonreactive bowl, combine vinegar, apricot nectar, oils, Worcestershire, and tarragon. Remove lobster from the refrigerator and pull claws from the body. Open body cavity and, with a spoon, remove the greenish colored tomalley. Spoon 1½ teaspoons of it into the vinaigrette and whisk thoroughly. Season to taste.

Remove all lobster meat from the tail and claws. Decoratively place greens and lobster meat on chilled salad plates. Garnish with cherry tomatoes. Drizzle whisked dressing over lobster and greens and serve.

SERVES 2 TO 4 AS AN APPETIZER OR LIGHT ENTRÉE

Chicken Paprika with Dried Peach and Almond Relish (Classic Pairing)

RECOMMENDED WINE: Viognier
ALTERNATIVE WINE: Riesling

THE OPULENT FLAVORS OF VIOGNIER MATCH WELL WITH THIS DISH, WHICH FEATURES THE SWEET-HOT PERFUME OF PAPRIKA ACCENTED BY A DRIED-FRUIT RELISH THAT EMPHASIZES THE NATURAL APRICOT-PEACH CHARACTER IN THE WINE. DON'T BE DISSUADED BY THE SLIGHTLY LONG LIST OF INGREDIENTS. THIS DISH IS REALLY QUITE EASY. FOR BEST RESULTS, USE BOTH HOT AND SWEET FORMS OF PAPRIKA. RIESLING, WITH ITS EXUBERANT FRUIT CHARACTER, IS AN ATTRACTIVE ALTERNATIVE.

RELISH

¾ cup chopped dried peaches or apricots

¾ tablespoon raspberry vinegar

¾ teaspoon honey

3 tablespoons toasted diced almonds

2 tablespoons chopped green onions

2 tablespoons chopped parsley

½ teaspoon caraway seed

½ teaspoon chopped lemon zest

—

4 large boneless, skinless chicken breasts

¼ teaspoon kosher salt

½ teaspoon hot paprika

¼ teaspoon ground sage

¼ teaspoon chopped lemon zest

1 tablespoon butter

1–2 tablespoons vegetable oil

1½ cups sliced yellow onions

2 cloves garlic, chopped

2 cups sliced button mushrooms (about 8 ounces)

1 teaspoon dried marjoram

¾ teaspoon sweet paprika

¾ teaspoon caraway seed

½ cup chicken stock

1¼ cups sour cream

Kosher salt and freshly ground black pepper

To make relish, in a small bowl, mix all ingredients together and refrigerate for 1 to 2 hours.

Rinse chicken breasts with cold water and pat dry. Season chicken with salt, hot paprika, sage, and lemon zest.

In a large sauté pan or skillet over medium heat, heat butter and 1 tablespoon oil. Add chicken and brown on both sides. Remove chicken from pan, place on paper towels, and pat dry.

Add the second tablespoon of oil to pan, if needed, and heat. Add onions and garlic and sauté for 3 to 4 minutes until onions are translucent. Add mushrooms, marjoram, sweet paprika, and caraway seed and continue cooking for 3 to 4 minutes. Add chicken stock and sour cream and stir thoroughly.

Return chicken to pan and cover. Simmer for 12 to 14 minutes. Season to taste.

To serve, remove chicken breasts from pan and top with hot sauce. Spoon relish on top of chicken. Serve with buttered noodles or spaetzle.

SERVES 4 AS AN ENTRÉE

Duck Breasts with Honey, Ginger, and Lavender

RECOMMENDED WINE: Viognier

ALTERNATIVE WINE: Pinot Noir

VIOGNIER IS AN INCREDIBLY AROMATIC WINE. THIS RECIPE INTENDS TO CAPTURE THIS CHARACTER WITH A COMBINATION OF EQUALLY AROMATIC INGREDIENTS—SNAPPY GINGER, EXOTIC LAVENDER, AND THE SWEET SCENTS OF VANILLA AND HONEY. THE SAUCE OFFERS LUSHNESS THAT WORKS TEXTURALLY WITH THE FULLNESS OF THE WINE AS WELL. THE RED MEAT AND INTRIGUING SPICE OF THE DISH CAN ALSO ACCENTUATE THE CHERRY-SPICE CHARACTER OF PINOT NOIR.

2 whole boneless duck breasts	1 teaspoon pure vanilla extract
⅛ teaspoon mixed whole peppercorns, crushed	¾ teaspoon honey
1 teaspoon white-wine Worcestershire	½ teaspoon chopped fresh tarragon (¼ teaspoon dried)
¾ teaspoon ground ginger	1 tablespoon unsalted butter at room temperature
1 teaspoon dried lavender (see NOTE)	Kosher salt
1 shallot, thinly sliced	1 teaspoon vegetable oil
½ cup white wine	GARNISH: tarragon sprigs
1¾ cups chicken stock	

Cut whole duck breasts into two halves lengthwise and trim all excess fat from the ends and sides of the breast. With the tip of a sharp knife, score the fat side of the breasts by cutting an X in the middle of the breast.

Marinate breasts in half of the crushed pepper, Worcestershire, ¼ teaspoon ginger, lavender, and shallot slices. Cover and refrigerate for 2 to 3 hours.

In a large sauté pan or skillet, combine wine, stock, vanilla, remaining ½ teaspoon ginger, reserved crushed pepper, and sliced shallots removed from the top of the duck breasts, and bring mixture to a boil. Reduce heat to a simmer and reduce liquid by half. Add honey and tarragon and reduce further to sauce consistency. Remove from heat and swirl in butter. Season to taste. Keep warm until ready to serve.

In another large sauté pan or skillet, heat oil over medium heat. Place duck breasts in pan, skin side down, and sauté for 5 to 6 minutes until lightly brown. Turn breasts and continue to cook on meat side for 2 to 4 minutes until medium rare. The juices should run pinkish. Do not overcook the duck.

Remove breasts from the pan and slice at an angle. Fan breasts on the plate and top with the sauce. Garnish with sprigs of tarragon. Serve with wild rice studded with dried cherries and minced green onions.

NOTE: Dried lavender is a delightfully aromatic herb that can be purchased at most health food stores. It is excellent on Grilled Lamb with Olive Sauce (page 172), and it keeps very well stored in an airtight jar.

SERVES 2 AS ENTRÉE

Almost without question, Chardonnay is the world's greatest white wine, although Riesling lovers would vigorously challenge this notion. Surely, Chardonnay's popularity is unquestioned. In the United States alone, about 24 million cases of Chardonnay are consumed each year; this amounts to about 300 million bottles a year, which is a lot of exposure!

That being said, Chardonnay as a partner to food is extremely challenging. In fact, of all wines, it is probably the single most difficult to match with food. The reasons are simple: Chardonnay is relatively high in alcohol, typically ranging from 13 to 14 percent, and it spends more time in oak barrels than any other white wine varietal. The combination of weight and body from alcohol and sometimes excessive oakiness from barrel aging presents problems for the Chardonnay lover who wishes to pair it successfully with foods. Nevertheless, few enthusiasts seem to care since the wine offers widespread pleasure and is positively delicious to drink.

Like some other varietals, Chardonnay is a bit of a chameleon and varies dramatically in style. It can be elegant, refined, and slightly austere as well as full and opulent, depending on its place of origin and the style that the winemaker expresses.

The "manipulation" of Chardonnay in its fermentation and barrel-aging regime is thought to be necessary because of the relatively one-dimensional character of the grape itself. Chardonnay tends to be somewhat innocuous, therefore most winemakers prefer to craft the wine in a manner that is appealing to consumers (and often to themselves). There are significant differences in style, for example, between the more full-blown California and Australian versions and their French counterparts, which tend to be more restrained and higher in acid.

There are fine examples of Chardonnay made with little or no oak aging, and these wines are far easier to match with food than their weightier counterparts. Americans, for the most part, seem to love their Chardonnay with the rich, buttery mouthfeel and layered flavors that result from malolactic fermentation (a secondary fermentation which converts tart malic acid to rounder, softer lactic acid) and extended barrel aging.

At times, Chardonnay can seem like a celebration of oak (the seasoning agent), not the fruit itself. Chardonnay made in this style is very delicious to drink as an aperitif, but it is unusually difficult to pair with food, unless it is matched with relatively simply prepared seafood and lighter meats.

There are solutions to this apparent problem, particularly through the use of "bridge" ingredients that can help marry the dish to the wine. Ingredients such as toasted nuts, tarragon, mushrooms, bacon, butter, cream, and even corn are surprisingly good connections to Chardonnay.

However, you'll find that most of the recipes in this chapter tend to focus on the textural elements of Chardonnay, offering dishes with similar weight and body to the typically viscous (fat, full-bodied) nature of Chardonnay. While flavor matching with Chardonnay's apple, pear, tropical fruit, and citrus character is possible, the pairing of textural elements tends to be the most successful.

CHARDONNAY

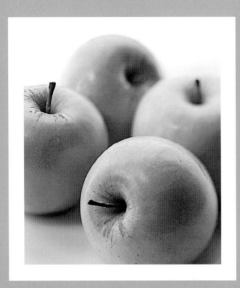

TYPICAL AROMAS & FLAVORS

Green Apple, Golden Delicious
Pear
Peach
Honeydew Melon
Citrus: Lemon, Lime, Orange
Tropical Fruit: Pineapple, Passion Fruit,
    Papaya, Guava, Banana, Coconut,
    Kiwi
Fig
Quince
Toast, Baked Bread, Yeast
Butter, Buttered Popcorn
Butterscotch
Vanilla
Honey
Oatmeal
Hazelnut, Toasted Hazelnut
Oak
Mineral

BASE INGREDIENTS

*Base ingredients refer to the main ingredient of
the dish: meat, poultry, game, seafood, shellfish,
or vegetable. These represent the core ingredients
that are most likely to be matched with a varietal,
although successful pairings result as much from
the other ingredients used in the dish as they do
the base ingredient.*

Crab, Shrimp, Clams, Scallops, Lobster, Halibut,
Sea Bass, Monkfish, Snapper, Trout, Grouper,
Swordfish, Salmon, Tuna, Chicken, Game Hen,
Turkey, Pheasant, Goose, Veal, Pork

BRIDGE INGREDIENTS

*Bridge ingredients help connect the food and the
wine through their interaction in flavor, body,
intensity, or basic taste.*

Citrus: Orange, Lime, Lemon, Citrus Zest
Pears
Apples
Fennel (roasted)
Corn
Avocado
Pumpkin
Squash
Coconut, Coconut Milk
Polenta
Herbs: Tarragon, Basil, Thyme
Spices: Nutmeg, Curry Powder, Ginger,
    Saffron
Toasted Nuts: Hazelnuts, Pine Nuts,
    Cashews, Almonds
Olive Oil
Butter
Cream, Milk, Sour Cream
Mushrooms: Shiitake, Oyster, Crimini,
    Chanterelle, Button
Cheeses: Brie, Parmesan, Swiss, Jack
Bacon, Pancetta
Sweet Onions
Roasted Garlic
Dijon Mustard
Tropical Fruit: Mango, Papaya, Pineapple

BEST SOURCE REGIONS
CHARDONNAY

The following is a list of countries, regions, and appellations (a wine word referencing specific growing locales) that produce the highest-quality versions of these wines.

This is not intended to be a complete list, only a reference for where the finest renditions can be found.

CALIFORNIA
  Napa Valley
    Carneros
  Sonoma
    Carneros
  Mendocino
  Santa Cruz
  Santa Barbara
  Santa Maria
  Monterey
NEW YORK
  Long Island
FRANCE
  Burgundy
    Côte de Beaune
      Meursault
      Puligny-Montrachet
      Chassagne-Montrachet
      Corton-Charlemagne
      Côte-Challonaise
      Côte-Mâconnais
  Chablis
ITALY
  Trentino-Alto Adige
  Friuli
AUSTRALIA
  Barossa Valley
  Hunter Valley
  Margaret River
  Yarra Valley
  Padthaway
NEW ZEALAND
CHILE
SOUTH AFRICA

CHARDONNAY STYLES

Lighter:
  Light-medium body; often fermented in stainless steel rather than oak barrels; more delicate and fruity; often lower in alcohol (12 to 13 percent)

Medium Barrel-Aged:
  Medium body; richer with toasty-oak flavors; slightly higher in alcohol

Full Barrel-Aged:
  Medium-full body; quite rich with mouth-filling buttery, toasty-oak flavors

TIPS TO SUCCESSFUL MATCHES WITH CHARDONNAY

1

With most Chardonnays, dishes with some richness help underscore the fuller body and creamy mouthfeel of the wine.

2

Spicy dishes (with chiles) accentuate the alcohol and oak in most Chardonnays, and therefore should be avoided.

3

In addition to a wide variety of appetizers, richer seafood, shellfish, and poultry dishes, Chardonnay pairs nicely with many veal and pork entrées, particularly when prepared more simply so that the wine doesn't fight with complex ingredients.

4

A sprinkling of toasted nuts will help draw many dishes to the oaky flavors of most Chardonnays.

5

Butter and cream love Chardonnay, but you may not love them every time you open a bottle.

Chilled Corn and Sun-Dried Tomato Chowder with Goat Cheese–Chive Croutons

RECOMMENDED WINE: Chardonnay
ALTERNATIVE WINE: Sauvignon/Fumé Blanc

TWO OF MY "SECRET INGREDIENTS" TO PAIR WITH CHARDONNAY ARE CORN AND TARRAGON. NOW THAT THE SECRET'S OUT: THE SWEET SUCCULENCE OF SUMMER CORN, COMBINED WITH THE INCOMPARABLE SWEET-TART QUALITY OF SUN-DRIED TOMATOES AND THE LICORICE-LIKE CHARACTER OF TARRAGON, FIND A READY, WILLING, AND ABLE COMPANION IN CHARDONNAY. THE GOAT CHEESE CROUTONS ARE AN ELEGANT ADDITION TO THE CHOWDER, OFFERING A CREAMY TEXTURE TO FURTHER ENHANCE THIS WINE AND FOOD FLIRTATION. THE CHOWDER CAN BE SERVED HOT, TOO. SAUVIGNON/FUMÉ BLANC WORKS AS WELL, FINDING PARTICULAR SYNERGY WITH THE GOAT CHEESE CROUTONS.

4 ears sweet corn, husks removed

1½ tablespoons olive oil

2 cups chopped sweet onions (Maui, Vidalia, or Walla Walla)

1 tablespoon chopped fresh tarragon (½ tablespoon dried)

1 teaspoon ground cumin

¼ teaspoon ground turmeric

1½ teaspoons minced lemon zest

2 14½-ounce cans, plus 6 ounces chicken stock

¾ cup white wine

1 tablespoon chopped roasted garlic (see page 164)

¾ tablespoon fresh lemon juice

1 cup sour cream

¾ cup sun-dried tomato halves (rehydrated in water and drained)

Kosher salt and freshly ground black pepper

4 ounces fresh goat cheese

1 tablespoon minced chives

1 sourdough baguette, cut on the diagonal into twelve ¼-inch slices

GARNISH: chopped fresh tarragon

Using a serrated knife, remove corn from cob by scraping down the cob (this will yield about 2 cups). Reserve the cobs. In a large soup pot, heat olive oil. Add onions, tarragon, cumin, turmeric, and 1 teaspoon lemon zest and sauté for 7 to 8 minutes. Add corn, reserved corn cobs, stock, and wine and bring to a full, rolling boil. Reduce heat to a simmer and cook, covered, for 12 minutes. Remove cobs with tongs.

Carefully transfer soup mixture to a food processor or blender. Add roasted garlic, lemon juice, and sour cream. Process soup in batches. Add sun-dried tomatoes and rough chop. Stir thoroughly. Season to taste and refrigerate for 3 to 4 hours. Soup can be thinned with a little extra chicken stock, if necessary.

Mix goat cheese, chives, and ½ teaspoon lemon zest together using both hands. Refrigerate until ready to serve.

When ready to serve, spread goat cheese–chive mixture on sourdough slices. Put under broiler for about 5 to 6 minutes, until goat cheese starts to turn color slightly. Divide soup evenly in large soup bowls. Place two crisscrossed croutons halfway into soup with the other halves resting against the edge of the bowl. Garnish with chopped tarragon.

SERVES 6 AS AN APPETIZER

Scallop and Smoked Salmon Cakes
with Rémoulade

RECOMMENDED WINE: Chardonnay
ALTERNATIVE WINE: Viognier

———————————

THE SWEET SUCCULENCE OF THESE LUSCIOUS SEAFOOD CAKES COMBINES WITH THE CREAMY TEXTURE OF THE RÉMOULADE TO MAKE FOR A PERFECT MATCH WITH CHARDONNAY. THIS IS A GOOD EXAMPLE OF HOW SIMILAR TEXTURES (MEANING WEIGHT OR BODY) CAN BRING A WINE AND FOOD COMBINATION TOGETHER. MATCHED WITH A FULL-FLAVORED VIOGNIER, THE DISH WORKS BEAUTIFULLY AS WELL.

RÉMOULADE

1 egg (briefly boiled, optional)

2 tablespoons fresh lemon juice

1½ tablespoons coarse-grained mustard

¼ teaspoon kosher salt

¼ teaspoon freshly ground black pepper

½ cup olive oil

2 teaspoons tomato paste

1 tablespoon chopped fresh parsley
    (½ tablespoon dried)

½ tablespoon minced fresh chives
    (¼ tablespoon dried)

½ tablespoon chopped fresh thyme
    (¼ tablespoon dried)

1 tablespoon chopped capers, drained

1½ tablespoons chopped cornichons
    or dill pickles, drained

1 teaspoon minced lemon zest

———

1 pound fresh sea scallops, drained

¼ pound smoked salmon pieces,
    skin removed

⅓ cup finely chopped yellow or
    green bell pepper

⅓ cup finely chopped red bell pepper

⅓ cup finely chopped yellow onions

2 teaspoons minced chives

¾ cup fresh bread crumbs

2 tablespoons finely chopped parsley

2 tablespoons unsalted butter

4 ounces mixed greens (optional)

GARNISH: chopped red and yellow
    bell pepper

To make rémoulade, in a food processor or blender, add egg, lemon juice, mustard, salt, and pepper. With the processor running, add oil in a slow, steady stream until the mixture emulsifies. Add tomato paste, herbs, capers, cornichons, and lemon zest and continue to process until well mixed. Scrape out with a spatula into a small bowl and refrigerate, covered, until ready to use.

Place scallops and smoked salmon in a food processor and pulse about 10 times so that scallops and salmon are in small chunks but are not overprocessed and mushy.

In a large bowl, combine chopped scallops and smoked salmon with peppers, onions, chives, and ¼ cup of the rémoulade, reserving the remainder to use with finished cakes.

In a separate bowl, mix bread crumbs and parsley together thoroughly. Add just enough bread crumb mixture to the seafood mixture to allow it to hold together when formed into small patties. Divide mixture into 12 equal portions, form into small patties, and place on waxed paper.

Preheat oven to 400°F. In a nonstick sauté pan, melt butter over low-medium heat. Sauté patties until golden brown, about 2 to 3 minutes. Turn carefully and press down slightly to flatten. Cook for an additional

RECIPE CONTINUES

2 to 3 minutes. With a spatula, place seafood cakes on a baking sheet and bake in the oven for 12 minutes, or until they are cooked through.

To serve, place a small amount of mixed greens on each plate. Place two seafood cakes on top of greens. Drizzle rémoulade over cakes and greens. Sprinkle chopped peppers over top and serve.

SERVES 6 AS AN APPETIZER

Crab, Jícama, and Mango Salad with Lemon-Curry Dressing (Classic Pairing)

RECOMMENDED WINE: Chardonnay

ALTERNATIVE WINE: Viognier

THIS COMBINATION WORKS BECAUSE THE RICHNESS OF THE SUCCULENT CRAB MEAT, THE TROPICAL FRUIT FLAVORS OF THE MANGO, AND THE LIGHTLY CURRIED CITRUS DRESSING HELP SHOWCASE THE RIPE TROPICAL FRUIT AND CITRUS FLAVORS FOUND IN MANY CHARDONNAYS. THE USE OF CURRY POWDER ENLIVENS THE DRESSING JUST ENOUGH TO PLAY INTO THE SPICE CHARACTER THAT COMES FROM THE WINE'S BARREL AGING. VIOGNIER, WITH ITS OPULENT TEXTURE, ALSO MARRIES WELL WITH THIS ELEGANT APPETIZER.

1 pound crab meat, picked over for shells

¾ cup diced fresh or frozen mango

2½ tablespoons minced fresh chives

1 cup peeled and diced jícama

DRESSING

Juice of 1 lemon (Meyer lemon, if possible)

1 teaspoon minced lemon zest

½ tablespoon white-wine vinegar

⅓ cup mayonnaise or sour cream

1½ teaspoons curry powder

⅛ teaspoon fresh ground black pepper

——

12 leaves butter lettuce, rinsed and dried

GARNISH: chopped chives, 6 lemon slices

In a medium nonreactive mixing bowl, combine crab meat, mango, chives, and jícama and mix well.

To make dressing, in a small mixing bowl, combine all ingredients and whisk thoroughly. Add dressing to crab mixture and combine thoroughly. Allow to sit, refrigerated, for at least 2 hours. Season to taste.

To serve, place 2 butter lettuce leaves side by side on each salad plate. Mix crab thoroughly. Spoon mixture equally onto lettuce leaves on each plate. Sprinkle with chopped chives and garnish with lemon slices.

SERVES 6 AS AN APPETIZER

Risotto with Squash, Oyster Mushrooms, and Peppered Jack Cheese

RECOMMENDED WINE: Chardonnay
ALTERNATIVE WINE: Sauvignon/Fumé Blanc

THIS RISOTTO COMBINES EARTHY OYSTER MUSHROOMS, SWEET SQUASH, AND CREAMY PEPPERED JACK CHEESE IN A FLATTERING FLAVOR AND TEXTURE MATCH WITH CHARDONNAY. THE SQUASH AND MUSHROOM FLAVORS MESH NICELY WITH THE WINE, WHILE THE TEXTURE OF THE RISOTTO ACCENTUATES THE FULL BODY OF THE WINE. THIS MÉLANGE IS PARTICULARLY WELL SUITED TO CHARDONNAYS WITHOUT A LOT OF OAK. IF THAT TASK BECOMES DIFFICULT, SAUVIGNON/FUMÉ BLANC WORKS QUITE EFFORTLESSLY, TOO.

1½ pounds seeded, sliced butternut squash (see NOTE)

4 tablespoons (¼ cup) unsalted butter or olive oil

8 ounces oyster mushrooms, sliced (about 2 cups)

¼ cup chopped shallots

2 large cloves garlic

2 teaspoons chopped fresh basil (1 teaspoon dried)

½ teaspoon dried summer savory

1 cup Arborio rice

¼ cup white wine

3 cups hot chicken stock

½ cup grated peppered Jack cheese

¼ cup chopped chives

Kosher salt and white pepper

GARNISH: 12 baby cherry tomatoes

In a preheated 375°F oven, bake squash for 40 to 45 minutes, until tender but not mushy. Cut squash away from skin and into ½-inch dice. Reserve 1¼ cups for risotto and keep warm in foil.

In a large sauté pan or skillet over medium heat, heat 1 tablespoon of butter or oil. Add mushrooms and sauté for 5 to 7 minutes, stirring occasionally, until slightly browned. Remove from pan and reserve.

In the same pan, heat remaining 3 tablespoons of butter or oil. Add shallots, garlic, herbs, and rice and sauté for 3 to 5 minutes, until rice is translucent. Add the wine and continue to simmer until wine is absorbed. Add ½ cup of chicken stock and cook until the liquid is absorbed, stirring constantly. Continue adding stock in small amounts and stirring until the liquid is absorbed in the rice each time before adding more liquid.

In the last 5 minutes, add the cheese along with reserved squash and mushrooms and stir thoroughly. When rice is al dente, remove from heat and stir in chives. Season to taste. Serve in warm bowls or on warm plates. Garnish with cherry tomatoes.

NOTE: Smaller portions of butternut squash can often be found pre-sliced and packaged in the produce section. This dish only requires 1½ pounds, so this might be a good way to purchase it.

SERVES 4 TO 6 AS AN APPETIZER OR 2 TO 3 AS AN ENTRÉE

Rigatoni with Shiitake Mushrooms, Fennel, and Oysters

RECOMMENDED WINE: Chardonnay
ALTERNATIVE WINE: Sauvignon/Fumé Blanc

OYSTERS, WHETHER FRESH FROM THE WATERS OF THE PACIFIC OR ATLANTIC OR BOTTLED (CALLED FOR IN THIS RECIPE), HAVE A LUSCIOUS, SILKY TEXTURE THAT BALANCES THE LUSH ELEGANCE OF CRISPER-STYLE CHARDONNAYS (SUCH AS CHABLIS), PARTICULARLY WITH THE ADDITION OF A HINT OF CREAM TO HELP MAKE THE TEXTURAL CONNECTION. SHIITAKE MUSHROOMS, WITH THEIR EARTHY FLAVOR, AND FRESH FENNEL ADD COMPLEMENTARY FLAVOR NOTES TO THIS PAIRING. SAUVIGNON/FUMÉ BLANC WILL PROVIDE A CRISP, CLEAN ACID COUNTERPOINT TO THESE FLAVORS AS WELL.

1 pound dried rigatoni or other small pasta

¼ cup olive oil

4 cloves garlic, chopped

¼ cup chopped shallots

1 pound shiitake mushrooms, thinly sliced

2 cups thinly sliced fennel (stalks removed)

¼ cup chopped fresh basil
   (2 tablespoons dried)

⅓ cup white wine

½ cup fish stock or clam juice

½ cup cream or half-and-half

2 10-ounce jars Pacific oysters, drained

¾ cup seeded, chopped plum tomatoes

Kosher salt and freshly ground white pepper

GARNISH: fresh basil leaves

In a large pot of salted water, boil pasta for 7 to 8 minutes, or until al dente. Drain thoroughly. Return to pot, drizzle with a little olive oil and keep warm.

In a medium sauté pan or skillet over medium heat, heat olive oil. Add garlic, shallots, mushrooms, fennel, and basil and sauté for 5 to 6 minutes. Add wine, fish stock, and cream and simmer for 8 to 10 minutes more, reducing liquid slightly. Add oysters and tomatoes and heat through. Season to taste.

Combine oyster-mushroom mixture with pasta and heat thoroughly. Serve on warm plates with basil garnish.

SERVES 4 AS AN ENTRÉE

Spinach Fettuccine with Sea Bass and Lemongrass-Coconut Cream Sauce

RECOMMENDED WINE: Chardonnay

ALTERNATIVE WINE: Viognier

CHARDONNAY SEEMS TO STRUT ITS STUFF MOST CONFIDENTLY WHEN IT'S PAIRED WITH RICHER FOODS. IN THE CASE OF THIS TASTY SEAFOOD PASTA, THE LEMONGRASS-SPIKED COCONUT CREAM SAUCE PROVIDES THE BODY, TEXTURE, AND FLAVOR SYNCOPATION THAT MAKES FOR MAMBO AS OPPOSED TO BALLET. VIOGNIER, TOO, ADAPTS WELL TO AROMATIC DISHES AND WORKS SEAMLESSLY WITH THESE FLAVORS.

1 stalk fresh lemongrass or 1 teaspoon minced lime zest

3 tablespoons olive oil

3 tablespoons chopped shallots

2 tablespoons peeled, chopped fresh ginger

¾ cup sliced shiitake mushrooms

⅔ cup white wine

¾ cup broccoli florets, steamed or microwaved

1¾ cups unsweetened coconut milk (see NOTE)

¼ teaspoon saffron threads

⅛ teaspoon ground turmeric

½ teaspoon kosher salt

⅛ teaspoon freshly ground black pepper

2 tablespoons minced fresh chives

1½ pounds fresh sea bass, cut crosswise into ½-inch slices

1 teaspoon cornstarch mixed with 1 teaspoon cold water (optional)

1 pound spinach fettuccine

2 tablespoons toasted pine nuts

½ cup seeded and chopped tomatoes

Remove outer leaves and top dark green parts of lemongrass and trim end. Mince light-green and white parts very finely as it is rather fibrous. Reserve 1½ tablespoons for sauce.

In a large sauté pan or skillet, heat oil over medium heat. Add shallots, ginger, and lemongrass and sauté for 2 minutes. Add mushrooms and continue sautéing for 4 to 5 minutes. Add white wine, increase heat, and reduce wine by half. Add broccoli, coconut milk, saffron, turmeric, salt, pepper, and 1 tablespoon of the chives and cook at a steady simmer for 5 to 6 minutes to reduce liquid slightly. Reduce heat to a low simmer and add sea bass. Cook, covered, for 10 minutes, stirring and turning sea bass once. Keep warm until ready to serve. Season to taste. If a thicker sauce is desired, add cornstarch mixture and simmer for two more minutes.

In a large pot of boiling salted water, cook fettuccine for 6 to 7 minutes, or until al dente. Drain in a colander, return to pot, and drizzle with a little olive oil. Keep warm until ready to serve.

To serve, combine sauce and sea bass with pasta and heat through. Divide equally into warmed soup bowls. Garnish with pine nuts, tomatoes, and remaining chives.

NOTE: Coconut milk can be found in most Asian sections of grocery stores. In some areas, it might be found only in Asian grocery stores.

SERVES 5 TO 6 AS AN APPETIZER OR 3 TO 4 AS AN ENTRÉE

Broiled Monkfish with Fennel, Hazelnuts, and Orange Sauce

RECOMMENDED WINE: Chardonnay
ALTERNATIVE WINE: Sauvignon/Fumé Blanc

COAXING THE DELICIOUS BUT DIFFICULT-TO-MATCH FLAVORS OUT OF CHARDONNAY, THIS SEAFOOD DISH WRAPS ORANGE, FENNEL, AND TOASTED HAZELNUT FLAVORS AROUND SIMILAR NOTES IN THE WINE. MONKFISH, WITH A MEATY TEXTURE THAT RESEMBLES LOBSTER (IT IS SOMETIMES REFERRED TO AS "THE POOR MAN'S LOBSTER"), IS AN EXCELLENT FISH TO MATCH WITH CHARDONNAY. SAUVIGNON/FUMÉ BLANC PICKS UP THE CITRUS AND FENNEL ACCENTS IN THIS SAUCE AND FINDS A FRIENDLY CONNECTION AS WELL.

2 pounds monkfish or sea bass or grouper fillets

2½ tablespoons olive oil

1½ teaspoons curry powder

1 tablespoon chopped fennel fronds (see NOTE)

Kosher salt and white pepper

2 tablespoons chopped shallots

3 cups thinly sliced fennel (about 2 bulbs with core removed)

1 teaspoon crushed fennel seed

1 cup fresh orange juice

½ cup white wine

1 cup fish or chicken stock

¾ teaspoon minced orange zest

½ teaspoon cornstarch mixed with ½ teaspoon cold water

GARNISH: toasted, peeled, and lightly chopped hazelnuts; thinly sliced orange; and remaining fennel fronds

Coat monkfish with 1 tablespoon olive oil. Sprinkle 1 teaspoon curry powder and 1 tablespoon chopped fennel fronds evenly on monkfish and season with salt and pepper. Place on a broiler pan.

In a large sauté pan or skillet over medium heat, sauté shallots, sliced fennel, fennel seed, and ½ teaspoon curry powder in 1½ tablespoons olive oil for 7 to 8 minutes, stirring frequently. Add orange juice, wine, fish stock, and zest and bring to a boil. Reduce heat to a simmer and reduce by half, about 8 minutes. Add cornstarch mixture and simmer until sauce thickens slightly. Season to taste.

Preheat oven to broil. Broil monkfish for 8 to 10 minutes, until cooked through but not overcooked.

To serve, place monkfish on plates and spoon sauce over the top. Garnish with hazelnuts, orange slices, and fennel fronds. Serve with herbed rice.

NOTE: Fennel fronds are the dark green leafy part of the fennel. They are delightfully fragrant and tasty with an intriguing licoricelike aroma and flavor.

SERVES 4 AS AN ENTRÉE

Cold Poached Salmon
with Tarragon-Mint Aïoli

RECOMMENDED WINE: Chardonnay
ALTERNATIVE WINE: Pinot Noir

WHEN THE DOG DAYS OF SUMMER CREATE A CRAVING FOR COLD FOOD, THIS SIMPLE POACHED SALMON REQUIRES VERY LITTLE TIME ON THE STOVE AND SUITS THE SEASON PERFECTLY. THE CREAMY, RICH AÏOLI FEATURES MINT AND TARRAGON, TWO FRAGRANT HERBS WHOSE FLAVORS COMPLEMENT CHARDONNAY. THE TEXTURE OF THE AÏOLI IS PERFECT FOR A FULL-BODIED CHARDONNAY. PINOT NOIR PROVIDES MORE OF A CONTRAST TO THESE FLAVORS, BUT IS A NATURAL MATCH WITH THE OILY RICHNESS OF THE SALMON.

½ cup white wine

2 cups fish stock, clam juice, or chicken stock

1 bay leaf

½ cup thinly sliced carrots

½ cup thinly sliced celery

½ cup chopped yellow onions

¼ teaspoon peppercorns

½ teaspoon kosher salt (if using unsalted stock)

4 salmon fillets (about 2 pounds)

AÏOLI

1½ tablespoons chopped fresh tarragon (¾ tablespoon dried)

2 tablespoons chopped fresh mint (1 tablespoon dried)

1 tablespoon fresh lime juice

1 teaspoon white-wine vinegar

1½ teaspoons capers, drained

2 briefly boiled egg yolks

1½ tablespoons chopped roasted garlic (see page 164)

½ teaspoon kosher salt

½ teaspoon freshly ground black pepper

½ cup (or more) extra-virgin olive oil

GARNISH: lime and lemon slices

In a large sauté pan or skillet, bring wine, stock, bay leaf, carrots, celery, onions, peppercorns, and salt to a steady simmer. Add salmon, skin side down, cover pan, and lightly simmer for about 12 minutes, or until salmon is cooked through. Remove salmon and chill for 2 to 3 hours. If quick chilling is required, it can be placed in the freezer.

To make aïoli, in a food processor or blender, combine tarragon, mint, lime juice, vinegar, capers, egg yolks, roasted garlic, salt, and pepper and process for 1 minute. With the machine running, slowly drizzle in olive oil and process until mixture is emulsified, adding slightly more if necessary. Refrigerate, covered, for an hour or until ready to serve.

To serve, place salmon on plates. Garnish with alternating thin lemon and lime slices. Top salmon with dollop of aïoli. This dish goes beautifully with the Preserved Lemon–Toasted Pine Nut Couscous (page 122). Leftover aïoli complements almost any seafood or poultry dish and is delicious as a sandwich spread.

SERVES 4 AS AN ENTRÉE

Three-Seed Crusted Ahi with Lima Beans, Corn, and Pancetta

RECOMMENDED WINE: Chardonnay
ALTERNATIVE WINE: Pinot Noir

I CALL AHI—THE TUNA THAT IS CAUGHT IN THE PACIFIC OCEAN (KNOWN AS YELLOWFIN ON THE EAST COAST)—"FILET MIGNON WITH FINS" BECAUSE THE BEAUTIFUL, GLISTENING RED MEAT IS SO SIMILAR TO FILET. PERFECTLY RARE AHI IS A MEAT EATER'S DREAM—JUICY, WITH A SILKEN TEXTURE THAT IS QUITE UNMATCHED BY ANY OTHER SWIMMING OR WALKING CREATURE. WHILE, TO MY TASTE, AHI TUNA IS USUALLY BEST PAIRED WITH PINOT NOIR (IT CAN BE A FOOD AND WINE EPIPHANY), THE ACCOMPANYING INGREDIENTS OF LIMA BEANS, CORN, AND PANCETTA GUIDE THIS DISH IN THE DIRECTION OF A GOOD, BARREL-AGED CHARDONNAY. THE CREAMY TEXTURE OF THE BEANS MESHES WITH THE LUSH BODY OF THE WINE, WHILE THE SMOKY PANCETTA ECHOES THE TOASTY OAK-SPICE FLAVORS THAT ARE ACQUIRED THROUGH THE BARREL-AGING PROCESS.

1 red bell pepper	2 pounds ahi steaks (4 steaks)
4 ounces pancetta or bacon	1½ tablespoons olive oil
1 teaspoon olive oil	1½ tablespoons sesame seed
1½ cups chicken or vegetable stock	1½ tablespoons poppyseed
2½ tablespoons minced shallots	1½ tablespoons mustard seed
1 pound shelled fresh or frozen lima beans	⅔ teaspoon kosher salt
¾ cup corn kernels	½ teaspoon freshly ground black pepper
	GARNISH: minced green onions

In a preheated 350°F oven, roast bell pepper for 30 minutes on a baking sheet. Remove from oven and place in a brown paper bag for 8 to 10 minutes. Remove pepper and peel off skin. Remove stems, seeds, and white ribs. Dice peppers and reserve for lima beans.

Chop pancetta into small pieces. In a medium, nonstick sauté pan or skillet, sauté pancetta in olive oil over medium heat for 8 to 10 minutes, stirring frequently, until lightly browned. Remove, pat dry, and reserve.

In a medium pot, bring stock and shallots to a boil, add lima beans and simmer uncovered for 15 to 17 minutes. Don't overcook; beans should be cooked to just past al dente so that they are cooked through but not overcooked and mushy. Discard most of remaining stock. Stir in corn kernels, pancetta, and roasted pepper with beans and keep warm until ready to serve.

Using hands, coat ahi with olive oil on all sides. Mix seeds, salt, and pepper together in a small bowl and coat ahi evenly on all sides with the mixture.

Heat a large sauté pan or skillet over high heat until very hot. Add ahi to pan. It will sizzle a lot when you first add the ahi because the pan is so hot. Sear for 2 to 3 minutes per side, making sure that you don't overcook the meat. It should be very rare inside; overcooking will completely change the texture of the meat and make it rubbery. Slice thinly.

To serve, spoon lima beans onto plates with a little of the remaining liquid. Top with thinly sliced ahi. Garnish with green onions.

SERVES 4 AS AN ENTRÉE

Herb and Spice Roasted Cornish Game Hens

RECOMMENDED WINE: Chardonnay
ALTERNATIVE WINE: Sauvignon/Fumé Blanc

THIS IS A VERY SIMPLE DISH THAT SHOWCASES THE FLAVORS AND BODY OF A FRUITY-STYLE CHARDONNAY QUITE EFFEC-TIVELY. THE GAME HENS ARE COATED IN A MIXTURE OF HERBS, SPICES, AND DIJON MUSTARD AND ARE SLOWLY ROASTED TO BRING OUT THEIR SUCCULENT FLAVOR. THIS COMBINATION IS MORE ABOUT GOOD, HOMEY FOOD MATCHING WITH WINE THAN ANY STARTLING PAIRING REVELATION, BUT IT WORKS EXTREMELY WELL. SAUVIGNON/FUMÉ BLANC PLAYS NICELY OFF THE HERB AND SPICE FLAVORS AS WELL.

3 Cornish game hens, livers and gizzards removed, and rinsed

3 whole cloves garlic, peeled

2 large shallots, peeled and quartered

3 large sprigs fresh rosemary

1 teaspoon kosher salt

1½ tablespoons Dijon mustard

1½ tablespoons coarse-grained mustard

2 teaspoons *fines herbes* (see NOTE)

1 teaspoon sweet paprika

1 teaspoon fennel seed, crushed

½ teaspoon freshly ground black pepper

¾ teaspoon red pepper flakes

Preheat oven to 350°F. Place game hens in a large ovenproof baking dish. Place 1 clove garlic, several pieces of shallot, and 1 rosemary sprig into the cavity of each game hen. Rub ½ teaspoon salt into the cavity of the hens.

In a small bowl, combine mustards, *fines herbes,* paprika, fennel seed, pepper, red pepper flakes, and remaining ½ teaspoon salt and whisk thoroughly. Coat game hens thoroughly with mixture.

Place in oven and roast for 1¼ hours, or until juices run clear. Remove from oven and serve with buttered corn and braised Swiss chard.

NOTE: *Fines herbes* is a classic French mixture of dried chervil, chives, parsley, and tarragon, available in the herb or gourmet sections of most supermarkets.

SERVES 3 TO 6 AS AN ENTRÉE, DEPENDING ON APPETITE

Braised Pork with Apples, Mushrooms, and Calvados

RECOMMENDED WINE: Chardonnay
ALTERNATIVE WINE: Pinot Noir

THIS FOOD AND WINE COMBINATION DESTROYS THE MYTH THAT WHITE WINES DON'T MATCH WELL WITH MEAT. IN FACT, PORK, HERALDED WIDELY AS "THE OTHER WHITE MEAT," IS A PERFECT COMPLEMENT TO THE RICH FLAVORS AND ROUND BODY OF BARREL-AGED CHARDONNAY, PARTICULARLY WHEN THE PORK IS BRAISED. THE FLAVORS OF APPLES, CALVADOS (APPLE BRANDY), AND MUSHROOMS, ALL FRIENDLY TO CHARDONNAY, SUPPORT THE PAIRING. THE ADDITION OF SOUR CREAM TO THE BRAISING LIQUID ADDS LUSHNESS AND BODY TO THE FINISHED DISH. THE TOASTED ALMONDS PROVIDE A NUTTY NOTE TO ECHO THE TOASTED, BARREL-AGED FLAVORS OF THE WINE. PINOT NOIR IS A CLASSIC MATCH WITH PORK SINCE THE TEXTURE OF THE WINE IS QUITE COMPLEMENTARY.

1 cup sliced shiitake mushrooms

1 cup chopped yellow onions

4 ounces pancetta or bacon, chopped

3 cloves garlic, minced

2 tablespoons unsalted butter

1½ pounds pork stew meat (from the shoulder), cut into 1-inch pieces

½ teaspoon kosher salt

¼ teaspoon freshly ground black pepper

1 tablespoon chopped fresh tarragon (½ tablespoon dried)

1 tablespoon chopped fresh thyme (½ tablespoon dried)

½ teaspoon poppyseed

¼ cup white wine

⅓ cup Calvados (apple brandy) or other brandy

1 cup chicken stock

½ cup sour cream

1 cup peeled, cored, and sliced McIntosh apples

Kosher salt and freshly ground black pepper

GARNISH: toasted, diced almonds; chopped parsley

In a large sauté pan or skillet over medium heat, sauté mushrooms, onions, pancetta, and garlic in butter until onions are translucent, about 5 to 7 minutes. Season pork with salt and pepper. Add pork, tarragon, thyme, and poppyseed and continue sautéing until pork is lightly browned, about 8 to 10 minutes. Add wine, Calvados, and chicken stock and bring to a boil. Reduce heat, cover pan, and simmer for 40 minutes. Stir in sour cream and continue simmering, covered, for 15 minutes to reduce liquid further. Add apples and continue cooking for 3 to 4 minutes to barely cook apples. They should still have some crunch. Season to taste. Spoon onto plates and garnish with almonds and parsley. Serve with spinach fettuccine or spaetzle.

SERVES 4 AS AN ENTRÉE

Veal Roast with Dijon-Tinged Vegetable Sauce

RECOMMENDED WINE: Chardonnay
ALTERNATIVE WINE: Pinot Noir

MUSTARD IS A FASCINATING INGREDIENT BECAUSE OF ITS EXTRAORDINARY VERSATILITY WITH MANY WINES. THE RICH, TANGY TASTE OF DIJON MUSTARD, WHEN USED SPARINGLY, SEEMS TO INTERMINGLE WELL WITH CHARDONNAY. SLOWLY ROASTING THE VEAL TENDERIZES IT AND ALLOWS THE VEGETABLES, HERBS, AND SPICES TO HARMONIZE NICELY. VEAL SHOWS ITSELF TO BE AN AMIABLE PARTNER WITH A FULL-BODIED CHARDONNAY BUT HAS THE VERSATILITY TO PAIR WITH PINOT NOIR AS WELL.

1 5-pound boneless leg of veal, rolled and tied

1 teaspoon kosher salt

¾ teaspoon freshly ground black pepper

1 teaspoon sweet paprika

1 teaspoon fennel seed, crushed

4 tablespoons (½ stick) unsalted butter

2 large yellow onions (about 1 pound), sliced

4 cloves garlic, chopped

2 stalks celery, diced

4 large carrots (about ¾ pound), sliced

1 tablespoon chopped fresh oregano (½ tablespoon dried)

1 tablespoon chopped fresh thyme (½ tablespoon dried)

2 bay leaves, halved

2 cups chopped and seeded fresh tomatoes

¾ cup chicken stock

¾ cup white wine

3 tablespoons Dijon mustard

GARNISH: chopped parsley, minced lemon zest

Season veal with salt, pepper, paprika, and fennel seed and let rest.

In a large sauté pan or skillet over medium-high heat, brown veal in 2 tablespoons of butter on all sides, including ends. Remove veal and let rest. Add remaining butter to pan and sauté onions, garlic, celery, carrots, oregano, thyme, and bay leaves for 5 minutes. Add tomatoes and continue cooking for 1 to 2 minutes more, stirring thoroughly.

Preheat oven to 325°F. In a large foil-lined roasting pan (13-by-9-by-2-inch), spoon vegetable mixture into the pan and top with veal roast. Pour chicken stock and wine over roast and spread 2 tablespoons mustard on top. (NOTE: Can be prepared up to 6 hours in advance to this point and refrigerated prior to roasting. Let the vegetable mixture cool first before adding veal, if preparing in advance.)

Put roast in oven and roast for 2½ hours, or until internal temperature is 165° to 170°F. Baste occasionally with liquid.

Remove roast from oven, cut string, and tent in foil to keep warm. Transfer vegetable sauce to a food processor or blender, add remaining 1 tablespoon mustard, and purée. Season to taste; sauce should have a fresh, slightly mustardy taste. Thin sauce with chicken stock if necessary. Return sauce to pan and heat thoroughly before serving.

Spoon hot sauce onto plates. Slice veal thinly and place on top of sauce. Sprinkle with parsley and lemon zest. Serve with roasted parsley-garlic potatoes.

SERVES 4 AS AN ENTRÉE

Grilled Rabbit with Preserved Lemon–Toasted Pine Nut Couscous

RECOMMENDED WINE: Chardonnay

ALTERNATIVE WINE: Sauvignon/Fumé Blanc

IN ONE OF MY PREVIOUS COOKBOOKS, *AMERICAN GAME COOKING,* COAUTHORED BY JOHN ASH, I HERALDED RABBIT'S EXTRAORDINARY VERSATILITY AS A FOOD. MY FEELINGS HAVE NOT CHANGED IN THE LEAST. THIS NEW RABBIT DISH INTEGRATES THE INCOMPARABLE FLAVOR OF PRESERVED LEMON, A STAPLE OF MOROCCAN COOKING, TO CONNECT WITH CHARDONNAY. PRESERVED LEMONS REQUIRE ADVANCE PREPARATION, BUT ONCE THEY'RE IN YOUR PANTRY, YOU'LL FIND UNENDING USES FOR THEM IN PASTAS, RISOTTOS, OR TO ACCENT SEAFOOD AND POULTRY DISHES. THE ADDITION OF TOASTED PINE NUTS TO THE COUSCOUS CREATES A CONDUIT TO THE BARREL-AGED, OAKY FLAVOR IN MOST CHARDONNAYS. IF RABBIT ISN'T YOUR PLEASURE OR ISN'T READILY AVAILABLE, THE DISH ALSO WORKS WELL WITH GRILLED CHICKEN.

PRESERVED LEMON–TOASTED PINE NUT COUSCOUS

3 cups cooked couscous (cooked according to package instructions)

3 tablespoons toasted pine nuts

1 cup seeded, chopped preserved lemons with skin on (recipe follows)

2 teaspoons chopped roasted garlic (see page 164)

2 tablespoons chopped fresh mint

3 tablespoons chopped green onions

1 ½ tablespoons olive oil

Kosher salt and freshly ground black pepper

GRILLED RABBIT

2 whole rabbits, rinsed and patted dry

1 ½ tablespoons olive oil

1 ½ tablespoons Dijon mustard

1 teaspoon ground cumin

½ cup white wine

2 tablespoons chopped fresh mint (1 tablespoon dried)

¼ cup chopped green onions

Kosher salt and freshly ground black pepper

In a large bowl, combine couscous, pine nuts, preserved lemon, garlic, mint, green onions, and olive oil and fluff with a fork to separate couscous. Season to taste. It can be reheated in a microwave prior to serving if it gets too cool, or it can be served at room temperature.

Remove giblets from rabbits. Cut leg pieces off rabbit and trim loins carefully by carving meat away from the carcass. (A good butcher will do this for you.) Place rabbit pieces in a large, sealable plastic bag. Combine oil, mustard, cumin, wine, mint, and green onions in a small bowl and whisk thoroughly. Season to taste. Marinate, refrigerated, for 2 to 3 hours, or up to overnight.

Remove rabbit from marinade and pat dry. Reserve marinade for basting. Over a charcoal fire with hot coals, place leg pieces on grill and cook for 12 to 15 minutes, turning once and basting. Add loins and cook for 4 to 6 minutes per side. They should remain juicy and be barely white inside. Remove loins and keep warm. Check leg pieces to see if the juices run clear when pricked with a knife or fork. If necessary, continue grilling leg pieces for a couple of minutes until just done.

To serve, cut loin into thin slices and place on side of a mound of couscous. Divide other rabbit pieces evenly on warm plates. Serve with green beans.

SERVES 4 AS AN ENTRÉE

Preserved Lemons

12 Meyer or other thin-skinned lemons

4½ tablespoons kosher salt

3 tablespoons fresh lemon juice

6 cinnamon sticks

12 whole cloves

18 black peppercorns

To make preserved lemons, rub lemons in cold water and soak in cold water in a nonreactive bowl for 3 days. Change the water daily.

Remove lemons. Cut 4 incisions lengthwise from just below the top and bottom of each lemon, being careful not to cut through the top or bottom.

Gently squeeze lemons open and sprinkle ½ teaspoon kosher salt into the center of each. Sterilize 6 canning jars. Place 2 lemons, ½ cinnamon stick, 2 cloves, and 3 peppercorns into each jar. Sprinkle evenly with remaining salt. Add ½ tablespoon lemon juice to each jar and add boiling water to cover lemons. Place lid on top, tighten to shut, and allow lemons to steep for 2 weeks or longer in a dark, cool place. They will keep indefinitely.

"When a man drinks at dinner he begins to be better pleased with himself."

PLATO

Red Wines

Pinot Noir in many ways represents the quintessence of winemaking. While many varietals almost make themselves, Pinot Noir requires constant nurturing and attention, both in the vineyard and in the winery. It can be a troublesome, moody, and demanding beast.

However, the agony is worth it to most winemakers. Pinot Noir is the most beguiling and sensual of all wines, offering an incomparable bouquet and graceful, elegant flavors.

The legend of Pinot Noir is long and deep. Often called the "heartbreak grape" because of the difficulty in making it, Pinot Noir is described artfully by Marq deVilliers in his wonderful account of the trials and tribulations of Josh Jensen of the tiny Calera winery: "They called it the heartbreak grape because it was so stubborn, so particular, so elusive, so damn difficult to get right. And also because when it was at its best it made the most sublime wine of all. The heartbreak grape? You cannot break a heart without having captured it first."

Pinot Noir, grown on the terraced slopes of the Côte d'Or in Burgundy in France, is the model by which all others (principally from California and Oregon) are made. When produced from vintages when the often-inclement weather cooperates, Burgundies are the ultimate in liquid pleasure, but they can be frustratingly inconsistent. Unfortunately, because these wines are quite expensive, this inconsistency comes at a high price.

Quick to learn after some early mistakes, vintners in California and Oregon have begun to identify the proper grape clones (there are several hundred), the perfect soils, and the optimum climate (near ocean breezes and protected from too much heat) to make great Pinot Noir.

Occasionally, the results are magnificent, other times ordinary.

Two styles of Pinot Noir seem to emerge: a lighter-bodied "fruit bomb" (which is particularly food-friendly) or a fuller, more concentrated version in which oak and some tannin are assertive when the wine is young. Because of good natural acidity, either of these styles will age quite gracefully in the bottle for three to six years. Some French Burgundies show extraordinary aging potential and offer captivating bouquets and flavors even after ten to fifteen years and, in great vintages, beyond that.

Part of the varietal's appeal is its extraordinary compatibility with food. Offering seductive aromas and juicy, fruit-driven flavors, Pinot Noir is the epitome of a "food wine." It has delicacy and grace, charm and appeal, yet it tantalizes with complexity. While effective with more delicate and subtle dishes, fruity styles of Pinot Noir work magic with more highly seasoned, smoked, and even spicy dishes (see Grilled Ahi with Ginger–Black Bean Sauce on page 133).

Pinot Noir is, in a word, a wonder. It is a mysterious and seductive wine that echoes the smell of the earth from which it comes. It beckons to be enjoyed at the table, and we wholeheartedly seek to unveil its varied pleasures, searching for that ultimate connection in food, wine, and spirit.

PINOT NOIR

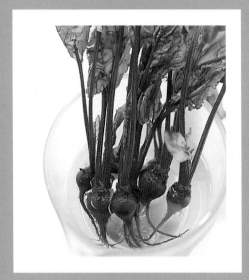

TYPICAL AROMAS & FLAVORS

Black Cherry, Dried Cherry
Currant
Blackberry, Blackberry Jam
Raspberry, Raspberry Jam
Strawberry, Strawberry Jam
Cranberry
Rhubarb
Pomegranate
Plum
Mushroom
Earth: Wet Leaves, Barnyard
Smoke
Vanilla
Oak
Spices: Cinnamon, Clove
Mint
Licorice
Cola
Coffee
Violet
Rose
Tea
Roasted Tomato

BASE INGREDIENTS

Base ingredients refer to the main ingredient of the dish: meat, poultry, game, seafood, shellfish, or vegetable. These represent the core ingredients that are most likely to be matched with a varietal, although successful pairings result as much from the other ingredients used in the dish as they do the base ingredient.

Beef, Lamb, Pork, Veal, Sweetbread, Kidneys, Liver, Chicken, Game Hens, Squab, Pheasant, Duck, Rabbit, Quail, Salmon, Tuna (Ahi)

BRIDGE INGREDIENTS

Bridge ingredients help connect the food and the wine through their interaction in flavor, body, intensity, or basic taste.

Berries
Cherries, Dried Cherries
Mushrooms: Shiitake, Portobello,
    Crimini, Porcini, Chanterelle, Morel
Truffles
Onions, Sweet Onions
Shallots
Garlic, Roasted Garlic
Cheese: Brie, Teleme, Aged Goat
    Cheese, Aged Cheddar
Pesto
Black Beans
Lentils
Eggplant
Beets
Roasted Red Bell Peppers
Black Olives
Spices: Cinnamon, Clove, Star Anise,
    Ginger, Fennel Seed, Pepper
Herbs: Mint, Basil, Tarragon, Thyme,
    Rosemary, Lavender, Oregano
Roasted Tomato, Sun-Dried Tomato
Dijon Mustard

BEST SOURCE REGIONS
PINOT NOIR

The following is a list of countries, regions, and appellations (a wine word referencing specific growing locales) that produce the highest-quality versions of these wines.

This is not intended to be a complete list, only a reference for where the finest renditions can be found.

FRANCE
- Burgundy
  - Fixin
  - Gevrey-Chambertin
  - Morey-St.-Denis
  - Chambolle-Musigny
  - Vougeot
  - Echézeaux
  - Vosne-Romanée
  - Nuits-St.-Georges
  - Pernand-Vergelesses
  - Aloxe-Corton
  - Beaune
  - Pommard
  - Volnay

CALIFORNIA
- Mendocino
  - Anderson Valley
- Sonoma
  - Russian River
  - Carneros
- Napa
  - Carneros
- Santa Barbara/Central Coast
  - Santa Maria Valley
  - Edna Valley
  - Santa Ynez Valley
- Monterey

OREGON
- Willamette Valley

PINOT NOIR STYLES

Light/Medium:
Light garnet; medium body; simpler, bright, juicy fruit with hints of spice from barrel aging; good acidity, zesty

Medium/Medium-full:
Darker ruby; more jammy, ripe cherry, and stone fruit; fuller tannins and oak impression, lush

TIPS TO SUCCESSFUL MATCHES
WITH PINOT NOIR

1

Pinot Noir is the most flexible red wine in terms of matching with meat, poultry, vegetarian dishes, and even some seafood, such as salmon and ahi tuna.

2

Foods with light aromatic spices will harmonize with fruitier versions of Pinot Noir.

3

Because of its delicacy, don't overwhelm Pinot Noir with dishes that are too powerful or assertive.

Risotto with Roasted Shallots, Portobello Mushrooms, Radicchio, and Parmesan

RECOMMENDED WINE: Pinot Noir
ALTERNATIVE WINE: Chardonnay

THE EARTHY, SLIGHTLY BITTER FLAVORS OF THIS RISOTTO ARE HEIGHTENED BY THE FORWARD FRUIT AND SIMILAR EARTHY NOTES OF THE PINOT NOIR. INTERESTINGLY, THIS DISH MATCHES ALMOST EQUALLY WELL WITH CHARDONNAY, PROVIDING A PLEASING TEXTURAL CONNECTION TO THE WINE.

8 ounces whole shallots

3 tablespoons olive oil

Kosher salt and freshly ground black pepper

1 tablespoon unsalted butter

½ pound portobello mushrooms, diced (about 2 cups)

½ cup chopped yellow onions

1½ cups Arborio rice

1 tablespoon chopped fresh thyme (½ tablespoon dried)

½ cup white wine

4–5 cups hot chicken stock

1¾ cups loosely packed chopped radicchio

1 cup seeded, chopped tomatoes

¾ cup grated Parmesan cheese

GARNISH: minced chives

Preheat oven to 350°F. Trim ends of shallots. Peel off outer brown layer and discard. Halve shallots, coat with 1 tablespoon olive oil and sprinkle lightly with salt and pepper. Wrap shallots loosely in foil and roast for 65 minutes. Keep wrapped in foil until ready to serve.

In a large sauté pan over medium heat, heat remaining olive oil and butter. Add mushrooms and onions and sauté for 2 to 3 minutes, stirring frequently. Add rice and thyme and continue cooking for 4 to 5 minutes, stirring frequently. Carefully add wine (it may steam up when poured into hot pan) and simmer to evaporate. Start adding stock in ½-cup increments and slowly stir until mostly evaporated. Cook until al dente.

Stir in radicchio and tomatoes. Cook for 1 to 2 minutes more to wilt radicchio slightly. Stir in Parmesan.

Serve very hot in soup bowls, garnished with shallots and minced chives.

SERVES 6 AS AN APPETIZER OR 4 AS AN ENTRÉE

Grilled Salmon with Mushrooms, Sweet Onions, and Pinot Noir Sauce (Classic Pairing)

RECOMMENDED WINE: Pinot Noir
ALTERNATIVE WINE: Zinfandel

SALMON, ALONG WITH AHI, IS A TERRIFIC FISH TO MATCH WITH PINOT NOIR. THE OILY TEXTURE AND MEATY FLESH OF THE FISH BLEND SEAMLESSLY WITH THE WINE; IT OFFERS ENOUGH FAT TO COAT THE TONGUE AND BALANCE THE TANNIN IN THE WINE. WITH THIS DISH, PINOT NOIR BECOMES THE VEHICLE FOR A SILKY SAUCE THAT CARRIES FORWARD THE SWEET ONION AND EARTHY MUSHROOM FLAVORS FOUND IN THE SAUTÉED VEGETABLES.

MARINADE

¼ cup soy sauce

½ cup white wine

½ cup sliced yellow onions

½ tablespoon dry mustard

1 tablespoon chopped fresh thyme
(½ tablespoon dried)

½ teaspoon crushed black pepper

½ tablespoon olive oil

—

3 pounds fresh salmon fillets

3 cups sliced portobello mushrooms,
inner gills removed

3 cups sliced shiitake mushrooms

3 cups sliced sweet onions (Vidalia, Maui,
or Walla Walla)

2 tablespoons chopped fresh thyme
(1 tablespoon dried)

2 teaspoons mustard seed

4 tablespoons olive oil

Kosher salt and freshly ground black pepper

1 tablespoon chopped shallots

2 cups Pinot Noir

2½ cups chicken stock

1 tablespoon Dijon mustard

½ teaspoon cornstarch mixed with
½ teaspoon cold water

2 tablespoons unsalted butter

To make marinade, mix all ingredients together in a small bowl and whisk thoroughly. Marinate salmon for 2 hours. Remove salmon from marinade and pat dry.

In a large sauté pan or skillet over medium-high heat, sauté mushrooms, onions, 1 tablespoon thyme and mustard seed in 3 tablespoons oil for 7 to 8 minutes, or until onions are translucent. Season and keep warm.

In a medium sauté pan or skillet, heat 1 tablespoon olive oil. Add shallots and sauté for 2 to 3 minutes. Add wine and reduce by half. Add stock, 1 tablespoon thyme, mustard, and cornstarch mixture and reduce until sauce coats the back of a wooden spoon. Remove from heat and stir in butter. Season to taste. Keep sauce warm until ready to serve.

Prepare a hot charcoal fire and grill salmon for 4 to 5 minutes per side, depending on thickness, making sure not to overcook it. Alternatively, salmon can be broiled for about 6 to 7 minutes on a broiler pan.

To serve, divide mushroom-onion mixture on warm plates. Place salmon fillets on top. Spoon sauce over the salmon. Serve with brown sugar–glazed, parslied carrots.

SERVES 6 AS AN ENTRÉE

Grilled Ahi with Ginger–Black Bean Sauce

RECOMMENDED WINE: Pinot Noir
ALTERNATIVE WINE: Sauvignon/Fumé Blanc

MUCH LIKE SALMON, WHICH ALSO PAIRS EXTREMELY WELL WITH PINOT NOIR, AHI SEEMS TO ALMOST SEDUCE PINOT NOIR. THE SLIGHTLY SWEET, OILY MEAT AND FLESHY BODY OF THE WINE ARE SUBLIME WITH ONE ANOTHER. THIS ASIAN TREATMENT RELIES ON GINGER AND FERMENTED BLACK BEANS IN A FAIRLY INTENSE REDUCTION SAUCE THAT BRINGS OUT SOME OF THE SPICY AND FRUITY CHARACTERISTICS OF A YOUNG CALIFORNIA PINOT NOIR (PREFERABLY ONE EXHIBITING LESS OAK).

MARINADE

- ¼ cup soy sauce
- ¼ cup sake or dry white wine
- 1 tablespoon toasted sesame oil
- 2 tablespoons seasoned rice-wine vinegar
- 2 tablespoons chopped fresh ginger
- 2½ tablespoons minced green onions

- 4 ahi steaks (about 2 pounds)

SAUCE

- 1½ tablespoons chopped shallots
- 3 tablespoons peeled and chopped ginger
- 2 tablespoons vegetable oil
- 1½ cups Pinot Noir or other light-bodied red wine
- 1¾ cups fish or chicken stock
- 2½ tablespoons whole fermented black beans, rinsed in cold water, or 1 tablespoon Chinese black bean sauce
- 2 teaspoons rice-wine vinegar
- 1 teaspoon wasabi powder, mixed with 1 teaspoon cold water
- ½ teaspoon cornstarch mixed with ½ teaspoon cold water
- ¼ cup chopped cilantro
- 2 tablespoons unsalted butter at room temperature (optional)

GARNISH: toasted sesame seeds, cilantro sprigs

In a medium mixing bowl, combine soy sauce, sake, sesame oil, vinegar, ginger, and green onions with a whisk. Place ahi in a large, sealable plastic bag, add marinade, and refrigerate for 1 to 2 hours. Turn occasionally.

To make sauce, in a medium sauce pan over low-medium heat, sauté shallots and ginger in oil for 2 to 3 minutes. Add wine and increase heat to boil briefly. Reduce heat and simmer until liquid is reduced by three-fourths. Add stock, black beans, vinegar, and wasabi and reduce by half. Remove from heat, strain liquid, and discard solids. Return liquid to the pan, add cornstarch mixture and cilantro and reduce to thicken slightly. Whisk in butter. Keep sauce warm off direct heat.

Grill ahi over very hot coals for 2 to 3 minutes. Turn and cook for an additional 1 to 2 minutes. Do not overcook or the beautiful red meat of the fish will become chewy; ahi should be very rare inside. (Remember that top-quality ahi is served raw in sushi bars.) Cut ahi into thin slices.

To serve, spoon finished sauce onto plates and place sliced ahi on top. Sprinkle with sesame seeds and garnish with cilantro. Serve with jasmine rice and Chinese-Style Vegetables (page 79).

SERVES 4 AS AN ENTRÉE

Asian-Style Grilled Squab with Fennel, Bok Choy, and Chanterelle Mushrooms

RECOMMENDED WINE: Pinot Noir
ALTERNATIVE WINE: Chardonnay

SQUAB IS A DELECTABLE BIRD (ACTUALLY A YOUNG PIGEON, IF TRUTH BE TOLD) THAT IS PARTICULARLY WELL SUITED TO GRILLING. THIS ASIAN-STYLE MARINADE PLAYS SUPERBLY OFF THE ASIAN SPICE AROMAS AND FLAVORS THAT ARE COMMON TO MANY PINOT NOIRS. A RICH CHARDONNAY WILL ALSO PAIR VERY NICELY WITH THE JUICY SQUAB MEAT AS THE FULLNESS OF THE WINE SUPPORTS THE FAT IN THE BIRD.

4 whole squabs

MARINADE

1/3 cup soy sauce

1 1/2 tablespoons sesame oil

3 tablespoons rice-wine vinegar

1/4 cup olive oil

1/2 tablespoon five-spice powder (see page 72)

3 tablespoons lime juice

1/2 teaspoon minced lime zest

1 tablespoon peeled, chopped fresh ginger

1 1/2 tablespoons chopped shallots

———

1 sweet onion (Vidalia, Maui, or Walla Walla), peeled and thinly sliced

1 fresh fennel bulb, cored and cut into 1/2-inch pieces, with leafy fronds reserved for garnish

2 tablespoons olive oil

4 ounces fresh chanterelle mushrooms (or 1 ounce dried and reconstituted in warm water), lightly rinsed and sliced

1 tablespoon peeled, chopped fresh ginger

1/4 cup julienned red bell pepper

1/4 cup julienned yellow bell pepper

2 small bunches baby bok choy, ends trimmed, rinsed, and cut into 1/4-inch pieces

1/4 teaspoon mustard seed

1/2 teaspoon curry powder

Kosher salt and freshly ground black pepper

Bone squab by cutting in half through breastbone and backbone with a sharp knife. Carefully cut breast meat from bone, keeping breast meat in one piece. Cut leg-thigh pieces away from the carcass. Discard wings and bones or retain for use in stock.

To make marinade, combine all ingredients in a small mixing bowl and whisk thoroughly. In a large sealable plastic bag, place breast meat and leg-thigh pieces in marinade and refrigerate for 2 to 3 hours.

Remove squab from marinade and pat dry with paper towels. Reserve marinade for basting.

In a medium sauté pan or skillet over low-medium heat, sauté onions and fennel in olive oil for 6 to 7 minutes. Add chanterelles, ginger, and bell peppers and continue sautéing for 4 minutes. Add bok choy, mustard seed, and curry powder and cook for 3 to 4 minutes, stirring often. Season to taste. Keep warm.

Prepare a hot fire. When coals are ready, place squab leg-thigh pieces skin side down, and grill for 2 to 3 minutes. Add breasts, skin side down, and grill for 2 to 3 minutes. Turn leg-thigh pieces and breasts and cook for another 1 to 2 minutes, or until breasts are juicy rare. Remove breasts and keep warm in foil. Continue cooking leg-thigh pieces for another 2 to 3 minutes, or until rare to medium-rare. Overcooking results in dry, livery-tasting meat. Be sure to check breasts in particular.

To serve, spoon vegetables evenly onto dinner plates. Place 1 breast and 1 leg-thigh piece on top of veggies. Garnish with fennel fronds and serve with vanilla-scented jasmine rice.

SERVES 4 AS AN ENTRÉE

Grilled Pork Tenderloin with Pomegranate Sauce

RECOMMENDED WINE: Pinot Noir
ALTERNATIVE WINE: Merlot

———————

THIS POMEGRANATE SAUCE BRINGS OUT A SIMILAR FLAVOR IN MANY PINOT NOIRS–A SWEET-TART CHARACTER THAT IS QUITE INTRIGUING. THE USE OF STAR ANISE IN THE SAUCE PLAYS INTO THE EXOTIC ASIAN SPICE CHARACTER THAT CAN SHOW ITSELF IN BOTH THE BOUQUET AND FLAVOR OF MANY PINOT NOIRS.

MARINADE

⅓ cup red wine

¾ tablespoon olive oil

1 tablespoon crushed star anise pods

2 tablespoons chopped shallots

¼ teaspoon ground allspice

⅓ teaspoon kosher salt

¼ teaspoon freshly ground black pepper

———

2 pork tenderloins (about 2½ pounds)

SAUCE

2 tablespoons chopped shallots

1 tablespoon olive oil

½ cup Pinot Noir

½ cup port

2 tablespoons raspberry vinegar

¼ teaspoon whole mixed peppercorns

¼ cup pomegranate concentrate (see NOTE)

½ cup fresh orange juice

1½ cups chicken stock

3 whole star anise pods

1 teaspoon honey (or to taste)

2 tablespoons unsalted butter at room temperature

Kosher salt and freshly ground black pepper

GARNISH: mint sprigs, pomegranate seeds

To make marinade, combine all ingredients and whisk thoroughly. Put pork tenderloins in a large, sealable plastic bag and add marinade. Refrigerate for 3 to 4 hours. Remove pork and pat dry. Reserve marinade for basting.

To make sauce, in a large sauté pan or skillet over medium heat, sauté shallots in oil for 2 to 3 minutes. Do not brown. Add the red wine, port, vinegar, and peppercorns. Bring to a boil, then reduce heat and simmer until reduced by half. Add pomegranate concentrate, orange juice, stock, and star anise and continue simmering until reduced by half once again, or until sauce coats the back of a wooden spoon. Add honey to taste. Remove from heat, strain, and swirl in butter. Season to taste and keep warm.

Grill pork over hot coals for 5 to 6 minutes per side or until medium-rare. Baste occasionally. Slice pork and keep warm.

To serve, place pork on the plate and top with sauce. Garnish with mint sprigs and pomegranate seeds sprinkled around meat. Serve with couscous.

NOTE: Bottled pomegranate concentrate or molasses (not juice) is available in gourmet food stores and Middle Eastern groceries.

SERVES 4 AS AN ENTRÉE

Thai-Style Grilled Lamb with Raspberry-Mango Relish

RECOMMENDED WINE: Pinot Noir

ALTERNATIVE WINE: Zinfandel

THIS MÉLANGE OF FLAVORS, SOME EXOTICALLY ASIAN, SOME STEADFASTLY AMERICAN, CALLS OUT FOR A FRUITY, LOWER-TANNIN WINE SUCH AS PINOT NOIR TO COMPLEMENT IT. THE MARINADE FOR THIS DISH IS DECIDEDLY SPICY, SWEET, AND SALTY, SO HIGHLY OAKED OR TANNIC WINES TEND TO INTERFERE AND FIGHT WITH THESE TASTES.

MARINADE

- 3 tablespoons whole fermented black beans, rinsed in cold water, or 1 tablespoon Chinese black bean sauce
- 3 cloves garlic, chopped
- 1½ tablespoons peeled, chopped fresh ginger
- 3 tablespoons chopped lemongrass, outer leaves and stems removed (optional)
- 3 tablespoons minced green onions
- 1 teaspoon Thai chile sauce
- ¼ cup hoisin sauce
- ¼ cup seasoned rice-wine vinegar
- 2 tablespoons toasted sesame oil
- ⅓ cup white wine
- 1 tablespoon five-spice powder (see page 72)
- 2 tablespoons chopped fresh mint (1 tablespoon dried)

- 1 6- to 7-pound whole leg of lamb, boned, butterflied, and trimmed of excess fat (about 4½ pounds boned and trimmed)

RELISH

- ¾ cup diced fresh or frozen mango
- 1 cup fresh or frozen (drained) raspberries
- 1 teaspoon chopped roasted garlic (see page 164)
- 2½ tablespoons chopped pickled ginger (see page 78)
- 3 tablespoons chopped fresh cilantro
- ½ teaspoon five-spice powder
- ½ teaspoon honey
- ½ cup chopped sweet onions (Vidalia, Maui, or Walla Walla)
- 1 tablespoon seasoned rice-wine vinegar
- 1 teaspoon toasted sesame oil

GARNISH: cilantro sprigs

To make marinade, mix all ingredients together and whisk thoroughly. In a large sealable plastic bag, marinate lamb, refrigerated, for at least 3 to 4 hours, turning occasionally to ensure that all sides are exposed to marinade. Remove lamb from marinade and pat dry.

To make relish, mix all ingredients together and refrigerate for 2 to 3 hours so that flavors blend. Adjust to taste.

Over a hot (but not flaming) charcoal fire, cook lamb for 7 to 8 minutes per side, until medium rare. Be sure not to let fire char lamb too much—the sweet condiments in the marinade will tend to burn. The lamb can also be roasted in the oven at 450°F to desired doneness.

To serve, carve lamb into thin slices and place on plates. Spoon relish over the top. Garnish with cilantro sprigs. Serve with turmeric-infused couscous.

SERVES 6 AS AN ENTRÉE

Coffee- and Spice-Rubbed Lamb with Coffee-Vanilla Sauce

RECOMMENDED WINE: Pinot Noir
ALTERNATIVE WINE: Cabernet Sauvignon

AS PINOT NOIR AGES, IT PICKS UP SOME GRACEFUL, COFFEE-LIKE NOTES. THIS DISH WAS CREATED TO TRY TO MIRROR THIS CHARACTERISTIC AS WELL AS ACCENTUATE THE VANILLA CHARACTER THAT RESULTS FROM BARREL AGING. IF THE RECIPE SOUNDS A LITTLE "OVER THE TOP," DON'T BE INTIMIDATED. IT IS QUITE FLAVORFUL AND A WONDERFUL WAY TO HEIGHTEN THE CHARACTER OF ALMOST ANY RED WINE, PARTICULARLY THOSE THAT HAVE AGED FOR A WHILE.

MARINADE

- 2 teaspoons chopped garlic
- 1½ tablespoons chopped fresh mint
- 1 tablespoon finely ground coffee
- ¼ cup olive oil
- ⅓ cup red wine
- ¼ teaspoon whole mixed peppercorns
- ¼ teaspoon cumin seed
- ¼ teaspoon mustard seed
- ¼ teaspoon coriander seed
- 2 teaspoons chopped fresh rosemary (1 teaspoon dried)
- ¼ teaspoon kosher salt

- 4 boneless, tied lamb sirloin rolls (about 2 pounds) or 8 double-thick lamb chops (about 6 pounds), trimmed of fat

- 2 tablespoons olive oil
- 1 cup coarsely chopped shiitake mushrooms
- 2 tablespoons minced shallots
- 1½ cups red wine
- 1 6-inch vanilla bean, split lengthwise
- 1 tablespoon chopped fresh mint
- 2 cups lamb or chicken stock
- ¼ cup freshly brewed coffee
- ½ teaspoon honey
- 1 teaspoon cornstarch mixed with 1 teaspoon cold water
- 1 tablespoon unsalted butter at room temperature (optional)

Kosher salt and freshly ground pepper

GARNISH: mint sprigs

To make marinade, combine garlic, mint, coffee, olive oil, and wine in a small, nonreactive mixing bowl. Using a mortar and pestle (or electric coffee/spice grinder), grind peppercorns, seeds, rosemary, and salt. Add to coffee mixture and whisk thoroughly.

Place lamb in a large glass dish. Pour marinade over lamb and rub in thoroughly on all sides. Refrigerate, covered, for 3 to 4 hours. Remove from marinade and wipe off most but not all of coffee mixture with paper towels.

In a large sauté pan or skillet over medium heat, sauté olive oil, mushrooms, and shallots for 4 to 5 minutes. Add red wine, vanilla bean, and mint and bring to a boil. Reduce heat to a simmer and reduce wine by half. Stir in stock, coffee, and honey and reduce by half. Remove vanilla bean. Stir in cornstarch mixture to thicken sauce. Remove from heat, swirl in butter, and season to taste. Keep warm.

Prepare a hot grill. Cook lamb for 7 to 8 minutes per side, or until medium-rare.

To serve, place lamb rolls on plates and top with sauce. Garnish with mint sprigs.

SERVES 4 AS AN ENTRÉE

Roast Leg of Veal with Wild Mushroom Sauce and Walnuts

RECOMMENDED WINE: Pinot Noir

ALTERNATIVE WINE: Merlot

PINOT NOIR HAS AN UNMISTAKABLE AFFINITY FOR WILD MUSHROOMS. THE EARTHY AROMAS AND FLAVORS OF THE WINE ARE PERFECTLY ACCENTUATED BY THE MUSHROOMS. MOST OF THE MUSHROOMS IN THIS DISH ARE USED TO CREATE A FAIRLY THICK SAUCE, BUT IT'S NICE TO RESERVE A FEW OF THE PRETTIER ONES FOR GARNISH. WALNUTS ARE A USEFUL INGREDIENT TO HELP SOFTEN TANNINS IN MANY YOUNG WINES (ALTHOUGH PINOT NOIR IS NOT TYPICALLY THAT TANNIC) AND PROVIDE A PLEASING TEXTURAL CRUNCH. THE SOFT, JUICY FRUIT CHARACTER OF MERLOT HARMONIZES NICELY WITH BOTH THE RICH MUSHROOM SAUCE AND THE HERBED VEAL.

1 4- to 5-pound boned leg of veal, rolled and tied

2 teaspoons sweet paprika

1 teaspoon kosher salt

½ teaspoon freshly ground black pepper

1 red onion, peeled and thinly sliced

2 cups sliced portobello mushrooms, stems trimmed, inner gills removed

3 cups sliced shiitake mushrooms, stems trimmed

2 tablespoons fresh thyme (1 tablespoon dried)

1 tablespoon fresh sage (½ tablespoon dried)

1 tablespoon fresh rosemary (½ tablespoon dried)

3 tablespoons olive oil

1½ tablespoons unsalted butter

1 cup Pinot Noir or other red wine

1¼–1½ cups chicken stock

Kosher salt and freshly ground black pepper

⅔ cup toasted chopped walnuts

GARNISH: chopped parsley, whole roasted shiitake mushrooms

Coat veal roast evenly with paprika, salt, and pepper. Preheat oven to 325°F.

In a large sauté pan over medium heat, sauté onions, mushrooms, and herbs in olive oil for 4 to 5 minutes, until onions are translucent. Remove from pan with a spoon and place in a large, foil-lined roasting pan or dish big enough to hold the veal.

In the sauté pan, add butter and lightly brown veal roast on all sides over medium heat. Remove veal and place it on top of mushroom mixture. Pour wine and 1¼ cups stock over the roast. Place in oven and roast for 2 hours, or until internal temperature reaches 170°F. Baste occasionally with liquid.

Remove roast from oven, cut string, and tent in aluminum foil to keep warm. Transfer mushroom mixture to a food processor and purée until smooth. Thin slightly with chicken stock if desired. Season to taste. Keep warm until ready to serve.

To serve, slice roast. Divide mushroom sauce evenly on plates and top with sliced veal. Sprinkle walnuts over the top. Garnish with parsley and whole mushrooms. Serve with glazed, dilled carrots and roasted potato quarters.

SERVES 6 TO 8 AS AN ENTRÉE

SANGIOVESE

Sangiovese, born of hundreds of years of Tuscan tradition, is undergoing a major renaissance. These changes are happening on both Italian and California soil, and they are creating a booming new demand for one of the most distinguished wines of Italy.

Italian Sangiovese is produced most prominently in the Chianti Classico and Brunello di Montalcino regions of Tuscany where it is prized for its vibrant fruit character and racy spirit. Sangiovese from these parts can vary tremendously in style—from lighter-colored, simple, easy-drinking country wines (Chianti) to more complex renditions (Chianti Classico, Chianti Classico Riserva, Vino Nobile di Montepulciano, and Brunello di Montalcino).

Italian law up until very recently demanded that Chianti be produced from a blend of Sangiovese, Canaiolo Nero, and two white grapes, Malvasia and Trebbiano. This tradition began to be challenged a decade ago by more progressive wineries that felt that these age-old regulations and formulas prevented them from producing higher-quality, 100 percent Sangiovese wines. These rebel wineries began producing what were deemed "Super Tuscans," of either 100 percent Sangiovese or Sangiovese blended with Cabernet Sauvignon or Merlot. These wines were met with worldwide interest but could not use the prized "Chianti" nomenclature.

Echoing the changes taking place in Italy, Piero Antinori, whose family had been in the wine business for more than six hundred years in Tuscany and who was paving the way for innovation in Chianti, established the Atlas Peak winery in the hills of Napa Valley. Antinori created a new spark of interest in Sangiovese in California that is just beginning to be felt nationwide.

Sangiovese has a captivating character that makes it well suited to the table. It offers a sprightly cherry fruit personality, and its acidity and tannin (often called "grip") make it an amiable partner to higher-acid dishes, particularly tomato-based pastas, as well as grilled meats, sausage, poultry, and game. Sangiovese also stands up to "gusto food"—food that offers redolent waves of garlic, onions, olives, beans, tomatoes—the essence of Italian country cooking.

For the most part, Sangiovese is a fun wine. It demands to be drunk and to be surrounded by laughter. Although there are many very serious versions of 100 percent Sangiovese and blended Sangiovese with Cabernet Sauvignon or Merlot, Sangiovese is a wine that slides easily onto the table and makes its presence felt in a friendly, undemanding manner. That, in itself, is something.

SANGIOVESE

TYPICAL AROMAS & FLAVORS

Plum
Cherry, Dried Cherry
Raspberry
Strawberry
Cedar
Tobacco
Tea
Spices: Clove, Cinnamon
Roasted Tomato
Herbs: Thyme, Sage, Fennel
Dusty

BASE INGREDIENTS

Base ingredients refer to the main ingredient of the dish: meat, poultry, game, seafood, shellfish, or vegetable. These represent the core ingredients that are most likely to be matched with a varietal, although successful pairings result as much from the other ingredients used in the dish as they do the base ingredient.

Beef, Lamb, Veal, Pork, Chicken, Game Hen, Rabbit, Squab, Quail, Sausage

BRIDGE INGREDIENTS

Bridge ingredients help connect the food and the wine through their interaction in flavor, body, intensity, or basic taste.

Raspberries
Plums
Cherries, Sun-Dried Cherries
Oranges, Blood Oranges
Onions
Garlic
Mushrooms
Eggplant
Fennel
Roasted Red Peppers
Tomatoes, Roasted Tomatoes,
    Sun-Dried Tomatoes
Green Olives, Black Olives
Capers
Herbs: Basil, Rosemary, Thyme, Oregano
Nuts: Pecans, Walnuts
Dijon Mustard
Prosciutto, Pancetta

BEST SOURCE REGIONS
SANGIOVESE

The following is a list of countries, regions, and appellations (a wine word referencing specific growing locales) that produce the highest-quality versions of these wines.

This is not intended to be a complete list, only a reference for where the finest renditions can be found.

ITALY
Chianti Classico
Brunello di Montalcino
Vino Nobile di Montepulciano
Carmignano
CALIFORNIA
Napa Valley
Sonoma
Mendocino

SANGIOVESE STYLES

Light-medium:
Light-medium color; medium body with out a lot of fullness; direct fruit character with good acidity; often quite lean

Medium-full:
Medium-dark color; medium-full body; riper, more intense fruit; good acidity

Super Tuscans:
Medium-dark color; medium-full body; concentrated with more layered flavors, oaky, tannic; often shows character of Cabernet Sauvignon or Merlot, with which Sangiovese is blended

TIPS TO SUCCESSFUL MATCHES WITH SANGIOVESE

1

Sangiovese connects best with simpler, rustic dishes, particularly those that are grilled or roasted.

2

Steer away from rich, intense sauces, except with the more concentrated Super Tuscans and Brunellos.

3

Use fresh herbs to highlight Sangiovese's "country" personality.

4

Tomatoes are a particularly excellent bridge ingredient to Sangiovese.

White Bean Soup with Escargots and Olive Relish

RECOMMENDED WINE: Sangiovese

ALTERNATIVE WINE: Zinfandel

THIS IS A HEARTY COUNTRY SOUP THAT IS WELL SUITED TO A CHILLY WINTER EVENING, WHEN IT CAN BE A PERFECT MAIN COURSE ALONG WITH A LOAF OF WARM, CRUSTY SOURDOUGH BREAD. THE USE OF ESCARGOTS (SNAILS) MAY SEEM A BIT ODD, BUT THE COMBINATION OF THE BEANS, HERBS, AND ESCARGOTS COMPLEMENT THE RUSTIC FLAVORS OF SANGIOVESE BEAUTIFULLY.

12 ounces white beans (such as Great Northern), rinsed and picked over

1½ tablespoons olive oil

1 large carrot, peeled and chopped

1 stalk celery, chopped

1 cup chopped yellow onions

¾ cup cored, chopped fresh fennel

3 cloves garlic, chopped

6 cups vegetable or chicken stock

1 cup plum tomatoes, seeded and chopped

1 pound Yukon gold or new potatoes, diced

2 teaspoons chopped fresh rosemary (1 teaspoon dried)

½ teaspoon mustard seed

½ teaspoon fennel seed

Kosher salt and freshly ground black pepper

RELISH

¼ cup olive paste

1 teaspoon chopped shallots

2 teaspoons balsamic vinegar

¾ teaspoon chopped fresh rosemary (⅓ teaspoon dried)

---

1 tablespoon olive oil

1 teaspoon minced garlic

12 escargots, drained of liquid

1 tablespoon Pernod (anise liqueur) or Sangiovese

GARNISH: rosemary sprigs

In a large bowl, place beans in cold water and soak overnight. Drain beans and discard any remaining beans that are discolored. Reserve beans.

In a large soup or stockpot, heat oil. Add carrots, celery, onions, fennel, and garlic and sauté over medium heat for 5 to 6 minutes. Add beans, stock, tomatoes, potatoes, rosemary, mustard seed, and fennel seed and bring to a boil. Reduce heat, cover, and continue to simmer for 45 to 55 minutes, until beans are cooked al dente. Season to taste.

To make relish, in a small bowl, combine all ingredients. Reserve.

In a small sauté pan or skillet over medium heat, heat olive oil. Add garlic and escargots and sauté for 3 to 4 minutes, stirring frequently, until escargots are heated through. Add Pernod and continue cooking for 1 minute or until liquid evaporates. Keep warm.

To serve, divide soup evenly into large, heated soup bowls. Dollop portions of olive relish on top and place sautéed escargots carefully around the relish. Garnish with rosemary sprigs.

SERVES 6 TO 8 AS AN APPETIZER OR 4 AS AN ENTRÉE

Herb and Sun-Dried Tomato Calzone with Hot Sausage, Prosciutto, and Okra

RECOMMENDED WINE: Sangiovese
ALTERNATIVE WINE: Zinfandel

THE COMBINATION OF CAJUN INGREDIENTS IN THIS RECIPE, SUCH AS ANDOUILLE SAUSAGE, OKRA, AND FILÉ, MARRY WITH THE TRADITIONAL ITALIAN CALZONE IN A TUSCANY–MEETS–NEW ORLEANS CREATION. WHILE BEER IS A TRADITIONAL AND IMMENSELY POPULAR ALCOHOLIC BEVERAGE WITH PIZZAS AND CALZONES, MOST FOOD-LOVING WINE DRINKERS WILL TELL YOU THAT SANGIOVESE OR ZINFANDEL ARE THE ONLY WAY TO GO, PARTICULARLY WITH SPICY, TOMATO-BASED PIZZAS SUCH AS THIS ONE. THE INTENSE SPICY-BERRY FLAVORS AND GOOD ACIDITY OF THE WINE SWING WITH THE ZESTY STUFFING, INCLUDING THE HOT SAUSAGE.

CALZONE DOUGH

- 1 cup warm tap water (110° to 115°F on an instant-read thermometer)
- 2 teaspoons granulated sugar
- 1 envelope (¼ ounce) active dry yeast
- ¼ cup plus ½ tablespoon extra-virgin olive oil
- 3 cups all-purpose flour
- 1½ teaspoons kosher salt
- ¼ teaspoon white pepper
- 2½ tablespoons chopped mixed herbs (parsley, basil, oregano)
- 2½ tablespoons chopped sun-dried tomatoes packed in oil

FILLING

- 1 tablespoon olive oil
- 1 cup fresh or frozen okra, sliced in half lengthwise
- 1 cup sliced shiitake mushrooms
- 2 stalks celery, finely sliced
- 2 carrots, finely sliced
- ⅔ cup chopped yellow onions
- 2 cloves garlic, chopped
- 3 tablespoons chopped fresh basil (1½ tablespoons dried)
- 1 tablespoon chopped fresh oregano (½ tablespoon dried)
- 12 ounces hot Italian, andouille, or chorizo sausage, cut into ¼-inch slices
- 2 cups tomato sauce
- 2 tablespoons tomato paste
- ½ teaspoon filé powder (see page 61)
- ¼ teaspoon cayenne pepper
- ¼ cup chopped prosciutto
- 1 cup grated Asiago or Parmesan cheese
- Kosher salt and freshly ground black pepper

Sprinkling of cornmeal

GARNISH: basil leaves

To make dough, in a small mixing bowl, combine warm water, sugar, and yeast, stirring to make sure yeast dissolves. Let stand at room temperature until a foam begins to appear, about 8 to 10 minutes. The color will be a nutty beige. Add ¼ cup olive oil to yeast mixture while stirring for 15 to 20 seconds.

In a food processor fitted with a steel blade, place flour, salt, and pepper. Process for 10 seconds to mix. Add the herbs and sun-dried tomatoes and process for a few seconds. With the machine running, slowly pour in the olive oil–yeast mixture and process until the mixture comes together in a ball, about 30 to 45 seconds.

Remove dough from the food processor and place on a lightly floured surface. Knead the dough by pressing it down and away from you with the back of your hand for about 5 to 8 minutes, or until dough is smooth and elastic. This can be tested by pressing your thumb in the middle of the dough. The dough should rise back up slowly. If it is too dry, add more warm water and knead until dough achieves the proper consistency. If it is too sticky, add small amounts of flour.

Place dough in a large mixing bowl coated with ½ tablespoon olive oil. Roll dough in oil so that a thin layer covers it. Cover bowl with plastic and let dough rise in a warm place for about 1½ hours (an unheated oven works well), or until it has doubled in size.

To prepare filling, in a large sauté pan, heat oil over medium heat. Add okra, mushrooms, celery, carrots, onions, garlic, basil, and oregano and sauté for 7 to 8 minutes. Reserve.

In a separate nonstick sauté pan over medium heat, cook sausage for 5 to 6 minutes, or until lightly browned. Pat dry with paper towels. Reserve.

In a small bowl, combine tomato sauce, tomato paste, filé powder, and cayenne. Whisk thoroughly. Add sausage, chopped prosciutto, cheese, and mushroom-okra mixture. Season to taste.

Preheat oven to 450°F. To prepare calzone, separate dough into four round balls on a lightly floured surface and punch it down several times to remove air bubbles. Roll into 8- to 9-inch circles. Brush each circle with a little olive oil. Divide filling onto half of each of the four circles. Carefully fold the other half over the filled portion and press the edges together. Roll the edges up to seal and crimp. Lightly press the edges with the tines of a fork to decorate. Brush lightly with olive oil. Prick the top of each turnover several times with a fork.

With a spatula, place turnovers on a baking sheet sprinkled with cornmeal. Bake on the top rack of the oven for 16 to 18 minutes, or until crust is golden brown. If edges start to burn, cover them with aluminum foil.

Serve garnished with whole basil leaves.

SERVES 4 AS AN ENTRÉE

"A man will be eloquent if you give him good wine."

RALPH WALDO EMERSON, *REPRESENTATIVE MEN*

Veal-Stuffed Manicotti with Roasted Yellow Pepper Pesto

RECOMMENDED WINE: Sangiovese
ALTERNATIVE WINE: Zinfandel

T HIS "COMFORT" DISH IS A PERFECT SHOWCASE FOR REVEALING THE FOOD-FRIENDLY CHARACTERISTICS OF SANGIOVESE. WITH ITS BRIGHT ACIDITY AND FORWARD FRUIT, SANGIOVESE WORKS PARTICULARLY WELL WITH SIMPLE, RUSTIC DISHES WHERE THE FLAVORS ARE DIRECT AND UNCOMPLICATED. THE WINE OFFERS SEAMLESS SUPPORT RATHER THAN CLAIMING CENTER STAGE ON ITS OWN. ZINFANDEL, WITH ITS INSISTENT FRUITINESS, ACHIEVES MUCH THE SAME EFFECT.

1 tablespoon olive oil

1 cup chopped yellow onions

3 cloves garlic, chopped

1 pound ground veal

1 tablespoon chopped fresh oregano
(½ tablespoon dried)

1 tablespoon chopped fresh marjoram
(½ tablespoon dried)

1 teaspoon fennel seed

1 teaspoon Worcestershire sauce

1 10-ounce package frozen chopped
spinach, thawed and well drained

2 beaten eggs

½ cup shredded mozzarella

½ cup ricotta cheese

½ cup bread crumbs

½ teaspoon kosher salt

½ teaspoon freshly ground black pepper

¼ teaspoon red pepper flakes

¼ teaspoon ground cinnamon

12 manicotti tubes

PESTO

2 roasted yellow bell peppers
(see page 116), peeled and seeded

1 shallot, peeled and quartered

¼ cup lightly toasted pine nuts

½ teaspoon white-wine Worcestershire

¼ cup extra-virgin olive oil
Kosher salt and freshly ground black pepper

SAUCE

½ tablespoon olive oil

1 cup finely chopped yellow onions

2 cloves garlic, chopped

½ cup dry sherry

3 cups tomato sauce

1 14½-ounce can chopped tomatoes,
drained

3 tablespoons tomato paste

1 tablespoon chopped fresh oregano
(½ tablespoon dried)

1 tablespoon chopped fresh basil
(½ tablespoon dried)

1 teaspoon sugar

¼ teaspoon red pepper flakes
Kosher salt and freshly ground black pepper

———

1 cup freshly grated mozzarella cheese
GARNISH: chopped fresh oregano

In a large sauté pan or skillet over medium heat, heat olive oil. Add onions and garlic and sauté for 4 to 5 minutes, until onions are translucent. Add veal, oregano, marjoram, fennel seed, and Worcestershire and continue cooking for 5 to 6 minutes, until veal is no longer pink. Drain fat from veal and return it to the pan. Stir in the spinach and beaten eggs and cook for 2 to 3 minutes. Remove from heat and stir in the mozzarella, ricotta, and bread crumbs. Season with salt, pepper, red pepper flakes, and cinnamon. Allow to cool.

In a large pot of salted boiling water, boil manicotti tubes for 7 to 8 minutes, or according to package instructions. Manicotti should remain relatively firm but be cooked through. Place manicotti in cold water so that they don't collapse. Remove manicotti from cold water bath, drain, and pat dry lightly with a paper towel. Stuff the manicotti with the meat mixture. Place in an oiled baking dish and refrigerate until ready to use.

To make pesto, in a blender or food processor, combine bell peppers, shallot, pine nuts, and Worcestershire and process until smooth. With machine running, add oil in a slow, steady stream and process until smooth. Season with salt and pepper. Cover and refrigerate. Bring to room temperature when ready to use.

To make sauce, in a large sauté pan or skillet, heat oil over medium heat. Add onions and garlic and sauté for 5 to 6 minutes or until onions are translucent. Add sherry, tomato sauce, chopped tomatoes, tomato paste, oregano, basil, sugar, and red pepper flakes and continue cooking for 7 to 8 minutes, stirring frequently. Season with salt and pepper. When sauce is cooked, pour over manicotti tubes. Cover baking dish with foil.

Preheat oven to 350°F. Bake manicotti, covered, for 30 minutes. Remove from oven, sprinkle with cheese, and return to oven, uncovered, for 15 minutes more.

To serve, place two manicotti on each plate. Top with a dollop of stirred pesto. Garnish with chopped oregano.

SERVES 6 AS AN ENTRÉE

"Smooth out with wine the worries of a wrinkled brow."

HORACE, *EPISTLES*

Chicken Cacciatore with Kalamata Olives and Fennel (Classic Pairing)

RECOMMENDED WINE: Sangiovese
ALTERNATIVE WINE: Zinfandel

THIS RUSTIC, TRADITIONAL ITALIAN DISH IS AN EXCELLENT SHOWCASE FOR THE VIBRANT, FRUITY CHARACTER OF SANGIOVESE, WHICH CONTRASTS THE SALTY OLIVES WHILE ACCENTUATING THE LICORICE CHARACTER OF THE FENNEL. THE HIGH FRUIT NOTE AND LIVELY ACIDITY IN THE WINE ALSO HELP TO CUT THROUGH THE TOMATO-BASED SAUCE WITH GREAT SUCCESS. ZINFANDEL, WITH ITS ZESTY FRUITINESS, IS EQUALLY ADEPT AT EMPHASIZING THE ROBUST QUALITY OF THIS DISH.

2 pounds boneless, skinless chicken breasts

2 pounds chicken thighs, skin removed

¼ teaspoon kosher salt

¼ teaspoon red pepper flakes

¾ tablespoon all-purpose flour plus more as needed

2 tablespoons unsalted butter

2 tablespoons olive oil

4 cloves garlic, chopped

1½ cups chopped red onions

2 cups sliced portobello mushrooms

1 fennel bulb, cored and thinly sliced (about 2 cups)

1 cup peeled, chopped carrots

1 tablespoon chopped fresh sage (½ tablespoon dried)

1 tablespoon chopped fresh rosemary (½ tablespoon dried)

1 cup chicken or beef stock

1 cup red wine

1 14-ounce can chopped tomatoes with juice

2 tablespoons tomato paste

½ cup pitted, chopped Kalamata olives

¼ teaspoon kosher salt

¼ teaspoon red pepper flakes

GARNISH: chopped parsley

Rinse and dry chicken and place on waxed paper. Sprinkle chicken with salt and pepper flakes and dust lightly with flour.

In a large stockpot over medium heat, heat butter and olive oil. Add chicken and brown on all sides. Remove with tongs and place on paper towels. In the same pot, add garlic, onions, mushrooms, fennel, carrots, sage, and rosemary and sauté for 7 to 8 minutes. Add chicken, stock, wine, tomatoes, tomato paste, and olives, cover pot and simmer for 50 to 55 minutes. Remove chicken with tongs and keep warm. Simmer and reduce sauce for 15 minutes. Add chicken back to pot and heat thoroughly before serving. Season to taste.

To serve, divide chicken and sauce into large soup bowls or plates. Garnish with chopped parsley and serve with wedges of baked polenta topped with Parmesan.

SERVES 4 AS AN ENTRÉE

Grilled Pork Tenderloin with Sun-Dried Cherry–Blood Orange Sauce

RECOMMENDED WINE: Sangiovese

ALTERNATIVE WINE: Pinot Noir

SUN-DRIED CHERRIES ARE ONE OF MY FAVORITE INGREDIENTS TO MARRY WITH RED WINES. THEY SEEM TO WORK WELL WITH SANGIOVESE, CABERNET SAUVIGNON, PINOT NOIR, ZINFANDEL, AND MERLOT ALIKE AS THEY AMPLIFY THE INHERENT SWEET-TART CHERRY FLAVOR IN MANY OF THESE WINES. BLOOD ORANGES HAVE A RADIANT, DARK RED COLOR AND A SIMILARLY SWEET-TART CHARACTERISTIC THAT MERGES WELL WITH THE CHERRIES AND HIGHLIGHTS SIMILAR FLAVOR NOTES IN SANGIOVESE. REGULAR ORANGES WILL DO.

MARINADE

- 1 cup red wine
- $2/3$ cup blood orange (or regular orange) juice
- $1/2$ teaspoon blood orange (or regular orange) zest
- 3 tablespoons chopped shallots
- 3 juniper berries, lightly crushed
- $1/2$ teaspoon toasted mustard seed
- 1 bay leaf
- $1/2$ teaspoon dried thyme
- $1/4$ teaspoon kosher salt
- $1/8$ teaspoon freshly ground black pepper

- 2 pork tenderloins (about $2½$ pounds)
- 1 tablespoon Dijon mustard
- $3/4$ cup chicken stock
- $1/2$ cup sun-dried cherries
- 1 teaspoon cornstarch mixed with 1 teaspoon cold water
- 1 tablespoon unsalted butter at room temperature (optional)

GARNISH: thin slices of blood orange

To make marinade, combine all ingredients in a nonreactive mixing bowl and whisk thoroughly. Place pork tenderloins in a glass dish and top with marinade. Refrigerate, covered, for 3 to 4 hours, turning once. Remove from marinade and pat dry, reserving marinade. Spread mustard evenly over pork.

Add reserved marinade to a large sauté pan or skillet along with chicken stock and sun-dried cherries and reduce until sauce covers the back of a wooden spoon, about 15 minutes. Add cornstarch mixture to thicken slightly. Whisk in butter, if desired, and keep sauce warm.

Prepare a hot charcoal fire and grill pork tenderloins over coals for 6 to 7 minutes. Turn and continue cooking for 4 to 5 minutes, or until pork is medium rare or to desired doneness. Meat should be juicy. To serve, slice pork, top with sauce, and garnish with blood orange slices.

SERVES 4 AS AN ENTRÉE

Zinfandel is a true mystery. Known as the quintessential California grape variety, Zinfandel's roots have always been in question. Some argue that Zinfandel is the Primitivo grape of southern Italy, while others are convinced that it originated on the Balkan Peninsula. Regardless of its true origin, Zinfandel was imported to California in the mid nineteenth century and has enjoyed periods of unpredictable popularity, which is currently at its zenith.

Early on, Zinfandel was blended with many other red grape varieties to create basic red table wines—relatively bland and innocuous. In the 1970s, as a varietal on its own, Zinfandel was often made in a robust, high-alcohol style that lacked charm and ultimately proved to be unpopular, except in the case of a few very fine versions.

Subsequently, much of the Zinfandel acreage in California was then used to produce "White Zinfandel," which eventually became the rage of California and still sells well over 20 million cases of wine a year. No small feat.

Like many other grapes, classic red Zinfandel varies fairly dramatically in style, ranging from forward, fruity bottlings to full-throttle, high-alcohol monsters. The real excitement in Zinfandel currently is in a medium-full style that favors exuberant berry fruits and a crackling snap of oak, pepper, and spice from barrel aging. These wines are extraordinarily delicious and are virtual chameleons on the table, offering compatibility that few other reds can.

One of Zinfandel's most pleasing attributes is its bright berry fruit character and lively acidity that allows it to partner with grilled meat dishes and spicier foods, particularly those done in a Latin-Hispanic style. Showing distinctive verve and an unmistakable racy streak, Zinfandel captivates and invites consumption.

Zinfandel is sometimes blended with a little Petite Syrah (a varietal that produces round, full-bodied wines) to soften its tartness. Zinfandels made from older vines, often noted on the label, are particularly noteworthy. One caveat: As the alcohol rises in some versions of Zinfandel, this drinkability can be a liability.

While Cabernet Sauvignon is regarded for its power, Pinot Noir for its elegance and grace, Syrah for its concentration, Merlot for its softness, and Sangiovese for its brightness, Zinfandel conjures up a little of all these characteristics. It is complex, yet highly approachable at the same time.

ZINFANDEL

TYPICAL AROMAS & FLAVORS

Blackberry, Blackberry Jam
Boysenberry, Boysenberry Jam
Raspberry, Raspberry Jam
Plum
Raisin
Prune
Rhubarb
Sweet Cherry, Sour Cherry
Pomegranate
Vanilla
Spices: Cinnamon, Clove, Black Pepper
Maple
Mushroom
Mint

BASE INGREDIENTS

Base ingredients refer to the main ingredient of the dish: meat, poultry, game, seafood, shellfish, or vegetable. These represent the core ingredients that are most likely to be matched with a varietal, although successful pairings result as much from the other ingredients used in the dish as they do the base ingredient.

Beef, Lamb, Pork, Venison, Buffalo, Chicken,
Game Hens, Squab, Duck, Sausage

BRIDGE INGREDIENTS

Bridge ingredients help connect the food and the wine through their interaction in flavor, body, intensity, or basic taste.

Tomatoes, Sun-Dried Tomatoes
Mushrooms: Portobello, Shiitake
Herbs: Mint, Bay Leaf, Rosemary,
    Oregano, Thyme
Spices: Black Pepper, Cinnamon, Clove,
    Fennel Seed, Juniper
Nuts: Walnuts, Pecans, Hazelnuts
Black Beans
Eggplant
Garlic, Roasted Garlic
Onions
Shallots
Balsamic Vinegar
Green Peppercorns
Kalamata Olives, Green Olives
Cheeses: Parmesan, Peppered Goat
    Cheese, Dry Jack, Manchego,
    Smoked Gouda, Buffalo Mozzarella

BEST SOURCE REGIONS
ZINFANDEL

The following is a list of countries, regions, and appellations (a wine word referencing specific growing locales) that produce the highest-quality versions of these wines.

This is not intended to be a complete list, only a reference for where the finest renditions can be found.

CALIFORNIA
Sonoma
Russian River
Dry Creek
Mendocino
Napa Valley
Mount Veeder
Howell Mountain
Santa Cruz Mountains
Sierra Foothills
Lake County
ITALY
Apulia
AUSTRALIA
Western Australia
South Australia

ZINFANDEL STYLES

White Zinfandel:
Rose-colored; light, semi-sweet

Medium-full:
Medium-full body; expressive fruit with some barrel influences; often spicy

Full:
Fuller body; ripe; higher alcohol; often more tannic and oaky

Late Harvest:
Full-bodied; sweet, port-like; high-alcohol; dessert wines

TIPS TO SUCCESSFUL
MATCHES WITH ZINFANDEL

1

Zinfandel pairs very well with spicier meat dishes, although too much chile heat will combat the high alcohol in some Zinfandels.

2

Zinfandel works better with saltier dishes than most red wines as its forward, sweet berry fruit contrasts saltiness effectively.

3

Match Zinfandel with weightier, medium- to full-bodied dishes, particularly those that are braised, grilled, or smoked.

4

Zinfandel pairs well with many fruit-based sauces, particularly those with berry fruits.

Paella with Peppered Chicken, Spicy Sausage, and Escargots

RECOMMENDED WINE: Zinfandel

ALTERNATIVE WINE: Syrah

PAELLA, ONE OF THE CLASSIC DISHES OF SPAIN, WAS PROBABLY NOT INVENTED WITH ZINFANDEL IN MIND SINCE THE GRAPE IS PRINCIPALLY GROWN IN CALIFORNIA, BUT IT'S A GREAT COMBINATION ANYWAY. THE COMBINATION OF PEPPERY CHICKEN, SPICY SAUSAGE, AND ESCARGOTS (SNAILS) HARMONIZES WITH THE GUSHING, BERRY-FRUIT INTENSITY AND PEPPERY NOTES OF MANY ZINFANDELS. SIMILAR CHARACTERISTICS IN SYRAH MAKE IT RUN A CLOSE SECOND. THIS DISH IS ADAPTED FROM TWO OF MY FOOD AND WINE HEROES, DAVID ROSENGARTEN AND JOSH WESSON, WHO INCLUDED IT IN THEIR GREAT BOOK, *RED WINE WITH FISH*, TO GO WITH A SPANISH RED.

4 large chicken thighs, skin on

½ teaspoon kosher salt

¼ teaspoon freshly ground black pepper

2½ tablespoons olive oil

2 spicy sausages (spicy Italian, andouille, or chorizo), cut in ½-inch slices

12 large canned escargots

4 medium garlic cloves, chopped

⅔ cup chopped yellow onions

1⅓ cups Arborio rice

½ teaspoon saffron threads

½ teaspoon hot paprika

¼ teaspoon turmeric

½ cup white wine

1¾ cups chicken stock

8 ounces mussels, debearded and rinsed (see page 58)

1 large roasted red pepper, diced (see page 116)

3 tablespoons chopped Italian parsley

¾ cup fresh or defrosted frozen peas

GARNISH: chopped Italian parsley

Rinse chicken thighs in cold water and pat dry. Rub thoroughly with ¼ teaspoon salt and pepper and let rest for a few minutes before cooking.

In a nonstick sauté pan or skillet over medium heat, heat ½ tablespoon olive oil. Add chicken and cook on both sides until browned. Remove from pan and place on paper towels.

In a large paella or sauté pan, sauté sausage and escargots in remaining 2 tablespoons olive oil for 3 to 4 minutes, stirring frequently. Add garlic and onions and continue sautéing for 3 minutes. Add rice, remaining ¼ teaspoon salt, saffron, paprika, and turmeric and stir to coat thoroughly with oil. Sauté for 5 minutes.

Add wine and reduce until liquid has evaporated, stirring occasionally. Add chicken stock, raise heat slightly, and bring stock to a boil. Reduce heat to a simmer and place reserved chicken and mussels evenly throughout the pot on top of the rice. Cover the pot and cook for 17 to 18 minutes, until the chicken is cooked through and the rice is al dente. Sprinkle roasted peppers, parsley, and peas evenly over the top of the paella. Cover and continue to cook for 2 to 3 minutes just to warm through without allowing the peas to lose their bright green color. Season to taste.

Garnish with additional sprinkling of Italian parsley. Serve at table in paella pan or divide servings in kitchen with one thigh per person plus evenly divided mussels and escargots.

SERVES 4 AS AN ENTRÉE

Basil Fettuccine with Sun-Dried Tomatoes, Olives, and Prosciutto

RECOMMENDED WINE: Zinfandel

ALTERNATIVE WINE: Sangiovese

THIS HEARTY, MEDITERRANEAN-STYLE PASTA IS A CLASSIC MATCH FOR THE FORWARD, SPICY BERRY FLAVORS OF YOUNG ZINFANDEL. WHILE ZIN'S VERSATILITY ON THE TABLE IS UNQUESTIONED, THIS KIND OF RUSTIC DISH SEEMS TO HARMONIZE WITH THE LIVELY QUALITIES OF THE GRAPE. THE USE OF WALNUTS IN THE DISH HELPS BALANCE THE TANNINS IN THE YOUNG WINE. THE ITALIAN CHARACTER OF THE DISH ALSO SUGGESTS SANGIOVESE, WHICH WILL COMPLEMENT THE SALTIER TASTE OF THE OLIVES AND PROSCIUTTO.

2 tablespoons olive oil

¾ tablespoon chopped garlic

1 cup sliced yellow onions

1¼ cups sliced crimini or shiitake mushrooms

¾ cup Zinfandel or other red wine

1 cup julienned sun-dried tomatoes packed in oil

¾ tablespoon tomato paste

¾ cup tomato sauce

⅔ cup pitted, chopped Kalamata olives

3 tablespoons chopped fresh basil (1½ tablespoons dried)

1 tablespoon toasted fennel seed

1 tablespoon balsamic vinegar

Kosher salt and freshly ground black pepper

1¼ pounds fresh or dried basil fettuccine noodles

½ cup freshly grated Parmesan cheese

3 ounces prosciutto, julienned

¼ cup chopped toasted walnuts

GARNISH: chopped fresh basil

In a medium sauté pan or skillet, heat olive oil over medium heat. Add garlic, onions, and mushrooms and sauté for 3 to 4 minutes, until onions are translucent. Add wine, tomatoes, tomato paste, tomato sauce, olives, basil, fennel seed, and balsamic vinegar and simmer, stirring frequently, until sauce begins to thicken slightly, about 8 minutes. Reduce heat and keep warm. Add a little more wine if the sauce thickens too much. Season to taste, being careful not to add too much salt since prosciutto will add saltiness to the dish.

In a large pot of salted boiling water, cook fettuccine for 3 to 5 minutes, or until cooked al dente. Drain water from pot and then transfer fettuccine back to the pot and place over medium heat.

Divide noodles evenly on plates. Spoon sauce over noodles. Top with evenly divided Parmesan, prosciutto, and walnuts. Garnish with fresh basil. Serve immediately.

SERVES 5 TO 6 AS AN APPETIZER OR 2 TO 4 AS AN ENTRÉE

"Best Ever" Moussaka

RECOMMENDED WINE: Zinfandel
ALTERNATIVE WINE: Syrah

Moussaka, the signature dish of greek cooking, has a natural affinity for zinfandel. the deep fruit intensity of this wine, or similar fruit intensity and full body of syrah, helps cut through the hearty, rich flavors. this recipe has been in my family's repertoire for years and has always been a crowd-pleaser.

2 medium globe eggplants

2 teaspoons kosher salt

2 pounds ground lamb

2 yellow onions, peeled and chopped

3 cloves garlic, chopped

1 teaspoon freshly ground black pepper

¼ teaspoon ground nutmeg

½ tablespoon ground cinnamon

1 teaspoon *fines herbes* (see page 36) or dried oregano

¼ cup minced parsley

1 6-ounce can tomato paste

¾ cup red wine

½ cup plain bread crumbs

¾ pound feta cheese

SAUCE

4 tablespoons (½ stick) unsalted butter

6 tablespoons all-purpose flour

2 cups whole (or low-fat) milk

¼ teaspoon ground nutmeg

¼ teaspoon kosher salt

1 egg yolk, beaten

½ cup grated Parmesan cheese

GARNISH: chopped parsley

Preheat oven to 375°F. Cut tops off eggplants and cut lengthwise in ¼-inch-thick slices. Sprinkle with 1 teaspoon salt and place on paper towels for 30 minutes to absorb the moisture. Rinse, wipe eggplant dry, and place in a single layer on a lightly oiled baking sheet. Roast for 30 minutes.

In a large sauté pan or skillet over medium-high heat, cook the lamb, onions, and garlic, crumbling the lamb with a fork and stirring frequently until browned. Remove with a slotted spoon and drain thoroughly in a strainer. Place meat mixture on paper towels and pat dry to further remove fat.

Return the meat to the cleaned pan and add remaining 1 teaspoon salt, pepper, nutmeg, cinnamon, *fines herbes*, parsley, and tomato paste. Stir well. Add wine and simmer for 10 minutes.

Grease the bottom of a 9-by-13-inch ovenproof baking dish and dust with all but 3 tablespoons of bread crumbs. Reserve remaining bread crumbs for sauce.

To make sauce, in a medium sauté pan over low-medium heat, melt butter and whisk in flour. Stir in milk, nutmeg, and salt and stir until thickened. In a separate mixing bowl, spoon a little of the hot sauce into the egg yolk and add the 3 tablespoons of reserved bread crumbs. Then, blend the egg–bread crumb mixture into the sauce. Mix thoroughly.

Layer dish first with eggplant, then meat, and then with a generous portion of feta cheese. Repeat layers and top with sauce.

Preheat oven to 350°F. Top with Parmesan and bake for 50 to 60 minutes or until top of cheese is golden brown. Cut into square servings. Garnish with chopped parsley.

SERVES 6 AS AN ENTRÉE

Coq au Zin

RECOMMENDED WINE: Zinfandel
ALTERNATIVE WINE: Pinot Noir

THIS IS A CONTEMPORARY SPIN ON THE CLASSIC FRENCH DISH, COQ AU VIN, WHICH WAS TRADITIONALLY MADE WITH ROOSTER AND A REDUCTION OF RED WINE, TYPICALLY CABERNET FRANC FROM THE LOIRE REGION. I'VE ELIMINATED THE ROOSTER BLOOD AND COGNAC, WHICH ARE OFTEN USED IN THE ORIGINAL VERSION, AND FOCUSED INSTEAD ON RICH, HEARTY FLAVORS REDOLENT OF GARLIC, ONIONS, PANCETTA, HERBS, AND, OF COURSE, ZINFANDEL. THIS PAIRING IS QUITE OBVIOUS SINCE NEARLY A BOTTLE OF ZINFANDEL IS USED IN THE STEW. THE RECIPE COULD BE MADE WITH PINOT NOIR AND TIED TOGETHER WITH A PINOT NOIR PAIRING WITH ALMOST EQUAL SUCCESS.

$4\frac{1}{2}$ pounds chicken breasts, thighs, and legs

$\frac{1}{2}$ teaspoon kosher salt

$\frac{1}{3}$ teaspoon freshly ground black pepper

3 tablespoons all-purpose flour

2 tablespoons unsalted butter

4 ounces pancetta, chopped

2 cups chopped yellow onions

1 cup sliced shiitake mushrooms

4 cloves garlic, chopped

$\frac{3}{4}$ teaspoon dried thyme

$\frac{1}{2}$ teaspoon dried chervil

2 bay leaves

2 cups Zinfandel

2 cups seeded, chopped tomatoes

2 tablespoons tomato paste

$\frac{3}{4}$ cup chicken stock

10 ounces peeled pearl onions

$\frac{1}{2}$ cup pitted, sliced Spanish green olives

1 tablespoon cornstarch mixed with
1 tablespoon cold water

2 tablespoons Dijon mustard

Kosher salt and pepper

GARNISH: chopped parsley

Rinse chicken in cold water and pat dry with paper towels. In a small bowl, mix together salt, pepper, and 2 tablespoons flour and sprinkle mixture on chicken on all sides.

In a large stockpot over medium heat, melt butter. Add pancetta and sauté for 5 to 6 minutes. Add chicken pieces skin side down and brown for about 5 minutes per side in batches. Remove with tongs and place on paper towels to dry.

Add remaining 1 tablespoon flour to the stockpot and brown for 1 to 2 minutes. Add onions, mushrooms, garlic, and herbs and sauté for 5 minutes. Add wine, tomatoes, tomato paste, and stock along with chicken and bring to a boil. Reduce heat, cover, and simmer for 30 minutes. Add pearl onions and green olives and continue cooking for 10 minutes.

Remove chicken from pot to a large bowl and cover with aluminum foil. Keep warm.

Add cornstarch mixture to cooking liquid and mix in mustard. Raise heat and boil rapidly for 6 to 7 minutes so that liquid reduces and thickens. Season to taste.

To serve, place chicken on plates or in large soup bowls and top liberally with sauce. Garnish with parsley. Serve with rice or pasta and crusty garlic bread.

SERVES 4 TO 6 AS AN ENTRÉE

Clove-Infused Pork—Black Bean Stew with Tomatillo—Roasted Red Pepper Salsa

RECOMMENDED WINE: Zinfandel

ALTERNATIVE WINE: Sangiovese

THIS FULL-FLAVORED, LATIN-BASED PORK AND BLACK BEAN STEW IS UNDERSCORED BY THE SPICY KICK OF CLOVES AND OTHER AROMATIC INGREDIENTS. TEXTURALLY, THE DISH IS HEARTY AND RICH, CALLING FOR A SIMILARLY HEARTY, ROBUST ZINFANDEL TO HELP AMPLIFY THE SPICY FLAVORS. SANGIOVESE KICKS A LITTLE ACIDITY INTO THE DISH TO CONTRAST THE HEARTINESS OF THE STEW AND TO MATCH THE TARTNESS OF THE TOMATILLOS.

1 pound dried black beans

1 tablespoon chili powder

2 teaspoons toasted cumin seed, crushed

¼ teaspoon cayenne pepper

¼ teaspoon achiote, optional (see NOTE)

1 teaspoon dried basil

½ teaspoon freshly ground black pepper

1 teaspoon kosher salt

2 pounds cubed pork stew meat (from the shoulder or roast)

4 ounces pancetta or bacon, chopped

1½ tablespoons vegetable oil

3 cloves garlic, chopped

1 medium yellow onion, chopped

2 stalks celery, ends trimmed and diced

1 large red bell pepper, cored, seeded, and chopped

2 jalapeños, seeded and minced

2 tablespoons chopped fresh oregano (1 tablespoon dried)

1 cup red wine

2½ cups chicken stock

½ cup chopped cilantro

1 bay leaf

10 whole cloves

TOMATILLO SALSA

1 tablespoon vegetable oil

12 ounces tomatillos, husked, rinsed, and cut into quarters

1 medium yellow onion, sliced

1 shallot, chopped

1 clove garlic, chopped

1 jalapeño, seeded and minced

1 roasted red pepper, seeded and chopped (see page 116)

½ teaspoon toasted cumin seed

⅓ cup chopped cilantro

Kosher salt and freshly ground black pepper

GARNISH: sour cream, cilantro sprigs

Soak beans in a large bowl of cold water for 8 hours or overnight. Strain and rinse. Pick out any discolored beans. Alternatively, beans can be placed in cold water, brought to a boil, and then allowed to sit for 1 hour in hot water before draining.

In a large mixing bowl, mix together chili powder, cumin, cayenne, achiote, basil, black pepper, and salt. Add pork and mix thoroughly to coat the meat.

In a large, heavy-bottomed stockpot, cook pancetta over medium heat until very lightly browned. Remove pancetta with a slotted spoon and discard fat. Add oil to the same pot over medium-high heat. Add pork, garlic, onion, celery, red pepper, jalapeños, and oregano and sauté for 7 to 8 minutes, until pork is lightly browned. Add reserved pancetta, red wine, chicken stock, beans, cilantro, bay leaf, and cloves

RECIPE CONTINUES

Clove-Infused Pork–Black Bean Stew with Tomatillo–Roasted Red Pepper Salsa
CONTINUED

and bring to a boil. Reduce heat to simmer. Cover and cook for 1 hour.

To make salsa, in a large sauté pan or skillet, heat oil over medium heat. Add tomatillos, onion, shallot, garlic, jalapeño, roasted red pepper, and cumin seed and sauté, stirring often, for 10 to 12 minutes, until tomatillos begin to soften and onions turn translucent. Remove from heat and cool. Add cilantro, salt, and pepper and mix thoroughly.

To serve, place pork and black beans in large soup bowls. Top with tomatillo salsa and a small dollop of sour cream to the side of the salsa. Garnish with cilantro sprigs. Serve with crusty garlic bread or corn tortillas.

NOTE: Achiote is ground annatto seed and is found in Latin sections of grocery stores or specialty food stores.

SERVES 6 AS AN ENTRÉE

"God made only water, but man made wine."

VICTOR HUGO

Grilled Lamb with Roasted Garlic–Mint Sauce (Classic Pairing)

RECOMMENDED WINE: Zinfandel
ALTERNATIVE WINE: Cabernet Sauvignon

ZINFANDEL, GIVEN ITS INIMITABLE FLEXIBILITY WITH HEARTY FOOD, SHOWS ITS VERY BEST SIDE WITH THIS FULL-FLAVORED GRILLED LAMB. ROBUST AND RUSTIC, THIS DISH FEATURES A FAIRLY INTENSE SAUCE, REDOLENT OF FRESH MINT AND ROASTED GARLIC, WHICH IS MIRRORED BY THE FULL-THROTTLE, BERRY-TINGED FLAVORS OF ZINFANDEL.

MARINADE

¼ cup reduced-salt soy sauce

½ cup red wine

1 tablespoon olive oil

½ cup sliced yellow onions

1 tablespoon chopped fresh mint

1½ tablespoons chopped fresh oregano
   (¾ tablespoon dried)

⅛ teaspoon freshly ground black pepper

½ leg of lamb, boned, butterflied, and
   trimmed of most fat (about 2 pounds
   meat)

1 large whole head of garlic, unpeeled

½ teaspoon extra-virgin olive oil

Kosher salt and freshly ground black pepper

SAUCE

½ tablespoon olive oil

1 tablespoon minced shallots

1¼ cups red wine

1½ cups beef or chicken stock

3 tablespoons chopped fresh mint

1 tablespoon chopped roasted garlic

¾ teaspoon Dijon mustard

Kosher salt and freshly ground black pepper

GARNISH: chopped fresh mint

To make marinade, mix all ingredients together in a small bowl. Place lamb in a large, sealable plastic bag and add marinade. Marinate in the refrigerator for at least 2 to 3 hours, turning bag occasionally. Remove lamb from marinade and pat dry.

Preheat oven to 350°F. Cut off just the very top of whole garlic head so that the cloves of garlic are barely exposed. Drizzle top with olive oil and sprinkle lightly with salt and pepper. Cover in aluminum foil, leaving a small area open at the top. Roast garlic head for 45 to 50 minutes. Remove from oven and let cool slightly. Squeeze the roasted garlic cloves out of the head. Discard the skin. Will keep, covered, in refrigerator for up to a week.

To make sauce, in a medium sauté pan or skillet, heat olive oil. Add shallots and sauté for 2 to 3 minutes. Add wine, bring to a simmer, and reduce by half. Add stock, mint, roasted garlic, and mustard and simmer until sauce is reduced by half. Season to taste.

Prepare a hot charcoal fire and grill lamb for 8 to 9 minutes per side, or until cooked medium-rare. With butterflied lamb, it may be necessary to remove thinner sections at ends before removing thicker middle section in order to achieve proper doneness throughout.

To serve, slice lamb and spoon sauce over the lamb. Garnish with mint.

SERVES 4 AS AN ENTRÉE

Grilled Flank Steak with Roasted Corn–Pancetta Salsa

RECOMMENDED WINE: Zinfandel

ALTERNATIVE WINE: Sangiovese

———————

HERE'S A SPECIAL SUMMER DISH WITH SASSY KICK TO GET YOUR JUICES GOING. WHILE CHILE HEAT AND RED WINES ARE NOT NECESSARILY ALWAYS A MATCH, THIS COMBINATION WORKS DUE TO THE RESTRAINT OF THE MARINADE AND SALSA. A ZINFANDEL THAT'S A LITTLE LOWER IN ALCOHOL (UNDER 13.8 PERCENT) HELPS IMMEASURABLY IN MAKING THE CONNECTION WORK. THE JUICY, CHERRY-FRUIT FLAVORS AND GOOD ACIDITY OF SANGIOVESE WILL ALSO SUPPORT THIS PAIRING QUITE CAPABLY.

MARINADE

⅓ cup dry sherry

3 tablespoons reduced-salt soy sauce

1 tablespoon toasted sesame oil

1 teaspoon Worcestershire sauce

½ cup sliced yellow onions

⅛ teaspoon freshly ground black pepper

1 rehydrated dried chipotle pepper, stemmed and minced, or ¼ teaspoon chipotle chiles in adobo (see page 175)

———

2 pounds flank steak, trimmed

SALSA

4 ears fresh (or frozen) corn, husks removed

Olive oil

2 ounces pancetta or bacon, chopped

½ cup chopped roasted red bell pepper (see page 116)

1½ teaspoons minced roasted garlic (see page 164)

½ teaspoon white-wine Worcestershire sauce

2 teaspoons minced jalapeños

2 teaspoons sherry wine vinegar

2 tablespoons chopped fresh basil (1 tablespoon dried)

Kosher salt and freshly ground black pepper

To make marinade, combine all ingredients in a small mixing bowl and whisk thoroughly. Place steak in a large, sealable plastic bag and add marinade. Refrigerate for 4 to 5 hours, turning bag occasionally. Remove steak from marinade and reserve marinade for basting.

To make salsa, preheat oven to 350°F. Rub corn lightly with olive oil and place on a baking sheet. Roast in the oven for 45 minutes. Remove corn and scrape kernels off cobs (should produce 2 cups of corn). Place in a medium mixing bowl.

In a medium sauté pan or skillet over low-medium heat, cook pancetta for 8 to 10 minutes until lightly browned. Pour pancetta into a small strainer over the sink and drain oil. Pat the pancetta dry and combine with the corn. Add bell pepper, garlic, Worcestershire, jalapeños, vinegar, and basil to the corn. Mix thoroughly, season to taste, and refrigerate. Bring to room temperature before serving.

To grill flank steak, prepare a hot fire. Place flank steak flat over the heat and grill for 5 minutes per side, until rare. Remove from grill and let rest under foil for 5 minutes. Slice steak on the angle against the grain.

To serve, place a portion of corn salsa on each plate. Top with several slices of flank steak. This dish is nicely preceded by Radish Slaw with Rémoulade and Pistachios (page 41).

SERVES 4 AS AN ENTRÉE

If you were to be offered a big, bold red wine with gobs of flavor, considerable fullness and weight, relatively low acidity, and smooth, polished tannins, you'd probably say "that's worth trying," right? The time may have come for Syrah, a remarkable red wine that is not terribly well known in the United States—yet. All signs point to a very bright future for this noble grape, which is thought to have originated in the ancient city of Shiraz in Persia.

Syrah is most well known for producing wines of great concentration, depth, and character in the northern Rhône region of France where wines from Côte Rôtie, Hermitage, Crozes-Hermitage, Cornas, and St. Joseph appellations are considered to be quintessential statements of the varietal. Further south in the Rhône, in Châteauneuf-du-Pape, Syrah is blended with Grenache, Mourvèdre, Carignane, and up to ten other varietals (including the white grape Viognier) to create wines that can be quite stunning.

The grape is also highly revered in Australia, where it is called Shiraz and accounts for almost as much acreage as Chardonnay. Shiraz is often blended with Cabernet Sauvignon in Australia, making for a flavorful blend that can pack a wallop.

In California, Syrah is just beginning to vie for the consumer's attention. A rebel band of wineries going by the name of the "Rhône Rangers" has been promoting interesting blends that are similar in style to Châteauneuf-du-Papes along with very good unblended Syrahs. Both French and California styles of blended wines are different from Syrah in that they are typically less tannic and more round when they are released.

For the sake of clarification, Syrah is not the same grape as Petite Syrah (or Petite Sirah), which has an even longer history in California. Petite Syrah is thought to be the French Durif grape and has similar (but not the same) qualities as Syrah, such as a deep, dark color, concentrated fruit, and a hint of pepper. While different, it can be thought of as similar to Syrah in terms of food matching.

While the styles of Syrah and Syrah blends can vary dramatically, most of these wines feature a softer, rounder, and fuller body than most other reds, without the rougher tannins or bracing acidity found in many young Cabernet Sauvignons.

Syrah's voluptuous flavors feature an interesting array of stone fruits (black cherry and plum) and currants along with hints of smoke, violets, tar, licorice, and an often gamey character, which make for intriguing pairing opportunities with meat, game, and other full-flavored fare. Wimpy wines these are not! The talented wine writer

Karen MacNeil compares Syrah to "a tuxedo-clad Clint Eastwood with a five o'clock shadow."

As a total turnabout from this blockbuster style, dry rosés are produced principally in the Tavel, Lirac, and Bandol areas of the Rhône. These pink wines grace the tables of southern France during the hot summer. They provide spectacular refreshment with spicier foods (see Roast Pork with Holy Mole Sauce on page 174) and with cold summer dishes. These are made principally from Grenache, Cinsault, and Mourvèdre. California also produces a very small amount of dry rosé that is quite quaffable.

Syrah offers considerable interest for its ability to partner with robust braised foods and a diverse array of grilled meats, with which it particularly shines. You need not be timid with Syrah, nor with its associated blends. These are gutsy, in-your-face wines that take their strength seriously and are capable of tackling most any full-flavored dish, but they maintain a certain charm and grace just the same.

SYRAH AND RHÔNE BLENDS

TYPICAL AROMAS & FLAVORS

Blackberry, Blackberry Jam
Boysenberry
Blueberry
Plum
Prune
Ripe Cherry
Currant
Smoke
Black Pepper, White Pepper
Leather
Violet
Orange Zest
Vanilla
Chocolate
Mint
Spices: Clove, Cinnamon,
    Sandalwood
Roasted Meat, Game

BASE INGREDIENTS

Base ingredients refer to the main ingredient of the dish: meat, poultry, game, seafood, shell-fish, or vegetable. These represent the core ingredients that are most likely to be matched with a varietal, although successful pairings result as much from the other ingredients used in the dish as they do the base ingredient.

Beef, Lamb, Veal, Venison, Buffalo, Pork,
Squab, Salmon, Tuna

BRIDGE INGREDIENTS

Bridge ingredients help connect the food and the wine through their interaction in flavor, body, intensity, or basic taste.

Blackberries
Plums
Currants
Prunes
Garlic, Roasted Garlic
Onions
Mushrooms: Portobello, Shiitake, Porcini
Nuts: Walnuts, Pecans
Cheeses: Parmigiano-Reggiano, Dry Jack,
    Peppered Goat Cheese, Feta
Herbs: Rosemary, Thyme, Mint,
    Lavender, Bay Leaf
Green Olives, Black Olives
Roasted Tomato, Sun-Dried Tomato
Eggplant
Fennel
Chocolate
Green Peppercorns
Black Pepper, White Pepper
Dijon Mustard, Coarse-Grained Mustard

BEST SOURCE REGIONS
SYRAH AND RHÔNE BLENDS

The following is a list of countries, regions, and appellations (a wine word referencing specific growing locales) that produce the highest-quality versions of these wines.

This is not intended to be a complete list, only a reference for where the finest renditions can be found.

FRANCE
Rhône
Côte Rôtie
Hermitage
Crozes-Hermitage
St.-Joseph
Cornas
Gigondas
Châteauneuf-du-Pape
Vacqueyras
Côtes-du-Rhône
Provence
Côte de Provence
Bandol
Languedoc-Roussillon
AUSTRALIA
Barossa Valley
McLaren Vale
Coonawarra
CALIFORNIA
Santa Barbara
Santa Maria
Napa Valley
Mendocino
Sonoma

SYRAH AND RHÔNE
BLEND STYLES

Medium:
Medium-dark color; often made with high proportions of grapes other than Syrah; round, soft, and full of fruit

Full:
Dark purple/inky; round and full-bodied; full flavored and often intensely concentrated with fruit; sometimes quite tannic when young; typically requires some bottle age

TIPS TO SUCCESSFUL
MATCHES WITH
SYRAH AND RHÔNE BLENDS

1
The full body and weight of Syrah and Rhône blends make them ideal partners for robust, hearty foods.

2
Rhône blends are softer, rounder, and less tannic than Syrah, and they will pair with spicier dishes than Syrah.

3
These wines match particularly well with full-flavored grilled meats and game.

4
Dry rosés are great warm-weather quaffing wines and are particularly well suited to complementing alfresco fare and spicy foods. Serve them very chilled.

Penne with Sausage, Porcini and Portobello Mushrooms, and Syrah

RECOMMENDED WINE: Syrah
ALTERNATIVE WINE: Zinfandel

THIS PASTA OFFERS INTENSE FLAVORS THROUGH THE COMBINATION OF SAUSAGE, EARTHY PORCINI MUSHROOMS, PORTO-BELLO MUSHROOMS, AND THE TOMATO-BASED RED WINE SAUCE, MAKING IT AN IDEAL PARTNER FOR THE FULL-FLAVORED INTENSITY OF SYRAH. TRY IT ON A COLD WINTER NIGHT WHEN YOU NEED TO WARM YOUR INSIDES. ZINFANDEL WORKS HERE AS IT OFFERS MUCH THE SAME FORWARD BERRY AND STONE FRUIT FLAVORS TO COMPLEMENT THE INTENSE SAUCE.

2 ounces dried porcini mushrooms

12 ounces Italian sausage, cut into ½-inch slices

1½ cups chopped yellow onions

3 cloves garlic, chopped

1½ cups chopped portobello mushrooms

¾ teaspoon crumbled dried rosemary

1 teaspoon dried thyme

¼ teaspoon kosher salt

¼ teaspoon freshly ground black pepper

1½ cups Syrah

2 14½-ounce cans chopped tomatoes, drained

1 tablespoon tomato paste

Kosher salt and freshly ground black pepper or red pepper flakes

1 pound dried penne or other small dried pasta

GARNISH: shredded Asiago cheese, chopped parsley

Soak porcini in hot water for 2 to 3 hours. Drain.

In a medium, nonstick sauté pan or skillet over medium-high heat, sauté sausage for 6 to 7 minutes, turning to brown on both sides. Remove with slotted spoon, place on paper towels, and pat dry.

In a large sauté pan or skillet over medium-high heat, sauté onions and garlic for 4 to 5 minutes, until onions are translucent. Add porcini, portobellos, rosemary, thyme, salt, and pepper and continue sautéing for 3 to 4 minutes. Add wine and bring to a boil. Reduce heat and simmer to reduce by half. Add tomatoes and tomato paste and simmer for 8 to 10 minutes. Add reserved sausage and heat through. Season to taste.

Bring a large pot of salted water to a boil. Carefully add penne and cook according to package directions or until it is al dente. Drain and return penne to pot. Add sauce to pasta and mix thoroughly. Reheat, if necessary.

To serve, divide pasta among 4 large pasta or soup bowls. Top with cheese and parsley.

SERVES 4 AS AN ENTRÉE

Grilled Lamb with Olive Sauce (Classic Pairing)

RECOMMENDED WINE: Syrah or Syrah blend
ALTERNATIVE WINE: Zinfandel

WHEN MY WIFE AND I TRAVELED IN THE SOUTH OF FRANCE IN 1995, I HAD A CONSTANT CRAVING FOR GRILLED LAMB WITH OLIVES, A DISH THAT I IMAGINED WOULD BE PERFECT IN THE RUSTIC VILLAGES OF GORDES OR MENERBES—PETER MAYLE COUNTRY. I NEVER QUITE FOUND THE DISH I WAS LOOKING FOR, SO WHEN I RETURNED HOME I CREATED MY OWN VERSION OF WHAT I HAD HOPED TO TASTE DURING OUR TRAVELS. THE FLAVORS OF GRILLED LAMB, ACCENTUATED BY BRINY OLIVES AND AROMATIC HERBS, PROVIDE THE PERFECT CONTRAST FOR THE SWEET, JUICY FRUIT OF A GOOD SYRAH OR RHÔNE BLEND (SYRAH BLENDED WITH GRENACHE AND MOURVÈDRE). SYRAH, BY NATURE, IS AN INTENSELY FLAVORED VARIETAL WITH A GREAT CONCENTRATION OF FRUIT; THIS DISH DOES IT JUSTICE. ZINFANDEL'S BERRY-LIKE FRUIT IS ALSO A GOOD CONTRAST TO THE BRINY FLAVORS.

MARINADE

- $\frac{1}{3}$ cup olive oil
- 1 tablespoon balsamic vinegar
- $\frac{3}{4}$ teaspoon dry mustard
- 2 bay leaves
- $\frac{3}{4}$ teaspoon hot paprika
- $\frac{1}{4}$ cup chopped mint leaves
- 4 cloves garlic, chopped
- $\frac{1}{3}$ cup red wine
- $\frac{1}{4}$ teaspoon fresh ground black pepper
- $\frac{1}{2}$ teaspoon kosher salt
- 1 tablespoon herbes de Provence

- 1 6- to 7-pound whole leg of lamb, boned, butterflied, and trimmed of excess fat (about $4\frac{1}{2}$ pounds meat)
- 2 shallots, chopped
- $5\frac{1}{2}$ ounces shiitake mushrooms, sliced
- 2 tablespoons olive oil
- $\frac{3}{4}$ cup red wine
- 3 cups lamb or chicken stock
- 1 tablespoon chopped fresh rosemary ($\frac{1}{2}$ tablespoon dried)
- 1 tablespoon Dijon mustard
- $\frac{1}{4}$ cup pitted, sliced green olives
- $\frac{1}{4}$ cup pitted and sliced Kalamata olives

GARNISH: rosemary or mint sprigs

In a medium, nonreactive mixing bowl, combine marinade ingredients and whisk thoroughly. Place marinade in a large, sealable plastic bag with lamb. Marinate for 4 to 6 hours, turning occasionally.

In a medium sauté pan or skillet over medium heat, sauté shallots and mushrooms in olive oil for 3 to 4 minutes. Add red wine and bring to a boil. Reduce liquid by half. Add stock and rosemary and reduce by half. Add Dijon mustard and olives, reduce heat, and continue simmering until sauce coats the back of a wooden spoon. Keep warm.

Prepare a charcoal fire. Remove lamb from marinade and pat dry. Reserve marinade for basting. When coals are very hot, grill lamb for 7 to 8 minutes per side to medium rare, occasionally basting lamb with reserved marinade. It may be necessary to remove the ends of the lamb first and continue cooking the thicker middle portion to desired doneness.

Remove lamb from fire. Let sit under tented foil for a few minutes. Slice thinly and place on warm plates. Spoon sauce over top. Garnish with fresh rosemary sprigs. Serve with oven-roasted potato quarters and whole tomatoes gratinée.

SERVES 6 AS AN ENTRÉE

Filet Mignon "Diana"

RECOMMENDED WINE: Syrah
ALTERNATIVE WINE: Zinfandel

I CREATED THIS RENDITION OF TRADITIONAL STEAK DIANE THE WEEKEND THAT PRINCESS DIANA DIED, AND IT IS THEREFORE DEDICATED TO HER. SYRAH, OF ALL RED WINES, IS THE MOST PEPPERY. BECAUSE OF THIS CHARACTERISTIC, THE MARRIAGE BETWEEN THE WINE AND THE INCREDIBLY INTENSE SAUCE IS PARTICULARLY SUCCESSFUL. ZINFANDEL OFTEN EXHIBITS THIS SAME PEPPERY CHARACTER AND IS AN EXCELLENT CHOICE AS WELL.

4 trimmed filets mignons (about 2 pounds)

1 tablespoon extra-virgin olive oil

¾ tablespoon whole mixed peppercorns, lightly crushed

¼ teaspoon kosher salt

1½ teaspoons Dijon mustard

SAUCE

1 tablespoon unsalted butter

1 tablespoon minced garlic

1½ cups red wine

¾ tablespoon balsamic vinegar

1 tablespoon Dijon mustard

1 teaspoon Worcestershire sauce

2 cups beef stock

3 tablespoons Cognac or brandy

2 teaspoons tomato paste

2 tablespoons cream or half-and-half

Kosher salt and freshly ground black pepper

Rub filets with olive oil on all sides. Mix peppercorns and salt together and press evenly on tops and sides of filets. Spread mustard evenly on top of filets.

To make sauce, in a large sauté pan or skillet over low-medium heat, melt butter. Add garlic and sauté for 3 to 4 minutes. Add red wine, vinegar, mustard, Worcestershire, stock, Cognac, and tomato paste and bring to a boil. Reduce heat and simmer until reduced by half. Add cream and continue to reduce to thicken slightly. Season to taste and adjust consistency as necessary.

Light a charcoal fire and allow coals to get very hot. Grill filets for 8 to 10 minutes. Turn and cook for an additional 5 to 6 minutes, until filets are rare or to desired doneness.

Spoon sauce onto plates and place filets on top of sauce. Serve with asparagus spears and sweet potato purée.

SERVES 4 AS AN ENTRÉE

Roast Pork with Holy Mole Sauce and Mexican Rice

RECOMMENDED WINE: Syrah blend
ALTERNATIVE WINE: Champagne/sparkling wine, preferably a *blanc de noir* (see page 21)

ONE OF THE MOST CHALLENGING TRICKS WITH FOOD AND WINE PAIRING IS MARRYING WINE TO THE SPICY HEAT OF CHILES. FINDING A RED WINE THAT WORKS IS EVEN MORE DIFFICULT. ADAPTED FROM MY COLLEAGUE JOHN ASH'S RECIPE, THIS TRADITIONAL MEXICAN MOLE PRESENTS INTERESTING OPPORTUNITIES DUE TO ITS RELIANCE ON UNSWEETENED CHOCOLATE, A FLAVOR NOTE FOUND IN MANY SYRAH-BASED WINES. THE BRIGHT FRUITINESS OF A *BLANC DE NOIR* OR A LIGHT, DRY FRENCH ROSÉ ARE TWO OTHER INTRIGUING OPTIONS. YOU'LL BE PLEASANTLY SURPRISED AT HOW WELL THIS INTENSE, RICHLY TEXTURED SAUCE CAN BE CONTRASTED BY THE BRIGHT, JUICY FRUIT IN EITHER THE CHAMPAGNE OR ROSÉ, WHICH CLEANSE THE PALATE OF THE BURST OF CHOCOLATE AND SPICE FLAVORS. THE EXTRA SAUCE AND RICE CAN BE USED WITH GRILLED OR ROASTED CHICKEN AS LEFTOVERS. THIS DISH IS WELL WORTH TRYING DESPITE THE SLIGHTLY LONG INGREDIENT LIST.

1 4-pound pork roast, rolled and tied

½ teaspoon kosher salt

⅓ teaspoon crushed black peppercorns

½ teaspoon ground cinnamon

½ teaspoon ground cumin

1 teaspoon dried oregano

½ teaspoon ground sage

3 tablespoons olive oil

MOLE

1⅓ cups sliced yellow onions

1½ tablespoons chopped garlic

1½ tablespoons toasted sesame seeds

½ teaspoon ground cinnamon

½ teaspoon ground cloves

½ teaspoon coriander seed, toasted and crushed

1½ tablespoons chopped, seeded pasilla chiles (see NOTE)

1 tablespoon chopped chipotle chiles in adobo (see NOTE)

2 tablespoons chopped fresh cilantro

3½ cups chicken stock

¼ cup smooth peanut butter

4½ tablespoons tomato paste

7 tablespoons raisins

2¼ ounces unsweetened chocolate, chopped (see NOTE)

1 tablespoon fresh lime juice

Kosher salt and freshly ground black pepper

MEXICAN RICE

1½ tablespoons unsalted butter

2 tablespoons vegetable oil

2 tablespoons minced shallots

1 cup chopped yellow onions

2 cups basmati rice

2½ teaspoons ground cumin

2 teaspoons ground oregano

1 teaspoon toasted fennel seed

3 cups chicken stock

1 14-ounce can chopped tomatoes with juice

8 ounces feta cheese (tomato-basil, if available), cut into ¼-inch cubes

1 cup chopped, roasted, peeled, and seeded peppers (yellow and red bell peppers, Anaheim chiles)

GARNISH: cilantro sprigs, lime slices

Sprinkle pork roast with salt, pepper, cinnamon, cumin, oregano, and sage, and rub into roast on all sides.

In a large sauté pan or skillet over medium heat, heat olive oil. Place pork roast in pan and lightly brown on all sides, including ends. To brown ends, hold pork roast upright with a large fork. When browned, remove pork from pan and put in a glass baking dish. Reserve oil for mole sauce. Refrigerate pork roast, covered, until ready to cook.

In a preheated 350°F oven, roast pork for 1½ hours, until it reaches an internal temperature of 165°F. (The roast can also be cooked on a gas grill over indirect medium heat with great results.)

Meanwhile, to make mole, using the same pan that was used for searing the pork, sauté onions and garlic over medium heat for 5 to 6 minutes, until onions are translucent. Add sesame seeds, cinnamon, cloves, coriander seed, pasilla chiles, *chipotle,* and cilantro and continue cooking for 3 to 4 minutes, stirring frequently. Add stock and bring to a boil. Reduce heat and simmer for 10 minutes, stirring occasionally.

Pour stock mixture into a food processor or blender. Add peanut butter, tomato paste, raisins, chocolate, and lime juice and process until smooth. Return sauce to pan and simmer, covered, for 35 to 40 minutes. Thin with additional stock, if necessary. Sauce should be fairly thick. Season to taste.

To make Mexican rice, in a medium sauté pan or skillet over medium heat, heat butter and oil. Add shallots and onions and sauté for 4 to 5 minutes, until onions are translucent. Add rice, cumin, oregano, and fennel seed, and sauté for 2 to 3 minutes, stirring frequently.

Add stock and tomatoes. Bring to a boil, then reduce heat and simmer, covered, for 10 to 12 minutes or until most of liquid is absorbed in rice. Stir in feta and peppers, cover, and continue to cook for 5 to 7 minutes. Remove from heat and allow the rice to rest for 10 minutes. Fluff with a fork thoroughly prior to serving.

To serve, slice pork and place on plates. Top with mole and serve rice on the side. Garnish with cilantro sprigs and lime slices.

NOTES: Pasilla peppers are dried chiles that can be found in most grocery stores. Chipotle in adobo is a fiery Latin condiment made with smoked jalapeño peppers that are pickled in vinegar. It can be found canned in the ethnic foods aisles of many supermarkerts. For the chocolate, try to find Mexican Ibarra unsweetened chocolate available in the gourmet or international sections of many grocery stores.

SERVES 6 TO 8 AS AN ENTRÉE

If the eighties was the decade of Chardonnay, then surely the nineties marked the emergence of Merlot as the darling of American wine consumers. This is not altogether surprising since Merlot, when grown in the proper areas and made with judicious viticultural practices and a knowing palate, can be a very attractive wine.

Merlot is often better suited to the table than its widely heralded kissing cousin, Cabernet Sauvignon. Blended with Cabernet, Merlot tones down some of big brother's rougher tannic qualities and tames the savage beast.

Merlot has a great deal going for it. First off, it's red. The wine boom of the 1990s, fueled in large part by the wide-reaching news of the health benefits of moderate red wine consumption, saw Merlot come of age. It has become the greatest benefactor of this positive health news, and this has sparked a feverish effort to plant new Merlot vineyards in virtually all parts of the world in order to capitalize on the new worldwide demand. The results of this boom have produced a lot of very drinkable Merlot along with many relatively mediocre and nondescript bottles.

In French, *merlot* means "little blackbird," probably due to the similarities in color between the grape and the bird. Stylistically, Merlot can be very attractive for its soft, supple texture and forward fruit. Merlot's most endearing qualities are its smoothness, roundness, and radiance. It displays a bright fruit character, which allows it to be partnered with a fairly wide range of foods.

In Bordeaux, Merlot dominates the varietal blend in the St. Emilion and Pomerol regions. In California, Merlot is often blended with the other great varieties of Bordeaux—Cabernet Sauvignon, Cabernet Franc, Petit Verdot, and Malbec—and bears the name "Meritage," a term that is occasionally used by American producers for wines that are made from combinations of the five great Bordeaux varieties.

Rather than being called "Meritage" specifically on the label, many producers choose to give these wines proprietary names and list the varietal percentages on the back label. These wines have similar food affinities to both Cabernet Sauvignon and Merlot, depending on the percentage of the blend.

As with so many other varietals, the persona of Merlot can change greatly depending on the style preferred by the winemaker. Extended skin contact during fermentation and longer barrel aging can produce wines of dark color and considerable oak and tannin, making them more difficult to pair with foods initially, but well suited to aging in the cellar. Unfortunately, only experience (or a good wine merchant) can be your guide here as there's no way of knowing what style of Merlot you are purchasing by reading the label.

Great Merlot can be a truly distinctive wine, but greatness is rare. More often than not, Merlot is a highly drinkable red wine—an amiable table partner to many foods, without any notable deficiencies.

MERLOT

TYPICAL AROMAS & FLAVORS

Blackberry
Boysenberry
Raspberry
Blueberry
Plum
Cranberry
Ripe Cherry
Currant
Cedar
Tea
Cocoa
Cigar/Tobacco
Green Olive
Vanilla
Smoky
Herbs: Bay Leaf, Mint

BASE INGREDIENTS

Base ingredients refer to the main ingredient of the dish: meat, poultry, game, seafood, shellfish, or vegetable. These represent the core ingredients that are most likely to be matched with a varietal, although successful pairings result as much from the other ingredients used in the dish as they do the base ingredient.

Beef, Lamb, Veal, Venison, Pork, Squab, Duck, Salmon, Tuna

BRIDGE INGREDIENTS

Bridge ingredients help connect the food and the wine through their interaction in flavor, body, intensity, or basic taste.

Blackberries
Blueberries
Cranberries
Currants
Mushrooms: Portobello, Shiitake
Onions, Garlic, Roasted Garlic
Herbs: Rosemary, Thyme, Mint,
    Tarragon
Nuts: Walnuts, Pecans
Tomatoes: Fresh, Dried, and Smoked
Eggplant
Fennel
Beets
Cheeses: Camembert, Smoked Gouda,
    Cheddar, Parmesan
Bacon, Pancetta
Dijon Mustard

BEST SOURCE REGIONS
MERLOT

The following is a list of countries, regions, and appellations (a wine word referencing specific growing locales) that produce the highest-quality versions of these wines.

This is not intended to be a complete list, only a reference for where the finest renditions can be found.

CALIFORNIA
  Napa Valley
  Sonoma
  Monterey
WASHINGTON
  Columbia Valley
NEW YORK
  Long Island
ITALY
  Trentino-Alto Adige
  Tuscany
  Veneto
  Friuli
FRANCE
  Bordeaux
    Saint-Emilion
    Pomerol
AUSTRALIA
CHILE

MERLOT STYLES

Light:
  Light body; soft, smooth, and very fruity with little apparent oak

Medium:
  Medium body; smooth, soft tannins, more oak, some complexity

Full:
  Medium-full body; oaky, more tannic, complex flavors, aging required

TIPS TO SUCCESSFUL
MATCHES WITH MERLOT

1

Use Merlot in marinades and sauces to help mirror the wine. You need not use the same wine as is to be served if you choose to cook with a less expensive one.

2

Medium-weight dishes, rather than extremely heavy food, complement Merlot the most.

3

If the Merlot is particularly tannic, a little sprinkling of chopped walnuts or pecans as a garnish in the dish will help reduce the impression of the tannin.

Sautéed Duck Breasts
with Smoked Tomato Sauce

RECOMMENDED WINE: Merlot
ALTERNATIVE WINE: Pinot Noir

THIS BEGUILING SMOKED TOMATO SAUCE WAS INSPIRED BY MY COLLEAGUE JOHN ASH, WITH WHOM I'VE COLLABORATED ON TWO BOOKS. THIS SAUCE IS INCREDIBLY FRIENDLY TO A LOT OF DIFFERENT FOODS—SEAFOOD, SHELLFISH, POULTRY, PORK, LAMB, AND PASTAS—AND IS EQUALLY ADEPT AT CAJOLING THE SMOKY QUALITIES, WHICH ARE INHERENT TO BARREL AGING, OUT OF MERLOT, PINOT NOIR, AND ZINFANDEL. THE EXTRA SAUCE CAN BE FROZEN AND USED IN OTHER COMBINATIONS.

SAUCE

7½ pounds vine-ripened tomatoes

2 pounds red onions, halved

3 red bell peppers, halved and seeded

2 whole shallots, halved

¼ cup olive oil

¼ cup chopped fresh oregano

¼ cup chopped fresh basil

1 cup dry sherry

3 tablespoons balsamic vinegar

3 tablespoons tomato paste

2 tablespoons chopped roasted garlic
(see page 164)

2 teaspoons kosher salt

½ teaspoon freshly ground black pepper

½ teaspoon red pepper flakes

---

4 halved duck breasts

1½ tablespoons extra-virgin olive oil

1 teaspoon Worcestershire sauce

10 drops hot sauce

⅛ teaspoon kosher salt

⅛ teaspoon freshly ground black pepper

1 teaspoon chopped fresh basil
(½ teaspoon dried)

1 teaspoon chopped fresh oregano
(½ teaspoon dried)

GARNISH: basil leaves, grated Parmesan cheese

To make sauce, in an electric smoker or gas grill using wet fruitwood, oak, or hickory chips, heat wood until it begins smoking. Place aluminum foil on each of the racks. Place tomatoes, onions, peppers, and shallots on the foiled racks. Smoke for 2 to 3 hours, replacing the wood chips with new ones, if necessary, to maintain a good smoking source. Remove the tomatoes, onions, peppers, and shallots and place in a large bowl. Peel, seed, drain, and chop tomatoes. Peel and chop shallots and onions. Seed and chop peppers.

In a large pot over medium heat, heat oil. Add onions, peppers, shallots, and herbs and sauté for 8 to 10 minutes, until onions are translucent. Add tomatoes, sherry, vinegar, tomato paste, and roasted garlic and continue simmering, uncovered, for 15 minutes. Add salt, pepper, and red pepper flakes. Adjust seasoning to taste.

Remove from heat and transfer in small batches to a food processor or blender. Process for about 45 seconds until smooth. Reserve 2 cups for the dish. Transfer the rest to a nonreactive bowl or to glass jars for freezing.

Prepare duck breasts by trimming all excess fat from the sides of the breasts. Cut two or three small X-shaped incisions into the fatty part of each breast. Place duck breasts skin side down in a glass dish and drizzle top of each breast with olive oil, Worcestershire sauce, and hot sauce. Sprinkle evenly with salt, pepper, basil, and oregano. Marinate, refrigerated, for 3 to 4 hours.

In a large sauté pan or skillet over medium-high heat, sauté duck breasts skin side down for 5 to 6 minutes. Turn and continue searing for 3 to 4 minutes. Meat should be medium rare inside. Do not overcook.

Let duck rest for a few minutes before cutting. Slice duck breasts at an angle and top with tomato sauce. Garnish with basil leaves and cheese. Serve with sautéed spinach with garlic.

SERVES 4 AS AN ENTRÉE

"The best kind of wine is that which is pleasant to him that drinks it."

PLINY THE ELDER, *NATURAL HISTORY*

Grilled Pork Tenderloin with Roasted Beet–Cranberry Sauce (Classic Pairing)

RECOMMENDED WINE: Merlot
ALTERNATIVE WINE: Zinfandel

TWO VERY DIFFERENT BUT COMPLEMENTARY FLAVORS (BEETS AND CRANBERRIES) MINGLE IN THIS DISH TO PROVIDE THE CONNECTION TO THE RIPE BERRY QUALITIES FOUND IN MOST MERLOTS. THIS DISH IS VERY, VERY RED AS WELL, WHICH ESTABLISHES A SUBLIMINAL COLOR LINK TO THE WINE. IT'S INTERESTING HOW COLOR CAN ALSO HELP TO ESTABLISH A CONNECTION BETWEEN FOOD AND WINE. THE BERRY FLAVORS OF ZINFANDEL ALSO SUPPORT THE CONCENTRATION OF THE DISH.

MARINADE

⅔ cup red wine

½ cup orange juice

1 teaspoon minced orange zest

½ cup sliced yellow onions

½ teaspoon toasted mustard seed, crushed

½ teaspoon toasted aniseed, crushed

1 bay leaf

1 teaspoon chopped fresh thyme
   (½ teaspoon dried)

½ teaspoon kosher salt

¼ teaspoon freshly ground black pepper

2 pork tenderloins (about 2 pounds)

SAUCE

8 ounces beets, ends trimmed

Vegetable oil for beets

¾ cup cranberry juice

1¾ cups chicken stock

1 tablespoon balsamic vinegar

1 teaspoon cornstarch mixed with
   1 teaspoon cold water

2 tablespoons unsalted butter (optional)

Kosher salt and freshly ground black pepper

GARNISH: sprigs of Italian parsley

To make marinade, in a medium mixing bowl, combine wine, orange juice and zest, onions, mustard seed, aniseed, bay leaf, thyme, salt, and pepper and whisk thoroughly. Place pork tenderloins in a large, sealable plastic bag and add marinade. Marinate, refrigerated, for 3 to 4 hours. Remove pork from marinade and pat dry. Reserve marinade for sauce.

To make sauce, preheat oven to 350°F. Wash, pat dry, and lightly oil the beets. Place beets on a roasting pan and roast for 55 to 60 minutes, until cooked through and skins begin to shrivel. Cool, pull off skin, and cut into ¼-inch dice. Set aside for use in sauce.

In a medium sauté pan or skillet, add reserved marinade, except bay leaf, and bring to boil. Reduce heat and continue to simmer until reduced by half. Add cranberry juice, chicken stock, vinegar, and beets and simmer until sauce is reduced by half. Add cornstarch mixture and continue to reduce until sauce thickens. Remove from heat and swirl in butter, if desired. Season to taste. Keep warm.

Grill pork over a hot fire for about 8 to 9 minutes. Turn and continue to cook for 5 to 6 minutes, or until pork is medium-rare and juicy inside. Do not overcook. Keep warm in aluminum foil.

To serve, spoon sauce evenly onto plates. Slice pork and place on top of sauce. Garnish with Italian parsley. Serve with horseradish mashed potatoes.

SERVES 6 AS AN ENTRÉE

Grilled Venison with Cherry Sauce and Crispy Corn Noodles

RECOMMENDED WINE: Merlot
ALTERNATIVE WINE: Cabernet Sauvignon

———————————————

YOUNG MERLOT HAS A PARTICULARLY EFFUSIVE, VIBRANT SWEET-CHERRY CHARACTER, WHICH IS NICELY MIRRORED BY THIS SWEET-CHERRY SAUCE. THE LITTLE TRICK WITH THIS SAUCE IS MAKING SURE THAT THE SAUCE DOESN'T GET SWEETER THAN THE WINE OR IT WILL MAKE THE WINE SEEM DRY AND LIFELESS. THIS CAN BE ADJUSTED DEPENDING ON HOW NATURALLY SWEET THE CHERRIES ARE AND HOW MUCH PORT IS USED IN THE SAUCE REDUCTION. IF THE CHERRIES SEEM PARTICULARLY SWEET, CUT BACK A LITTLE ON THE PORT. PORK TENDERLOIN COULD BE SUBSTITUTED FOR VENISON, IF DESIRED. CABERNET SAUVIGNON IS A SUPERB MATCH FOR THIS DISH AS WELL AND MAY REQUIRE A LITTLE LESS PORT IN THE SAUCE.

MARINADE

¾ cup red wine

1½ tablespoons chopped shallots

6 juniper berries, crushed

1 tablespoon chopped fresh tarragon leaves (½ tablespoon dried)

½ teaspoon mustard seed

⅛ teaspoon kosher salt

⅛ teaspoon freshly ground black pepper

1 pound venison loin

CRISPY CORN NOODLES

6 ounces chow mein noodles

4 green onions, ends trimmed and minced

⅔ cup corn kernels

1 tablespoon chopped fresh tarragon (1½ teaspoons dried)

½ teaspoon chopped lemon zest

1½ tablespoons olive oil

¼ teaspoon kosher salt

⅛ teaspoon freshly ground black pepper

2 tablespoons vegetable oil

SAUCE

1⅔ cups beef or lamb stock

1 cup pitted and halved fresh cherries

2 tablespoons port or to taste

1½ teaspoons Dijon mustard

2 tablespoons unsalted butter (optional)

To make marinade, in a small, nonreactive mixing bowl, combine all ingredients and whisk thoroughly. Transfer marinade to a sealable plastic bag and place venison in the bag. Marinate, refrigerated, for 3 to 4 hours.

To make crispy noodles, add chow mein noodles to a large pot of salted boiling water. Bring back to the boil and cook for 1½ minutes, stirring to make sure that noodles fully separate and cook. Drain noodles and submerge them in cold water. Drain when cooled. In a medium bowl, mix noodles with green onions, corn, tarragon, lemon zest, olive oil, salt, and pepper.

In a 12-inch, nonstick pan, heat vegetable oil over medium heat until hot (test with a small piece of noodle). Add all of the noodle mixture to pan and press down slightly to evenly cover pan. Cook for 6 to 7 minutes. Carefully turn the noodle mixture with a spatula. Cook on the second side for an additional 5 to 6 minutes, or until golden brown and crispy on the outside. Remove from pan and drain on paper towels. Cut into quarters and keep warm until ready to serve.

When ready to make sauce, remove venison from the marinade and pat dry. Transfer marinade to a large sauté pan or skillet. Add stock and cherries. Bring to a boil, then reduce heat and simmer until mixture is reduced by half and coats the back of a wooden spoon. Add port and mustard, mix thoroughly and continue simmering for 5 minutes until sauce thickens a little more. Season to taste. Remove from heat, swirl in butter, and keep warm.

Prepare a very hot charcoal fire. When coals are red hot, grill venison for 3 to 4 minutes per side, making very sure that it does not overcook. Meat should be cooked rare to medium-rare, otherwise it takes on a "livery" quality as it is cooked longer. Cut into thin slices and serve with cherry sauce and noodle cake.

SERVES 4 AS AN ENTRÉE

Braised Veal with Portobello Mushrooms, Celery Root, and Toasted Pecans

RECOMMENDED WINE: Merlot
ALTERNATIVE WINE: Chardonnay

THE SOFT, SUPPLE QUALITY OF MERLOT MAKES IT AN IDEAL CHOICE FOR BRAISED DISHES THAT COMBINE A LOT OF COMPLEMENTARY FLAVORS. THE SOFTER TANNINS AND MEDIUM WEIGHT OF THE WINE BLEND WELL WITH THE SAVORY VEAL, EARTHY MUSHROOMS AND CELERY ROOT, AND THE TOASTED NUTS. AS A WHITE WINE ALTERNATIVE, IT'S SURPRISING HOW WELL THE RICHNESS OF A FULL-BODIED CHARDONNAY PAIRS WITH THIS DISH.

1¾ pounds veal stew meat	4 cloves garlic, chopped
1 tablespoon all-purpose flour	1 tablespoon sweet paprika
¼ teaspoon kosher salt	1 teaspoon caraway seed
⅛ teaspoon freshly ground black pepper	1 teaspoon *fines herbes* (see page 36)
3 tablespoons unsalted butter	1¾ cups veal or chicken stock
1½ ounces pancetta, chopped	⅓ cup white wine
2 cups sliced portobello mushrooms	Kosher salt and freshly ground black pepper
2 cups peeled and diced celery root	¼ cup toasted pecan halves
1 cup chopped yellow onions	½ cup shredded smoked mozzarella cheese

Cut veal into 1-inch cubes. Sprinkle with flour, salt, and pepper. In a large sauté pan over medium heat, sauté veal in butter and pancetta for 6 to 7 minutes, or until lightly browned. Add mushrooms, celery root, onions, garlic, paprika, caraway, and *fines herbes* and continue cooking for 8 minutes. Add stock and wine and bring to a boil. Reduce heat, cover, and simmer for 1¼ hours. Season to taste.

Spoon veal stew onto plates while very hot. Top with pecans and mozzarella. Serve with wild rice and sautéed spinach.

SERVES 4 AS AN ENTRÉE

When all is said and done, when wine drinkers have toyed with trendy varietals or tried new blends from the Rhône, Italy, or California, Cabernet Sauvignon raises its noble head and reminds us that it—and it alone— is the king of wines. Cabernet, particularly when it has had time to age peacefully in a good, cool cellar, offers grandeur that is not achieved by any other wine.

However, despite its greatness, Cabernet Sauvignon remains a troublesome mate to food, not unlike the queen of whites, Chardonnay. The very qualities that make Cabernet great—power, muscle, concentration, and flesh—are not easy on food, at least until these elements harmonize in the bottle with the ripe fruit and oak of the wine. Cabernet Sauvignon is grown virtually throughout the winemaking world, although it achieves greatness principally in France and California and often in Italy, Australia, Chile, and Washington. To tame the rough, coarse tannins of Cabernet, it is often blended with Merlot, which softens it, as well as with Cabernet Franc, Petite Verdot, and Malbec. These other varietals add both aromatic and flavor components to Cabernet Sauvignon that are quite pleasing as the wine evolves in the bottle. When Cabernet drops below 75 percent in a blend, the wine is often given a proprietary name or is called "Meritage" (to rhyme with "heritage"), the name generally agreed upon in the United States to signify a blend of typical Bordeaux varietals.

While Cabernet Sauvignon argues for the longest aging of any red wine, many producers seek to make the wine in a style that is more open and accessible. This is accomplished through various technical methods—less skin contact during fermentation and more aeration as the wine is moved from tank to barrel or from barrel to barrel—with the goal of softening the often harsh, youthful tannins that are typical of the varietal.

Young Cabernet Sauvignon is ripe, powerful, and concentrated, while aged Cabernet takes on a certain elegance and grace that is quite extraordinary. The aging process brings out nuance and complexity in the wine that make it far more compatible as a food partner.

Cabernet generally does poorly with seafood, although a red wine–based seafood stew is not

totally out of the question. Cabernet is also difficult with spicy foods and with vinegar (with the
exception of judicious use of balsamic vinegar—
see Grilled Veal Chops with Balsamic Mushroom
Sauce on page 193).

Cabernet Sauvignon, matched with high-
quality meat, game, or cheese, offers unparalleled
pleasure and is often an exquisite partner on the
table. Because of the complexity of the varietal,
particularly as it ages, it's helpful to match
Cabernet to dishes with focused flavors, such as
those found in this chapter. This lets the food
showcase the wine, allowing it to be the star that
it can be.

As Warren Winiarski of Stag's Leap Wine
Cellars once said of Cabernet, it is an "iron fist in
a velvet glove."

CABERNET SAUVIGNON

TYPICAL AROMAS & FLAVORS

Black Currant, Cassis
Cherry
Blackberry
Blueberry
Vanilla
Mint
Eucalyptus
Bay Leaf
Green Olive
Bell Pepper
Cedar, Cigar Box, Tobacco
Chocolate
Oak
Mushroom
Truffle

BASE INGREDIENTS

Base ingredients refer to the main ingredient of the dish: meat, poultry, game, seafood, shellfish, or vegetable. These represent the core ingredients that are most likely to be matched with a varietal, although successful pairings result as much from the other ingredients used in the dish as they do the base ingredient.

Beef, Lamb, Pork, Veal, Venison,
Buffalo, Squab, Duck

BRIDGE INGREDIENTS

Bridge ingredients help connect the food and the wine through their interaction in flavor, body, intensity, or basic taste.

Currants
Walnuts, Pecans
Mushrooms: Portobello, Porcini, Morel
Truffles
Dijon Mustard
Black Olives, Green Olives
Balsamic Vinegar
Cheeses: Camembert, Gorgonzola, Aged
    Jack, Parmesan
Herbs: Mint, Rosemary, Thyme,
    Oregano, Basil
Black Pepper
Eggplant
Roasted Tomato
Butter

BEST SOURCE REGIONS
CABERNET

The following is a list of countries, regions, and appellations (a wine word referencing specific growing locales) that produce the highest-quality versions of these wines.

This is not intended to be a complete list, only a reference for where the finest renditions can be found.

FRANCE
  Bordeaux
    Pauillac
    Margaux
    Graves
    St. Julien
    St. Estèphe
    Pomerol
    Medoc
    Haut-Medoc
CALIFORNIA
  Napa Valley
  Sonoma
  Mendocino
  Santa Cruz Mountains
WASHINGTON
  Columbia Valley
AUSTRALIA
  Coonawarra
  McClaren Vale
  Clare Valley
  Barossa Valley
  Hunter Valley
  Margaret River
CHILE
  Maipo Valley
  Rapel Valley
ITALY
  Tuscany

CABERNET STYLES

Medium:
  Medium body; fruity, less tannic, softer, and rounder

Medium-full:
  Medium-full to full body; slightly more concentrated, oaky, and tannic

Full:
  Full body; concentrated, oaky, tannic, and less forward fruit when young; requires bottle aging of five to seven years from vintage date to showcase its typically complex flavors

TIPS TO SUCCESSFUL MATCHES WITH CABERNET SAUVIGNON

1

Cabernet Sauvignon is a perfect match with meats containing some fat. The fat from the meat coats the palate and protects against youthful tannins in the wine.

2

As Cabernet ages, it becomes less intense, thereby altering the type of dish that is best suited to it. Intense reduction sauces are no longer as successful a match with older Cabernets.

3

Dishes with a keen flavor focus are often quite successful with Cabernet. Walnuts and pecans are particularly useful when pairing dishes to younger Cabernet, as the tannins in the nuts will help lessen the impression of the tannins in the wine.

New York Steaks with Gorgonzola-Walnut "Butter" and Minted Tabbouleh

RECOMMENDED WINE: Cabernet Sauvignon
ALTERNATIVE WINE: Syrah Blend

THIS "BUTTER" DOESN'T ACTUALLY USE BUTTER BUT HAS A SIMILAR CONSISTENCY, WHICH COMES FROM THE CREAMY, RICH GORGONZOLA CHEESE. THIS IS A KEY ELEMENT IN TAMING THE INTENSITY, CONCENTRATION, AND TANNIN IN A FINE, YOUNG CABERNET SAUVIGNON. THE ADDITION OF WALNUTS, CONTAINING A FAIRLY HIGH BITTER TANNIN LEVEL OF THEIR OWN, HELPS TONE DOWN THE TANNINS IN YOUNG CABERNET AS WELL. A MINTED TABBOULEH HELPS WEAVE THE RICHER ELEMENTS TOGETHER AND PROVIDES REFRESHING CONTRAST. A YOUNG SYRAH BLEND WITH CONCENTRATED FRUITINESS CAN ALSO ADD THE RIGHT TEXTURAL ELEMENT TO THE PAIRING.

4 New York steaks (about 2 to 2½ pounds)

¼ cup olive oil

4 cloves garlic, thinly sliced

2 teaspoons balsamic vinegar

1 tablespoon chopped fresh rosemary
   (½ tablespoon dried)

¼ teaspoon kosher salt

   Freshly ground black pepper

   "BUTTER"

8 ounces Gorgonzola cheese, cut into
   small chunks

1 teaspoon white-wine Worcestershire

2 teaspoons green peppercorns

¼ cup lightly toasted walnut halves

1½ tablespoons minced chives

6 drops Tabasco

   TABBOULEH

1 cup bulgur wheat

1½ cups chicken stock

¾ cup seeded, diced tomatoes

¼ cup chopped fresh mint

1 tablespoon chopped fresh chives

¾ tablespoon chopped roasted garlic
   (see page 164)

3 tablespoons minced green onions

1 teaspoon sweet paprika

2 tablespoons herb-flavored (basil or
   oregano) or extra-virgin olive oil

   Kosher salt and freshly ground black pepper

Place steaks in a glass dish. In a small bowl, whisk together olive oil, garlic, vinegar, rosemary, salt, and pepper. Marinate in refrigerator, covered, for 2 to 3 hours. Remove steaks from marinade when ready to grill.

To make "butter," combine all ingredients in a food processor or blender and process for about a minute until mixed thoroughly. Can be refrigerated, but plan to serve at room temperature.

To make tabbouleh, place bulgur wheat in a large nonreactive bowl. Bring stock to a boil. Pour hot stock over bulgur wheat. Cover with foil and let stand for about 30 minutes, or until stock is absorbed into bulgur. Mix in tomatoes, mint, chives, garlic, green onions, paprika, and oil. Season to taste. Set aside.

Prepare a hot fire and grill steaks for 5 to 6 minutes per side or until cooked to desired doneness. Shortly after turning, sprinkle a mound of Gorgonzola butter on steaks and allow it to melt slightly while the steaks finish cooking. Serve with tabbouleh and additional Gorgonzola butter in a small dish on the table.

SERVES 4 AS AN ENTRÉE

Grilled Filets with Roasted Eggplant and Cherry Tomato Ragout

RECOMMENDED WINE: Cabernet Sauvignon
ALTERNATIVE WINE: Merlot

THIS IS A CLASSIC OUTDOOR SUMMER DISH, BUT IT CAN BE DONE VIRTUALLY YEAR-ROUND IF WEATHER COOPERATES. THE SIMPLICITY OF THE JUICY GRILLED FILETS SHOWCASES THE INTENSE FRUIT OF A GOOD, YOUNG CABERNET OR LAYS THE FOUNDATION FOR APPRECIATION OF AN OLDER, MORE MATURE WINE AS WELL. THE EGGPLANT RAGOUT IS A SIMPLE ACCOMPANIMENT THAT SUPPORTS THE PAIRING BY OFFERING THE SLIGHT BITTERNESS OF EGGPLANT TO OFFSET THE TANNIN IN THE WINE. THE PAIRING WILL WORK ALMOST EQUALLY WELL WITH MERLOT FOR THE SAME REASONS.

MARINADE

5 tablespoons soy sauce

2 teaspoons dry mustard

Freshly ground black pepper

———

4 filets mignons (about 2 pounds)

RAGOUT

2 medium globe eggplants, cut horizontally in ½-inch slices

2½ tablespoons olive oil

Kosher salt

½ cup chopped yellow onions

1 pound whole cherry tomatoes

2 teaspoons chopped roasted garlic (see page 164)

½ cup chopped fresh basil

2 tablespoons chopped fresh oregano (1 tablespoon dried)

½ teaspoon fennel seed, toasted and crushed

Freshly ground black pepper

To make marinade, whisk all ingredients together in a small mixing bowl. Spoon over filets. Allow to marinate, covered, in refrigerator, for 2 to 3 hours before cooking.

To make ragout, preheat oven to 350°F. Lightly rub eggplant slices with 1 tablespoon of olive oil and sprinkle with salt. Place eggplant in an ovenproof skillet or baking sheet and roast for 40 minutes. Chop into ½-inch cubes.

In a medium sauté pan or skillet, heat 1½ tablespoons oil over medium-high heat. Add onions and sauté for 3 to 5 minutes, until translucent. Add tomatoes, garlic, herbs, fennel seed, and eggplant and sauté for 8 to 10 minutes, stirring occasionally. Season to taste. Keep warm.

To cook filets, prepare a hot charcoal fire. When the coals are very hot, grill filets for 5 to 7 minutes per side, cooked medium-rare or to taste.

To serve, spoon ragout evenly onto plates with filets on the side.

SERVES 4 AS AN ENTRÉE

Grilled Veal Chops
with Balsamic Mushroom Sauce

RECOMMENDED WINE: Cabernet Sauvignon

ALTERNATIVE WINE: Syrah

BALSAMIC VINEGAR INTENSIFIES AND DEVELOPS A DEEP, CONCENTRATED FLAVOR AS IT REDUCES. THIS SAUCE CAPTURES THIS QUALITY ALONG WITH THE EARTHY FLAVORS OF DRIED MOREL AND CRIMINI MUSHROOMS. THE RESULT IS AN INTENSE, FULL-FLAVORED DISH THAT MARRIES PARTICULARLY WELL TO THE RIPE FRUIT OF CABERNET SAUVIGNON OR TO THE CONCENTRATION OF A GOOD SYRAH. THIS PAIRING IS A GOOD EXAMPLE OF FINDING PARALLEL INTENSITY IN BOTH THE DISH AND THE WINE.

MARINADE

2 tablespoons olive oil

1 tablespoon chopped shallots

¼ cup red wine

1 tablespoon Dijon mustard

2 tablespoons chopped fresh basil
   (1 tablespoon dried)

¼ teaspoon kosher salt

¼ teaspoon freshly ground black pepper

---

2 large veal chops (about 1½ pounds)

SAUCE

2½ tablespoons olive oil

2 tablespoons chopped shallots

1½ cups sliced crimini or shiitake mushrooms

1 teaspoon green peppercorns, chopped

¼ cup balsamic vinegar

½ cup red wine (preferably Cabernet Sauvignon)

1½ cups beef or chicken stock

¼ ounce dried morel or porcini mushrooms (rehydrated in cold water, drained, and halved)

2 tablespoons chopped fresh basil
   (1 tablespoon dried)

½ tablespoon Dijon mustard

½ teaspoon cornstarch mixed with
   ½ teaspoon cold water

Kosher salt and freshly ground black pepper

GARNISH: chopped fresh basil

To make marinade, combine all ingredients in a nonreactive mixing bowl and whisk thoroughly. Place veal chops in a glass dish and top with marinade. Refrigerate, covered, for 3 to 4 hours. Remove from marinade and pat dry.

To make sauce, in a large sauté pan or skillet over medium heat, heat oil. Add shallots and crimini mushrooms and sauté until shallots turn golden, about 3 to 4 minutes. Add green peppercorns, vinegar, and red wine and simmer until liquid is reduced by half. Add stock and morels and continue reducing until reduced by half. Add basil and stir in mustard and cornstarch mixture to thicken slightly. Sauce consistency should coat the back of a wooden spoon. Season to taste.

Prepare a hot charcoal fire. Grill veal chops for 8 to 10 minutes. Turn and continue grilling for another 7 to 8 minutes, until veal is medium-rare or cooked to desired doneness.

To serve, place veal chops on plates. Top with sauce. Garnish with chopped fresh basil. Serve with sautéed fresh peas.

SERVES 2 AS AN ENTRÉE

Grilled Lamb with Rustic Porcini Sauce

RECOMMENDED WINE: Cabernet Sauvignon

ALTERNATIVE WINE: Sangiovese

CABERNET SAUVIGNON IS NOT THE MOST VERSATILE WINE. OFTEN TANNIC WHEN YOUNG, IT RELIES ON VARIOUS INGREDIENTS TO HELP MAKE IT MORE FRIENDLY AND ADAPTABLE TO DIFFERENT FOODS. THE INTENSE EARTHINESS OF PORCINI MUSHROOMS HELPS TAME KING CAB, MELLOWING SOME OF ITS INHERENT TANNIN. THE JUICY LAMB PROVIDES THE RIGHT AMOUNT OF FLAVOR AND FAT TO HELP PAIR AMIABLY WITH THE WINE.

MARINADE

½ cup red wine

¼ cup soy sauce

1 bay leaf

1 tablespoon olive oil

1 teaspoon Worcestershire sauce

¼ cup chopped yellow onions

2 cloves garlic, chopped

2 juniper berries, crushed

1 tablespoon chopped fresh rosemary (½ tablespoon dried, crushed)

¼ teaspoon freshly ground black pepper

___

½ leg of lamb, butterflied and trimmed of excess fat (about 2 pounds net)

SAUCE

1 ounce dried porcini mushrooms

2 ounces pancetta, diced

1 tablespoon olive oil

½ cup chopped yellow onions

2 teaspoons chopped roasted garlic (see page 164)

2 tablespoons chopped fresh basil (1 tablespoon dried)

¾ cup red wine

1 cup beef stock

¾ teaspoon Dijon mustard

1 cup seeded, chopped fresh plum tomatoes

Kosher salt and freshly ground black pepper

GARNISH: chopped parsley

To make marinade, in a small mixing bowl, combine all ingredients and whisk thoroughly. Transfer marinade to a sealable plastic bag and add lamb. Marinate, refrigerated, for 2 to 3 hours. Remove lamb from marinade and pat dry.

In a small bowl, soak mushrooms in very hot water for 45 minutes until they are soft and reconstituted. Remove mushrooms from water, place in strainer, and gently squeeze water out of them. Slice in thirds and reserve.

To make sauce, in a medium sauté pan or skillet over medium heat, sauté pancetta in oil for 4 to 5 minutes, stirring often. Add onions, garlic, and basil and continue sautéing for 6 to 7 minutes, until onions are translucent. Add red wine and reserved mushrooms and simmer for 10 minutes, until wine is reduced by half. Add stock, mustard, and tomatoes and continue simmering for 15 minutes, until sauce is reduced to a consistency that coats the back of a wooden spoon. Season to taste.

Prepare a hot charcoal fire. Grill lamb over hot coals for 8 to 9 minutes and turn. Continue grilling for 7 to 8 minutes, or until medium-rare and juicy inside. Cut meat into thin slices.

To serve, spoon sauce on plates and place lamb slices on top. Garnish with parsley. Serve with polenta cakes and winter squash.

SERVES 4 AS AN ENTRÉE

Mustard- and Sourdough-Coated Venison with Currant Sauce (Classic Pairing)

RECOMMENDED WINE: Cabernet Sauvignon
ALTERNATIVE WINE: Syrah

THIS RECIPE PROVIDES A CLASSIC PAIRING FOR CABERNET SAUVIGNON. THE REDUCED RED-WINE MARINADE HELPS CREATE A SAUCE THAT ZEROES IN ON THE FLAVORS OF RARE VENISON AND MIRRORS THE WINE. THE INTENSELY FRUITY SAUCE ALSO AMPLIFIES THE CONCENTRATED FRUIT OF SYRAH.

MARINADE

¾ cup red wine

¼ cup chopped shallots

1 tablespoon chopped fresh sage
  (½ tablespoon dried)

1 tablespoon olive oil

¼ teaspoon kosher salt

¼ teaspoon freshly ground black pepper

¼ teaspoon mustard seed

—

2 pounds venison loin

COATING

3 slices sourdough French bread

1 tablespoon chopped shallots

1 tablespoon chopped fresh sage
  (½ tablespoon dried)

¼ teaspoon kosher salt

⅛ teaspoon freshly ground black pepper

1 tablespoon Dijon mustard

¾ tablespoon olive oil

SAUCE

¾ cup red wine

1½ cups beef or lamb stock

½ cup currants

1 tablespoon port or crème de cassis

¾ tablespoon Dijon mustard

2 tablespoons unsalted butter at room temperature

To make marinade, combine all ingredients in a sealable plastic bag. Add venison and marinate, refrigerated, for 3 to 4 hours, or up to overnight. Remove venison from marinade and pat dry. Reserve marinade for sauce.

To make coating, place bread in a food processor and process for about 1 minute. Add shallots, sage, salt, pepper, mustard, and olive oil and continue to process for 20 to 30 seconds. Remove coating from processor. Pat top and sides of venison with coating and carefully place on a broiler pan.

To make sauce, add reserved marinade and red wine to a large sauté pan or skillet and reduce by half. Add stock, currants, port, and mustard and reduce by half again, until sauce coats the back of a wooden spoon. Remove from heat, strain, and whisk in butter. Taste the sauce with the wine you plan to serve and add a touch of balsamic vinegar if sauce is too sweet. Keep warm.

Preheat oven to broil. Broil venison for 7 to 8 minutes, until rare. Don't overcook or the delicious meat will turn livery.

To serve, slice meat and place on plates. Top with currant sauce. Serve with corn fritters and sugar snap peas.

SERVES 6 AS AN ENTRÉE

Roast Prime Rib with Cabernet-Vegetable Jus and Herbed Yorkshire Pudding (Classic Pairing)

RECOMMENDED WINE: Cabernet Sauvignon
ALTERNATIVE WINE: Merlot

THERE'S NOTHING LIKE A PERFECTLY COOKED, FLAVORFUL ROAST PRIME RIB TO SHOWCASE THE INTENSITY AND COMPLEXITY OF CABERNET SAUVIGNON—AN EXCELLENT EXAMPLE OF HOW FAT HELPS COAT THE PALATE TO PROTECT AGAINST THE TANNIN IN RED WINE. THIS PARTICULAR RECIPE CALLS FOR COATING THE ROAST WITH DIJON MUSTARD AND ROSEMARY, TWO INGREDIENTS THAT ARE ESPECIALLY FLATTERING TO CABERNET. A REDUCTION SAUCE WITH CABERNET AND ROASTED VEGETABLES HELPS CORRAL ALL THE FLAVORS INTO PLEASING HARMONY. THE SOFT, ROUND MOUTHFEEL OF MERLOT PLAYS NICELY OFF THE ROAST BEEF AS WELL.

1 4½-pound prime rib roast of beef (2 ribs), trimmed and tied	2 eggs
1 tablespoon Dijon mustard	1 cup whole or low-fat milk
1 teaspoon prepared horseradish	¾ tablespoon minced chives
1¾ tablespoons chopped fresh rosemary	2 teaspoons minced fresh rosemary (1 teaspoon dried)
1½ teaspoons kosher salt	¾ teaspoon kosher salt
½ teaspoon freshly ground black pepper	2 tablespoons unsalted butter
1 large onion, quartered	2 tablespoons vegetable oil
1 large whole shallot	—
2 carrots, peeled	1 cup Cabernet Sauvignon
2 celery stalks, ends trimmed	1½ cups beef stock
6 ounces portobello mushrooms	Kosher salt and freshly ground black pepper
Olive oil	½ teaspoon cornstarch mixed with ½ teaspoon cold water
HERBED YORKSHIRE PUDDING	GARNISH: minced chives
1 cup all-purpose flour	

Preheat oven to 450°F. Place roast, fat side up, on a roasting rack in a large, flameproof roasting pan. In a small bowl, mix together ½ tablespoon Dijon mustard, ½ teaspoon prepared horseradish, ¾ tablespoon chopped fresh rosemary, kosher salt, and pepper with a whisk. Using hands or a pastry brush, coat entire roast with this mixture. Place roast in lower part of the oven and roast for 20 minutes to seal outside coating.

While roast is cooking, place onion, shallot, carrots, celery, and mushrooms in a large ovenproof baking dish and sprinkle with a little olive oil, salt, and pepper. After roast has cooked for 20 minutes, reduce heat to 350°F, and place vegetables on a rack below the roast. Continue roasting both the beef and vegetables for 1 hour.

To make Yorkshire pudding batter, in a food processor or blender, combine flour, eggs, milk, chives, rosemary, and salt and mix well so that mixture is smooth. Place in a small mixing bowl and refrigerate, covered, for at least 45 minutes.

Remove vegetables from the oven, roughly chop, and reserve for sauce. Continue cooking the roast

RECIPE CONTINUES

Roast Prime Rib with Cabernet-Vegetable Jus and Herbed Yorkshire Pudding

CONTINUED

for 10 minutes, until rare to medium-rare. Remove roast from the oven, place on a carving board and cover with foil for 20 to 30 minutes (it will continue to cook and increase in doneness). Set aside the roasting pan; do not soak.

To make Yorkshire pudding, while roast is resting under foil, preheat oven to 425°F. Place butter and oil in a shallow baking dish (copper works particularly well) and melt for 3 to 4 minutes. Immediately add chilled, whisked batter and bake for 18 to 20 minutes until pudding rises and becomes golden brown. Remove from oven and slice into four pieces.

Place roasting pan on the stove over medium heat. Add wine and deglaze the pan, simmering the wine and scraping up brown bits from the roast for 6 to 7 minutes, or until reduced by half. Add the stock and stir in ½ tablespoon Dijon mustard, ½ teaspoon horseradish, 1 tablespoon rosemary, and reserved roasted vegetables. Reduce by half. Add cornstarch mixture and season to taste. Keep warm until ready to serve.

To serve, slice beef into four servings, two of which will include ribs. Top with Cabernet vegetable sauce. Sprinkle with minced chives. Serve pudding slices alongside the beef.

SERVES 4 AS AN ENTRÉE

"Satisfy your hearts with food and wine, for therein is courage and strength."

HOMER, *THE ILIAD*

Dessert Wines

The rush of activity and flurry of flavors that make up the meal is over. Friends are relaxed and enjoying each other's company. Spirits have been raised. In short, life is good. So now is the perfect time for dessert and a wine that lifts dessert from the extraordinary to the sublime.

There are times when dessert wines might seem superfluous—at casual meals, when a lot of wine has already been consumed and friends have to drive, on weeknights, and other inappropriate occasions. Yet there are other times when it seems as though the meal can't possibly end without that last sip of liquid goodness. To some, dessert wine even replaces dessert.

Dessert wines range from great vintage ports from the Douro region of Portugal, to nectar-like golden Rieslings and Gewürztraminers from Germany and California, to the incomparable cigar-box smell of aged Sauternes made from Sauvignon Blanc and Sémillon in the Bordeaux region of France, to intensely fragrant Muscats of Italy, France, southern Portugal, Australia, and California, or to the nutty, sweet sherries of Jerez in the south of Spain.

What these wines all have in common is that they are picked at a time of maximum ripeness and sweetness, typically well after all other grapes are harvested. By hanging on the vine longer, the grapes develop a concentration of ripe flavor that is quite incomparable. Often these grapes (Riesling, Gewürztraminer, and Sauvignon Blanc/Sémillon in particular) are attacked by a "friendly fungus" known as *Botrytis cinerea* or "noble rot," which dehydrates the grapes and concentrates their sugars.

This is a magical process—one that offers much indulgent pleasure. Because of the scarcity of these grapes and the hand-picking that is always required, these wines are often quite expensive, making them a special treat. Many dessert wines, with the exception of port, are bottled in 375-milliliter bottles, which allows for easier consumption at smaller gatherings.

Port

Sauternes

Riesling

PORT

Port is truly the granddaddy of all dessert wines. Port has a long and illustrious history in Portugal, where the great port houses have dominated business for hundreds of years. These wines have been particularly prized in England for many years, but they've achieved virtually worldwide acclaim.

Port is a fortified wine, which is made by adding fermenting wine to 154-proof clear grape spirit. The finished wines range in alcohol from 18 to 20 percent and are quite sweet. The grape varieties used to make port are not well known:

Touriga Naçional, Tinta Roriz, Tinta Barocca, Tinto Cão, and Touriga Francesa.

Port is offered with a vintage date (the best indication of high quality because vintages are only declared in particularly exceptional years) or it can be non-vintage (blended from various years). Either way, port is magnificent with rich chocolate and coffee desserts and with nuts. The classic pairing with port is Stilton cheese, a salty, blue-veined cheese that provides a great contrast for the lush, sweet wine. True port lovers will be satisfied by this combination alone.

Port is unctuous, heady stuff that will cap off a meal with great success. It is traditionally accompanied by a cigar (but not in my house).

SAUTERNES

Sauternes, the famed liquid nectar of Bordeaux, is produced from Sémillon and Sauvignon Blanc, which are grown primarily in the Graves region. Recently, this style of wine has been produced in California with some success as well. It also has a following in Australia.

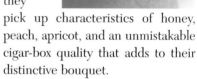

Sauternes ages magnificently, often for twenty to thirty years and beyond in the very best vintages. As these wines age, they pick up characteristics of honey, peach, apricot, and an unmistakable cigar-box quality that adds to their distinctive bouquet.

These intensely sweet wines are extremely harmonious with apple, pear, peach, and apricot desserts, although a classic match with Sauternes is to pair it with foie gras at the beginning of a meal. Sauternes is glorious decadence in a bottle.

RIESLING

As discussed in the Riesling chapter, this varietal produces wines in Germany, Austria, California, Australia, Alsace, and Washington. These wines range from bone dry to intensely sweet. The sweet dessert wines are made from late-harvest grapes with concentrated sugars. While very sweet, these wines tend to be low in alcohol, thus they are easier to drink at the end of a meal than port, for example.

Riesling stands up beautifully to more delicate desserts, such as fresh fruit, custards, and crème brûlée, as well as peach, apricot, and citrus-based pies and tarts. Late-harvest Riesling, whether from California, Australia, Alsace, or Beerenauslese and prized Trockenbeerenauslese from Germany, is truly liquid ambrosia—regal refinement of the highest order. Late-harvest Gewürztraminer offers much the same pleasure.

There are numerous other dessert wines that can top off a meal: late-harvest, sweet Tokay Pinot Gris from the Alsace region of France; sweet sherries from Spain; lush, nutty Madeira wines; and sweet Marsala. Time and space will not allow coverage in this book.

I am always amazed at how much people like dessert wines, no matter what the type. They are a special treat and a truly great way to end a great meal.

TIPS TO SUCCESSFUL MATCHES WITH DESSERT WINES

1
Try not to make the dessert very much sweeter than the wine as it will tend to dry out the wine.

2
Quick, simple matches: Fresh green apples with late-harvest Riesling; fresh mango or papaya with late-harvest Gewürztraminer; biscotti and fresh apricots with Sauternes and Sauvignon Blanc/ Sémillon blends; chocolate truffles with port; almonds with sweet sherries.

3
Only a 3- to 4-ounce pour per person (at most) is necessary with most dessert wines. Try seeking out 375-milliliter bottles of Riesling, Gewürztraminer, and Sauternes for smaller groups up to four people.

4
If the dessert is great, it will only taste better with a dessert wine.

Dried Apricot, Peach, and Pecan Tart

RECOMMENDED WINE: Port

ALTERNATIVE WINE: Sauternes

BASED ON AN ADAPTED *BON APPÉTIT* FILLING FROM MANY YEARS AGO THAT HAS EVOLVED IN OUR KITCHEN ALONG WITH A JIM DODGE CRUST CONCEPT, THIS IS A DENSE, CHEWY TART THAT SHOWCASES PECANS AND DRIED FRUITS WITH A THICK PORT FILLING. THE PAIRING IS A NATURAL DUE TO THE PORT USED IN THE PIE. A SAUTERNES WILL CAPTURE THE DRIED FRUIT FLAVORS OF THE TART QUITE EFFECTIVELY AS WELL.

TART CRUST

1 ⅛ cups all-purpose flour

1 ½ teaspoons sugar

1 ½ teaspoons ground cinnamon

¼ pound (1 stick) cold unsalted butter, cut into 1-inch pieces

⅛ teaspoon kosher salt

¼ cup cold water

FILLING

1 6-ounce package dried apricots, chopped

1 6-ounce package dried peaches, chopped

1 cup port

1 cup cold water plus more as needed for filling

½ cup brown sugar

2 tablespoons cornstarch

2 teaspoons fresh orange juice

1 cup chopped toasted pecans

GARNISH: crème fraîche or whipped cream, mint sprigs

Preheat oven to 400°F.

To make the crust, in a food processor fitted with a pastry blade, combine flour, sugar, and cinnamon. Blend in the butter until mixture resembles coarse meal, about the size of small peas. Mix the salt and water and add them to the flour mixture. Scrape down the sides of the bowl. Blend only until the dough comes together and is moist and smooth.

On a lightly floured board or pastry cloth, flatten dough into a circle. Roll out dough with a rolling pin to make an 11-inch circle about ⅛ inch thick. Gently fold dough into quarters and then transfer to a 10-inch tart pan with a removable bottom, placing point at center. Carefully unfold, easing dough from center out to rim, pressing dough gently into sides of tart pan. Place in refrigerator for 15 minutes to chill.

Remove tart crust from refrigerator. Using a fork, gently prick dough in several places along bottom and sides of pan to prevent shrinkage. Completely line bottom and sides of dough-lined pan with foil. Fill to top with weights (dried beans work quite well). Gently press weights into bottom and sides of pan to ensure that dough is weighted down.

Place pan on baking sheet on middle rack of oven. Bake for 15 to 20 minutes or until bottom and sides of dough are light golden. Place on wire rack and carefully remove foil and weights. Allow to cool completely at room temperature.

To make filling, in a large pot, combine apricots, peaches, port, and water. Bring to a simmer and cook until the dried fruit has softened, about 8 to 10 minutes. Strain fruit. Reserve cooking liquid and fruit. Add enough cold water to cooking liquid to make 1 cup.

In a mixing bowl, mix ¼ cup cooking liquid with brown sugar and cornstarch and whisk to dissolve cornstarch. Pour remaining ¾ cup cooking liquid back into the pot along with cornstarch mixture. Add orange juice.

Over medium heat, bring mixture to a boil, stirring often. Reduce heat and simmer to thicken liquid, stirring occasionally. Add reserved fruit and pecans, remove from heat, and cool. When thoroughly cooled, pour mixture into pre-baked crust.

Carefully remove tart from pan by pressing gently upward on the bottom of the pan. Place on serving plate.

Serve chilled or at room temperature with crème fraîche and garnish with mint sprigs.

SERVES 8

"It warms the blood, adds luster to the eyes, and wine and love have ever been allies."

OVID, *THE ART OF LOVE*

Apple, Cranberry, and Walnut Pie with Stilton

RECOMMENDED WINE: Port

ALTERNATIVE WINE: Sauternes

THIS IS A GREAT LATE FALL OR WINTER PIE THAT UNVEILS THE COMPLEMENTARY SEASONAL FLAVORS OF APPLES, CRAN-BERRIES, AND WALNUTS. THIS PIE OFTEN FINDS ITSELF ON OUR THANKSGIVING TABLE AND MAY DO JUSTICE TO YOURS AS WELL, PARTICULARLY WHEN SERVED WITH A WONDERFUL, INTENSE PORT ON THE SIDE. THE USE OF STILTON CHEESE IS A VARIATION ON THE CLASSIC MATCH OF THIS INTENSE CHEESE WITH THE HEADY PLEASURE OF PORT–VERY BRITISH, INDEED. SAUTERNES IS A REASONABLE ALTERNATIVE, BUT DOES NOT NEARLY DO THE JUSTICE OF PORT.

PIE CRUST

1⅛ cups all-purpose flour

1½ teaspoons sugar

1½ teaspoons ground cinnamon

¼ pound (1 stick) cold unsalted butter, cut into 1-inch pieces

⅛ teaspoon kosher salt

¼ cup cold water

FILLING

6 cups peeled, sliced green apples (about 4 to 5 medium apples)

1 cup cranberries (fresh or frozen)

1 cup lightly toasted walnuts

2 teaspoons finely grated orange zest

½ teaspoon ground cinnamon

¼ teaspoon ground ginger

½ cup sugar

2 tablespoons all-purpose flour, tapioca flour, or instant tapioca

⅛ teaspoon kosher salt

STREUSEL TOPPING

1 cup all-purpose flour

¼ cup packed brown sugar

2 tablespoons finely diced crystallized ginger

6 tablespoons (¾ stick) unsalted butter

GARNISH: small wedges of Stilton cheese

Preheat oven to 375°F. To make the crust, in a food processor fitted with a pastry blade, combine flour, sugar, and cinnamon. Blend in the butter until mixture resembles coarse meal, about the size of small peas. Mix the salt and water and add them to the flour mixture. Blend only until the dough comes together.

On a lightly floured board or pastry cloth, flatten dough into a circle. Roll out dough with a rolling pin to make an 11-inch circle about ⅛ inch thick. Gently fold dough into quarters and then transfer to a 9-inch pie pan, placing point at center. Carefully unfold, easing dough from center out to rim, pressing dough gently onto sides of pan. Trim any overhanging dough. Place in refrigerator for 15 minutes to chill.

In a large bowl, gently mix together all filling ingredients. In a small bowl, make streusel topping by combining flour, sugar, and ginger with a fork. With fingers, rub in butter until lumps are no longer distinguishable.

To assemble pie, transfer filling into pie shell. Sprinkle streusel topping over pie. Decoratively crimp edge of pie dough. Place on baking sheet and bake on middle rack of oven for 1 hour, or until the crust and topping are light golden and juices bubble. To prevent excessive browning of rim, wrap edge of crust with a strip of foil after 35 to 40 minutes of baking. Remove foil after 55 minutes.

Remove from oven and let cool. Serve with a small wedge of Stilton cheese.

SERVES 6 TO 8

Suzanne's Summer Apricot-Blackberry Pie (Classic Pairing)

RECOMMENDED WINE: Sauternes

ALTERNATIVE WINE: Riesling

M Y WIFE, SUZANNE, IS THE DESSERT MAKER IN OUR HOUSE AND PREFERS THAT, WHEN SHE'S BAKING, HER FOOD-LOVING HUSBAND REMAIN OUT OF THE KITCHEN SO THAT SHE CAN ENJOY HER HOBBY WITHOUT ANY "EXPERT ADVICE." THIS CLASSIC SUMMER PIE BRINGS TOGETHER BLACKBERRIES AND APRICOTS IN A MOUTH-WATERING AND TOTALLY DELICIOUS PAIRING THAT PROVIDES A FRAMEWORK FOR THE LIQUID GOLD NECTAR OF FINE SAUTERNES. RIESLING ALSO HAS A GREAT ABILITY TO WEAVE IN AND AROUND FRUIT DESSERTS.

PIE CRUST

2 $\frac{1}{4}$ cups all-purpose flour

1 tablespoon sugar

1 tablespoon ground cinnamon

$\frac{1}{2}$ pound (2 sticks) cold unsalted butter, cut into 1-inch pieces

$\frac{1}{4}$ teaspoon kosher salt

$\frac{1}{2}$ cup cold water

FILLING

5 cups apricots, pitted and quartered

3 cups blackberries or boysenberries

1 $\frac{1}{4}$ cups sugar

3 $\frac{1}{2}$ tablespoons cornstarch or tapioca flour

1 tablespoon fresh lemon or lime juice

$\frac{1}{4}$ teaspoon ground cinnamon

$\frac{1}{4}$ teaspoon ground cardamom

Preheat oven to 425°F. To make pie crust, in a food processor fitted with a pastry blade, combine flour, sugar, and cinnamon. Blend in the butter until mixture resembles coarse meal, about the size of small peas. Mix the salt and water and add them to the flour mixture. Blend only until the dough comes together. Divide the dough into equal halves and press lightly into two balls.

On a lightly floured board or pastry cloth, flatten dough into two rounds. Wrap one round in plastic wrap and place in refrigerator for use as lattice top. Roll out remaining dough with a rolling pin to make an 11-inch circle about ⅛ inch thick. Gently fold dough into quarters and then transfer to a 9-inch pie pan, placing point at center. Carefully unfold, easing dough from center out to rim, fitting dough gently onto pan sides. Place in refrigerator until ready to fill.

Combine apricots and berries in a large bowl. Add sugar, cornstarch, lemon juice, cinnamon, and cardamom. Gently mix together until well blended. Let mixture stand for at least 15 minutes before assembling.

To assemble the pie, pour filling into prepared pie shell. Roll out the remaining dough round into an 11-inch circle, about ⅛ inch thick. Using a sharp knife, cut 8 to 10 strips of dough about ½ inch wide to use as lattice. Using a crisscross pattern, arrange dough strips on top. Pinch the ends of the strips into the edge of the bottom dough. Then fold edges of bottom dough and flute decoratively between fingers or press with a fork to seal.

To prevent excessive browning of the rim, wrap rim with a strip of foil 2 to 3 inches wide. Place pie on middle rack of preheated oven. Remove foil from edge 15 to 20 minutes before pie is done. Bake for 55 to 60 minutes, or until crust is golden and juices are bubbling.

SERVES 6 TO 8

Fig and Raspberry Clafouti

RECOMMENDED WINE: Sauternes

ALTERNATIVE WINE: Port

CLAFOUTI IS NOT A TERRIBLY WELL-KNOWN DESSERT. ITS ORIGINS ARE IN THE SOUTH CENTRAL PART OF FRANCE WHERE A BATTER CAKE, TYPICALLY MADE WITH BLACK CHERRIES, IS A TRADITIONAL AND MUCH LOVED DELIGHT. THIS VERSION RESONATES WITH THE LUSH, HONEYED SWEETNESS OF LATE SUMMER FIGS AND SLIGHTLY TART RASPBERRIES, A TRULY MAGICAL COMBINATION THAT WRAPS ITS FLAVORS AROUND THE HONEY-LIKE QUALITY IN AGED SAUTERNES. PORT IS A SUITABLE ALTERNATIVE THAT WORKS WELL WITH THE FIG FLAVORS.

2 cups quartered figs

2 cups raspberries

½ cup sliced, blanched almonds

1 cup all-purpose flour

⅓ cup plus 2 tablespoons sugar

2 large eggs

1 cup milk

3 tablespoons port

2 tablespoons cold unsalted butter, cut into bits

Preheat oven to 400°F. Arrange figs cut side up in buttered 8-by-8-by-2-inch baking dish and sprinkle in raspberries. In a blender or food processor, finely grind the almonds with the flour. Add ⅓ cup sugar, eggs, milk, and port and blend well. Stop occasionally to wipe down sides as necessary. Pour the custard over the fruit, dot with butter, and sprinkle with the remaining 2 tablespoons sugar.

Bake on the middle rack of the oven for 30 to 40 minutes, or until the top is golden and the custard is set. Let cool for 20 minutes. Serve with a dusting of powdered sugar.

SERVES 6

Rhubarb and Berry Crisp

RECOMMENDED WINE: Sauternes

ALTERNATIVE WINE: Port

I LOVE THE COMBINATION OF FRESH RHUBARB, STRAWBERRIES, AND RASPBERRIES IN THE SPRING WHEN THESE INGREDIENTS FIRST START APPEARING IN THE MARKETS. IT IS SOMEHOW AN INVIGORATING SIGN OF THE SEASON BEGINNING TO CHANGE. THE SWEET FRUIT OF A GOOD SAUTERNES, WITH ITS LUSH MOUTHFEEL AND INSISTENT FRUIT, OR PORT WILL PUT THE FINISHING TOUCH ON THIS DESSERT AND YOUR MEAL.

1 ¼ cups sugar

¼ cup quick-cooking tapioca or tapioca flour

1 teaspoon ground cinnamon

1 teaspoon grated orange peel

4 cups diced rhubarb

1 cup sliced strawberries

1 cup raspberries or blackberries

2 tablespoons fresh lime juice

1 cup all-purpose flour

½ cup (1 stick) unsalted butter or margarine

½ cup brown sugar

⅛ teaspoon ground nutmeg

Lemon sorbet (optional)

Preheat oven to 375°F. In a shallow 2-quart baking dish, mix together the sugar, tapioca, cinnamon, and orange peel. Add the rhubarb, berries, and lime juice and mix together thoroughly. Let mixture sit for at least 30 minutes, mixing several times so that tapioca softens.

In a food processor or blender, add the flour, butter, brown sugar, and nutmeg. Blend until mixture forms lumps. Remove mixture from processor and crumble evenly over the top of the fruit.

Place on middle rack of preheated oven. Bake crisp until top is golden brown and juices are bubbling, about 35 minutes. Remove crisp from oven and place on wire rack. Let cool for 15 to 20 minutes before serving. Top with sorbet, if desired.

SERVES 6 TO 8

Peach and Banana Bread Pudding

(Classic Pairing)

RECOMMENDED WINE: Riesling
ALTERNATIVE WINE: Sauternes

THIS BREAD PUDDING IS AN ADAPTATION OF ONE I LEARNED YEARS AGO FROM GERRY KLASKALA, AN OUTSTANDING SOUTHERN CHEF WHO NOW RUNS THE VERY SUCCESSFUL CANOE RESTAURANT IN ATLANTA. THE FLAVORS OF PEACH AND BANANA COME TOGETHER IN THIS RICH, WONDERFUL DESSERT TO PROVIDE A SHOWCASE FOR A SWEET, LATE-HARVEST RIESLING. A LUSCIOUS SAUTERNES HIGHLIGHTS THESE FLAVORS AND PROVIDES A NICE TEXTURAL MATCH AS WELL.

5 ounces (10 tablespoons) unsalted butter at room temperature

1 pound brioche, challah, or egg bread, cut into ½-inch-thick slices

2 pounds fresh peaches, poached, skinned, pitted, and sliced or one 29-ounce can, drained

3 pounds bananas, peeled and sliced

6 eggs

1¾ cups sugar

3 cups whole milk

2 teaspoons cinnamon

GARNISH: mint sprigs

Preheat oven to 275°F.

Lightly butter both sides of bread and toast in oven on both sides. Puree one-half of peaches. Reserve half of puree for garnish. Combine remaining puree with sliced peaches and bananas and mix thoroughly.

In a separate large mixing bowl, whisk eggs, and then add ¾ cup of the sugar and the milk. Whisk vigorously for 2 minutes. Add peach-banana mixture and mix well.

Generously butter 3-inch-deep loaf pan and dust evenly with 2 tablespoons of the reserved sugar. Place a layer of bread on bottom of pan so that it covers it evenly. Cover with a layer of peach-banana custard so that fruit is evenly distributed. Repeat layering until pan is filled to ½-inch from the top. Allow to stand for 1 hour.

Combine cinnamon with remaining sugar and sprinkle on top. Cover with aluminum foil and bake in preheated oven for 1 hour and 15 minutes. Allow to rest for 2 hours at room temperature. Garnish with mint sprigs.

SERVES 10 TO 12

"Contrast is a primary principle throughout life from the moment of birth; light contrasts with dark, cold with warm, dry with wet, noise with silence, chaos with rhythm. Marriages are spiced by contrasts. Harmony and balance give pleasure. Balance in a meal is a studied achievement. In a wine it is a gift of Nature, tempered by the artistry of the winemaker. Four rich courses at a banquet infer long hours of gut-wrenching indigestion. On the other hand contrasting highs with lows, and rich with piquant, leaves a pleasant memory."

ANDRÉ SIMON, Australian Wine and Food Society, 1971

NEW YEAR'S DAY BOWL BUFFET
Shrimp and Avocado Salsa in Pita Toasts
Champagne/sparkling wine
Arugula, Smoked Trout, Roasted Beets, and Caramelized
Cashews with Ginger-Chile Dressing
Gewürztraminer
Clove-Infused Pork–Black Bean Stew with Tomatillo–Roasted
Red Pepper Salsa
Zinfandel

VALENTINE'S NIGHT DINNER
FOR TWO
Lobster Salad with Apricot-Walnut Vinaigrette
Viognier
Filet Mignon "Diana"
Syrah
chocolate-covered strawberries
port (in bed)

SPRING FLING
Risotto with Lemon Shrimp, Roasted Garlic,
and Goat Cheese
Sauvignon/Fumé Blanc
Grilled Salmon with Mushrooms, Sweet Onions,
and Pinot Noir Sauce
Pinot Noir
Rhubarb and Berry Crisp
Sauternes

TOTALLY CASUAL MEMORIAL DAY
Radish Slaw with Rémoulade and Pistachios
Sauvignon/Fumé Blanc
Penne with Sausage, Porcini
and Portobello Mushrooms, and Syrah
Syrah
ice cream topped with blueberries
and strawberries, biscotti
Late-Harvest Riesling

BASTILLE DAY IN PROVENCE
Roasted Eggplant-Garlic Soup (served cold)

Sauvignon/Fumé Blanc

Grilled Lamb with Green Olive Sauce

Syrah

raspberries with crème fraîche

Sauternes

FOURTH OF JULY BARBECUE/POOL PARTY
Marinated Mussels and Roasted Red Bell Peppers

Pinot Gris/Grigio

Grilled Flank Steak with Roasted Corn–Pancetta Salsa

Zinfandel

Suzanne's Summer Apricot-Blackberry Pie

Sauternes

LATE SUMMER GARDEN SUPPER
Chilled Corn and Sun-Dried Tomato Chowder
with Goat Cheese–Chive Croutons

Chardonnay

Grilled Lamb with Rustic Porcini Sauce

Cabernet Sauvignon

Fig and Raspberry Clafouti

Sauternes

HARVEST PARTY
Chilled Leeks with Green Olives, Capers,
and Sun-Dried Tomato Vinaigrette

Sauvignon/Fumé Blanc

Grilled Lamb with Roasted Garlic–Mint Sauce

Zinfandel

Peach and Banana Bread Pudding

Late-Harvest Riesling

RED WINE WITH FISH; WHITE WINE WITH MEAT
Grilled Ahi with Ginger–Black Bean Sauce
(small portions)

Pinot Noir

Veal Roast with Dijon-Tinged Vegetable Sauce

Chardonnay

chocolate mousse

port

PRE-THEATER SUPPER
Sid's Caesar

Sauvignon/Fumé Blanc

Basil Fettuccine with Sun-Dried Tomatoes, Olives,
and Prosciutto

Zinfandel

biscotti

TAKE THE CHILL OFF
Spicy Gingered-Carrot Soup

Gewürztraminer

Roast Leg of Veal with Wild Mushroom Sauce
and Walnuts

Pinot Noir

crème brûlée

Sauternes

A WINE LOVER'S THANKSGIVING
Shrimp-Scallop Pâté with Cilantro, Dill, and Pine Nuts

Sauvignon/Fumé Blanc

Herb and Spice Roasted Cornish Game Hens

Chardonnay (or Pinot Noir)

Apple, Cranberry, and Walnut Pie with Stilton

port

BACCHUS MEETS SANTA CLAUS
Wilted Red Cabbage Salad with Tangerines,
Bay Shrimp, and Almonds

Riesling

Roast Prime Rib with Cabernet-Vegetable Jus
and Herbed Yorkshire Pudding

Cabernet Sauvignon

Dried Apricot, Peach, and Pecan Tart

port

Bibliography

BALDY, MARIAN W.
The University Wine Course.
San Francisco: Wine Appreciation Guild, 1993.

BREITSTEIN, RON AND HENDRIK VAN LEUVEN.
Wine and Dine.
Santa Barbara, Calif.: Capra Press, 1996.

BUTLER, JOEL.
"Viognier Is an Opulent Pleasure,"
Contra Costa Times, July 13, 1994.

DE VILLIERS, MARQ.
The Heartbreak Grape.
San Francisco: HarperCollins West, 1994.

EVELY, MARY.
The Vintner's Table Cookbook—Recipes from a Winery Chef.
Healdsburg, Calif.: Simi Winery, 1998.

GOLDSTEIN, JOYCE.
Kitchen Conversations.
New York: William Morrow and Co., 1996.

GRAUSMAN, RICHARD.
At Home with the French Classics.
New York: Workman Publishing Co., 1988.

GREEN, JONATHON.
Consuming Passions.
New York: Fawcett Columbine, 1985.

"GUIDE TO UNDERSTANDING WINE AND FOOD."
Wine & Spirits Magazine, 1997.

HENDRA, TONY.
"The Best Damn Wine in the Whole Damn World,"
Forbes FYI, Winter 1997.

JOHNSON, HUGH.
Hugh Johnson's Modern Encyclopedia of Wine.
New York: Simon and Schuster, 1991.

KOLPAN, STEVEN, BRIAN H. SMITH, AND MICHAEL A. WEISS.
Exploring Wine.
New York: Von Nostrand Reinhold, 1996.

LAKE, DR. MAX.
Food on the Plate, Wine in the Glass.
Pokolbin, Australia: Max Lake, 1994.

MCINERNEY, JAY.
"The Cult of Condrieu,"
Home and Garden, May 1997.

RAMEY, BERN C.
The Great Wine Grapes and the Wines They Make.
Davis, Calif.: Great Wine Grapes Inc., 1977.

ROBINSON, JANCIS.
The Oxford Companion to Wine.
Oxford, England: Oxford University, 1994.

SHELFLIFE, ONLINE.
Vintage Trivia, May 28, 1998.

SIMON, JOANNA.
Wine with Food.
New York: Simon and Schuster, 1996.

ST. PIERRE, BRIAN.
A Perfect Glass of Wine.
San Francisco: Chronicle Books, 1996.

WESSON, JOSHUA, AND DAVID ROSENGARTEN.
Red Wine with Fish.
New York: Simon and Schuster, 1989.

WIEGAND, RONN, AND BRENDA BOBLITT.
Fine Wines of the World.
Napa, Calif.: TasteTour Publications and Seminars, 1996.

Table of Equivalents

THE EXACT EQUIVALENTS IN THE FOLLOWING TABLES HAVE BEEN ROUNDED FOR CONVENIENCE.

LIQUID/DRY MEASURES

U.S.	METRIC
¼ teaspoon	1.25 milliliters
½ teaspoon	2.5 milliliters
1 teaspoon	5 milliliters
1 tablespoon (3 teaspoons)	15 milliliters
1 fluid ounce (2 tablespoons)	30 milliliters
¼ cup	60 milliliters
⅓ cup	80 milliliters
½ cup	120 milliliters
1 cup	240 milliliters
1 pint (2 cups)	480 milliliters
1 quart (4 cups, 32 ounces)	960 milliliters
1 gallon (4 quarts)	3.84 liters
1 ounce (by weight)	28 grams
1 pound	454 grams
2.2 pounds	1 kilogram

LENGTH

U.S.	METRIC
⅛ inch	3 millimeters
¼ inch	6 millimeters
½ inch	12 millimeters
1 inch	2.5 centimeters

OVEN TEMPERATURE

FAHRENHEIT	CELSIUS	GAS
250	120	½
275	140	1
300	150	2
325	160	3
350	180	4
375	190	5
400	200	6
425	220	7
450	230	8
475	240	9
500	260	10

Index